praise for

# You'll Never Nanny in This Town Again

"[A] story that Hansen tells with real comic energy, sparing no unlibelous detail."—*Boston Globe*

"Accessible, hilarious, and sharp."—MSNBC.com

"Amusing . . . this entertaining book possesses a sincerity that other nannying tomes lack."—*Publishers Weekly*

"Plenty of dish."—*Working Mother*

"Loaded with juicy anecdotes and more than a few dirty diapers."—*Life*

"Thrillingly voyeuristic."—*The Times* (London)

"Funny and engaging enough to be a novel, that *You'll Never Nanny in This Town Again* is true takes it to another level—a stunning exposé of our culture's impossible expectations of mothers."
    —Ariel Gore, author of *The Hip Mama Survival Guide* and *The Mother Trip*

"Veterans of the serving class ourselves, we thought we'd seen it all, but *You'll Never Nanny in This Town Again* offers an intriguing peek into the never-before-revealed family lives of Hollywood's elite. Hansen's memoir poignantly proves that truth can be more powerful than fiction."
    —Leanne Shear and Tracey Toomey, authors of *The Perfect Manhattan*

"Just when you think you've heard everything about the behind-the-scenes world of celebrities, along comes *You'll Never Nanny in This Town Again*, a humorous yet down-to-earth account of the vagaries of warped Hollywood parenting. Author Suzanne Hansen's experiences as an L.A. nanny expose the absurd—and yet achingly funny—differences between the rich and famous and the rest of us."
    —Andrew Breitbart and Mark Ebner, authors of *Hollywood, Interrupted*

"A funny, absorbing true tale that will once again leave readers wondering why anyone would want to work in the insane asylum that is Hollywood."
    —Robin Lynn Williams, author of *The Assistants*

# Suzanne Hansen

the true adventures
of a hollywood nanny

# You'll Never Nanny in This Town Again

Three Rivers Press • New York

Published in the United States by Three Rivers Press, an imprint of the Crown
Publishing Group, a division of Random House, Inc., New York.
www.crownpublishing.com

Three Rivers Press and the Tugboat design are registered trademarks of Random
House, Inc.

Originally published by Ruby Sky Publishing, Beaverton, OR, in 2003. Subse-
quently published in hardcover in different form in the United States by Crown
Publishers, an imprint of the Crown Publishing Group, a division of Random
House, Inc., New York, in 2005.

Library of Congress Cataloging-in-Publication Data
Hansen, Suzanne.
  You'll never nanny in this town again : the true adventures of a Hollywood nanny /
Suzanne Hansen.—1st ed.
  Originally published: Beaverton, OR: Ruby Sky Pub., c2003.
  1. Hansen, Suzanne.   2. Nannies—California—Los Angeles—Biography.
3.  Hollywood (Los Angeles, Calif.)—Social life and customs—Anecdotes.
I. Title.
  HQ778.67.L7H35    2005
  649'.092—dc22          2005014810

ISBN  978-0-307-23768-2

Printed in the United States of America

10 9 8 7

First Paperback Edition

To my sisters, Cindy and Traci,

two of the greatest blessings in my life

# contents

# author's note

The decision to write this book, essentially the memoirs of a Hollywood nanny, didn't come easily. I agonized over whether this was my story to tell, especially since the children I loved and cared for are at the center of it. I began and ended this writing process with the clear intention of not divulging all that I observed. Carefully selecting the experiences was the balance and compromise that felt best in my heart.

Although this story is about my personal experiences, it is far from unique. Nannies don't have a union, but we do chat. I know that situations similar to the ones I experienced continue to take place in the homes of the wealthy, powerful, and famous all across America.

Often during media interviews, celebrity moms fail to mention—or barely mention—the help they have that makes their glamorous lives possible. I don't know whether I want to scream, laugh, or cry when they smile graciously, subtly implying that through their own super-human efforts they are able to pull off an Oscar-winning role and still drive the daily carpool. Are they really talented enough to juggle the high-gloss career, the splendid home, and the busy family all by them-selves? How do they have time to work such long hours, undergo a marathon of social obligations, and chair the PTA fund-raiser? Presumably, through superior multitasking genes! The reality is, when a member of the Hollywood elite explains that "we have a normal life just like everyone else," there is a little more to the story: they are not doing it all alone. What they do have is one heck of a secret support system.

It is sad that these famous families don't realize how hurtful it can be for a nanny to have her very existence denied while she labors endlessly to keep their world intact. In sharing my sometimes embarrassing tribulations as a nanny, I hope I provide a glimpse into the lives of the undervalued caregivers who wipe tears and devote their days to the love and comfort of children.

The amateur psychologist in me speculates that the reason Hollywood nannies are kept out of public view has much to do with society's expectation that a mother "should" be able to do it all. Since my nanny days, I've become a mother myself, and I often struggle with the overwhelming responsibility of motherhood. I know that it can be a real morale-destroyer for those of us in the diaper trenches to measure ourselves against the media perception, encouraged by the rich and famous, that having it all is just a matter of better management. If the megastars can manage the onslaught of minutiae in their lives, then what's keeping the rank-and-file mom from making time to sculpt the great body, pamper the flawless skin, mop the spotless floor, prepare nutritional meals, and bring home a paycheck? Oh, and don't forget scheduling date night to keep the romance alive!

For myself, there are many days I can barely keep my head above water. A nanny, a cook, a 24-7 housekeeper, a gardener, a car-washer, even a clone of myself—any help would be a godsend. I doubt that I'm alone on those days when pressing errands take precedence over a shower. Out comes the baseball cap on my way to the grocery store to buy last week's list of stuff, to the craft store for birthday invitations, and then to the bank to—oops, I'm already overdrawn. I can assure you that movie-star moms don't sacrifice the shower for taking the SUV in for an overdue oil change. Nor do they discover the load of forgotten wet laundry that didn't get to the dryer and has mildewed in the meantime.

I have shared my personal story in part to celebrate and commend the moms who really do "do it all" or attempt a reasonable facsimile thereof. If celebrity moms would acknowledge their personal limitations and their gratitude for their nannies' constancy, it would speak volumes to moms without any support staff.

My two favorite supporters of motherhood are Oprah and Maria Shriver, who both continually encourage moms to be proud of their important work. These two women of influence save many a mom's sanity by giving unwavering vocal support to the challenging job of motherhood, while continuing to remind us that motherhood is our highest calling.

Finally, I hope my misadventures in nannyhood will provide a little humor for all the mothers out there. After all, if you only have five minutes to sit and read, it's nice if you can laugh. And just so you know, many of the embarrassing scenarios in which I found myself as a nanny have continued to crop up in my mothering life. But I can only suffer so much embarrassment in one book.

A note about names: For the most part I have tried to use real names, but some of the names have been changed. The following names are pseudonyms: Mandie, Mr. and Mrs. Goldberg, and Sarah. I have changed the names of all children mentioned in the book, as well as many of the minor characters.

You'll

Never Nanny

in This

Town Again

If you want your children to turn out well, spend twice as much time with them, and half as much money.

—Abigail Van Buren

# prologue

When my boss told me that we were all going to Hawaii for Thanksgiving vacation, I tried not to panic. I was nineteen years old, and my vacation experience up to that point pretty much consisted of ten-hour trips in my family's cramped station wagon to visit my cousins in Canada. You'd think I would have been turning cartwheels down Sunset Boulevard. But as enticing as an all-expenses-paid stay at a posh Hawaiian beachfront resort would sound to most people, I was realistic enough—after almost a year of nannying for one of the most powerful families in Hollywood—to know that I'd be on duty for 192 hours straight. I had counted.

One hundred and ninety-two straight hours of running after three children under the age of seven, of sharing quarters a lot more cramped than the ten-thousand-square-foot home we normally occupied, where the air was already tense. Of no room to escape the kids or their parents for one minute.

This "vacation" sounded worse every time I thought about it. Good thing I didn't know about the other five kids.

The night after I was informed of our upcoming adventure, I decided to be more positive. *Come on, Suzy! You could never afford to travel to*

*Hawaii on your own. This is a great opportunity to soak up some paradise.*
I tried not to think about our previous "vacations." Surely this would
have a whole different, relaxed, tropical vibe? I called my friend and fellow nanny Mandie to tell her my news. She listened intently while I
borrowed scenes from postcards and spun my perfect vision of the
eight-day trip.

"I'll be basking on white-sugar beaches, with cute cabana boys constantly serving me fruity drinks in coconut halves. After I distribute the
beach toys and reapply sunscreen on the kids, I'll soak up the Polynesian
splendor. Just think, hula performances under torch-lit palms . . . leis
draped around me . . . luaus . . . lanais . . ." In my dream-dappled
mind, there would be grandparents, aunts, and uncles to lavish attention
on the kids. The gentle spirit of the island would permeate our hearts
and inner harmony would reign.

But then Mandie started laughing so hard that I was actually afraid
she'd lost control of her bladder.

We both knew it was far more likely that the actual scenario would
be similar to what a mutual nanny friend of ours had just undergone.
Her employer, a well-known baseball player, had brought her along to
the famous Pebble Beach golf course, where he was playing in a huge
charity golf tournament. The event was star-studded, and she couldn't
wait to rub elbows with some celebrities. But when the other baseball
players' wives realized someone had brought a nanny, they all dumped
their kids in her suite and headed off to the tournament unencum-
bered. She spent three days in a hotel room with nine—count 'em,
*nine*—kids. She never saw one moment of golf, beach, or sunshine.

I tried to be optimistic, but my spirits wavered when even getting
out of the driveway became a massive undertaking. Our traveling caravan
included me and my employers, Michael and Judy Ovitz; their three children (Joshua, Amanda, and Brandon); Michael's parents; his brother,
Mark, and Mark's wife, Linda, and their six-year-old son; and Michael's
business partner, Ron Meyer, along with Ron's date, Cyndi Garvey, and
their four combined daughters. It took two stretch limos just to get the
whole group to the airport. Altogether, the entourage totaled nine adults
and eight children. In addition, Michael's friend Al Checchi and his wife,
three kids, and nanny would be meeting us at the resort.

After we were greeted at LAX by a professional-looking woman waiting at passenger drop-off, the limo driver unloaded enough luggage to supply an army tank division. We were breezily escorted through security and down a long hall to a door marked THE CAPTAIN'S CLUB. Who knew that airlines provided these private little sanctuaries to their frequent fliers? And Creative Artists Agency, Michael's company—with his partners, staff, and clients—had probably racked up millions of such miles on the corporate American Express card. Michael waved the whole troupe over to the Captain's Club portal.

A stone-faced young woman at the desk stopped us. Airline policy was to allow the frequent flier and one guest, and she was here to enforce the rules. She was firm and implacable with a perfunctory pleasantness that was so calm it was irritating. Michael started arguing his case, but she repeated patiently that this was company policy, with no exceptions. No exceptions? Michael's face began to twitch as if a bug were trapped under his skin. The employee gave the impression of having weathered a few of these type A folks in her day. She repeated the policy clearly and identically several times. I recognized her "broken-record technique" from my childcare classes. But Michael wasn't six.

"I'm sorry, Mr. . . . ." She paused, waiting for him to fill in the blank.

He raised his eyebrows and lowered his face closer to hers. "Ovitz. Michael *Ovitz*," he pronounced emphatically, as though there was not a soul alive who would not recognize his name.

The woman didn't respond. She calmly kept typing on her computer as she stared into the monitor. I already had learned in my tenure with "the most powerful man in Hollywood" that there were several things that invariably irritated or angered him. One of them was not being recognized for the influential man he was. This was a bit of a contradiction, since he hated seeing his name in the papers and went to great lengths to keep his picture from being published. Whatever. Today was definitely a day he wanted to be recognized.

"Do you have any idea how many frequent-traveler miles my company has with this airline?" He smirked with the air of someone who always got his way. I thought about backing him up and rehearsed my part in my mind: *Please, miss, lighten up. I have a chubby baby on one hip and a heavy diaper bag on the other, and I would like to sit down.*

"I'm sorry, Mr. Ovitz. I don't know you, and it wouldn't matter if I did, because the rules are the rules," she replied with unsurpassed calm. "You can have only one guest come in with you." Oh dear, poor thing. Maybe if I wriggled my eyebrows frantically, she'd relent. I tried desperately to make eye contact, wondering what kind of expression would let her know that she was teetering on the verge of unemployment.

From my position just behind Michael, I could almost feel the steam start to rise off his neck. Why couldn't the woman see his rage? It was absolutely clear there was no way he was going to allow this irritating little bureaucrat to keep him from bringing his entire party into the Captain's Club. We had a full two hours before our flight left.

Once again, I tried to communicate the situation telepathically. *Girl, look at me. LOOK AT ME! Can't you see this guy is used to people quaking at the mere mention of his name? There's no way he is going to wait with his wife, parents, children, and friends with the riffraff at the gate! And now you've pissed him off, and the waiting is beside the point. You're messing with his ego. Save yourself!*

Without saying another word to the woman, Michael turned to us. "Take the kids and go sit over there," he ordered. "I'll be right back." With that, he disappeared through the door. By the time he had returned ten minutes later, the woman behind the desk had already been plucked from the room by a large man in a business suit and replaced by another woman wearing a big smile. Upon Michael's return, she personally ushered us into the elaborately decorated club and offered us lunch.

Michael may have won, but the rest of us certainly hadn't. It was beneath his dignity to use his sophisticated negotiation skills on such a nobody. His lips were tight and his upper body even stiffer than usual. I got the distinct impression that anyone who even dared to breathe too loudly around him would get a stinging tongue-lashing of their own. No, my boss was far from happy, and when Michael ain't happy, ain't nobody gonna be happy. I carefully avoided looking in his direction.

The two hours passed excruciatingly slowly.

Finally it was time to board the aircraft. And what an aircraft it was. Usually when we flew we took corporate jets—fancy but definitely cozy and compact. You could have put six of those on each wing of this plane.

I had a hard time comprehending such massive bulk. We had first-class tickets, obviously, so we boarded first. Good thing they started early because it took fifteen minutes for the entire group to get into the cabin. Between all of us, we took up a good portion of the first-class seats. The tickets alone must have cost almost $20,000. As we all jockeyed for position, the flight attendants helped us stow the carry-ons and find our seats, and I could see the faces of the aristocracy already ensconced in their rows giving us looks of combined disgust and fear. I knew what they were thinking: *How could anyone be so rude as to bring that many children, and so young, into first class? I paid a lot of money to sit here, and I'll be damned if I'm going to put up with a bunch of screaming brats.*

The airline billed this as a six-hour flight, and several of the children, including ten-month-old Brandon, were already either crying or fighting. The poor couple seated just behind us was settling down for their first flight as man and wife. What could they possibly think about the equivalent of a Chuck E. Cheese birthday party invading their honeymoon bliss? They were probably horrified enough to put off having their own kids.

I tried to avoid eye contact with them.

I did have plenty of distractions. First class alone stretched for two stories, connected by a large circular staircase that led to a lounge for first-class passengers. Well, not that I ever saw it, but that's what Grandpa Ovitz reported to me. It was like flying in a house; everybody had their own wing. Right after we got on, Michael, Judy, Ron, Cyndi, and all the rest of the adults dashed upstairs and left me with the various kids. When and how it had been decided that I would graciously govern all eight children, I didn't know. Nobody told me, that's for sure.

It could've been much worse. Years later I would hear about how one actress with two young children made her nanny take the kids on the twelve-hour flight to visit her parents in their native country. Somehow, the actress's busy work schedule always made it conveniently *impossible* to get tickets on the same flight as her toddlers. At least I wasn't flying *alone* with my charges. After all, the adults were just upstairs.

The other occupants and the flight attendants all eyed me accusingly, the glares suddenly much more menacing. I knew they were thinking:

*What gall to bring eight young children on board and be insufficiently pre-pared to amuse them for the duration.* Just who did I think I was?

Who was I?

I was the one changing diapers on the edge of the seat; the one wedg-ing herself into the bathroom with a preschooler. The one ducking fly-ing peanuts and consoling three little charges as they cried or screamed when the air pressure hurt their eardrums. The one needing the flexibil-ity of an Olympic gymnast to pull down the carry-ons in an attempt to find a replacement for root-beer-soaked shorts.

All of Ron and Cyndi's girls were very sweet and tried to help out, but this was ridiculous. I sent up a mayday by way of the flight atten-dant heading to the lounge. Evidently, the adults regarded this with some amusement, because Judy soon appeared at my side, laughing. "For goodness sakes, Suzy, what are you doing with these kids? Why didn't you come up and let us know you couldn't handle it?"

*Maybe because I knew you'd make a statement just like that one, for everyone in first class to hear. Maybe because I knew you'd roll your eyes, too, just so I'm sure to see how incompetent you think I am. Maybe because I wanted to avoid this humiliating scene we're having right now.*

Such was a glamorous day in the life of a Hollywood nanny.

I earn very good money, and I can have as much support as I need. But I'm not going to be a mother who uses a nanny to do all the hard work while I have fun.

—Angelina Jolie

# hotel california

"Sepple-veedah," I tried to sound out the word. My inflection was on the "veedah." Such an odd-looking name. "That's where our hotel is, on Sepple-veedah Boulevard," I told my mother during the plane ride. It was all so exciting. In just one short hour, she and I would be landing in Los Angeles. Home to Hollywood, Disneyland, and Tom Cruise! This would be my first visit to California. I grew up in a town that prided itself on being quite familiar with the movie industry: Cottage Grove, Oregon. Well, kind of familiar. Our claim to fame was that *Animal House* had been filmed there. Okay, not exactly Hollywood's rival. So you can see why I was nearly bursting out of the confines of my cramped economy-class seat.

The first disappointment was our hotel room on Snapple-whatever Boulevard. It was, to be kind, one step below a Motel 6. When the nanny placement agency had said they would find a reasonably priced hotel in the area, I didn't expect one you could rent by the hour.

We had a view, of a congested, dirty, and turbulent street somewhere in Los Angeles. By now—thanks to our cab driver, who wasted no time correcting my pronunciation in his own foreign accent—I learned it was Se-PUL-veda Boulevard. Either way you pronounced it, it was an ugly street in an ugly town. This was not the Los Angeles I had pictured. I couldn't imagine any movie stars living within a hundred miles. The street was lined with telephone poles, a morass of wires running in every direction. The exhaust from thousands of passing cars filtered into our room, and horns honked and sirens wailed throughout the night.

Everything seemed so flat and brown. I craned my neck out of the only window in the room, scanning above the rooftops of dingy discount liquor stores, laundromats, and porn shops to search for the Hollywood sign (how was I to know that we weren't even remotely close?). Not that I could have seen it, anyway, with the curtain of smog that hugged our windowsill, fighting the fumes from the street for entry. Cottage Grove didn't have much of a problem with smog, which I later discovered was a combination of smoke and fog. Based on the odor that pinched my nose and the sting that made my eyes water, there couldn't have been much fog in the formula.

My mother mostly kept quiet. She couldn't have missed my monumental disappointment, but she had always been good at making the best of even the worst situations. Of course, even she had limits. "Oh my, this motel is pretty shady," she trilled, inspecting the coin-operated, make-the-bed-vibrate thing attached to the headboard.

We hadn't even finished unpacking (well, as much as we dared) when the phone rang. It was three in the afternoon on a Thursday, and the nanny placement agency had my very first appointment "penciled in." Could I make it Friday morning? They'd "ink me in." The interview was in Hollywood. Maybe I'd even be able to see the sign. If it wasn't too smoggy.

I jumped up on the vibrating bed. "Hollywood, here I come!" I yelled, bouncing up and down wildly.

During my schooling at the Northwest Nannies Institute (NNI) in Portland, I had learned that nanny jobs came in two main varieties: live-out or live-in. In the live-out situation, you work for a couple during business hours, essentially nine to ten hours a day. These people want consistent care and want to avoid taking their children to a day-care center. Usually, both parents work outside the home, although you might get a stay-at-home mom who could afford a second pair of hands.

I was looking for a live-in job. Why? For one, I knew paying for housing in LA would eat up my whole paycheck. And two, odds were that families who had live-in help would also employ an official housekeeper. This was a must for me, based on the horror stories I'd heard. Some nannies had become a Jill of all trades, assuming the duties of maid, cook, and personal assistant. They were responsible for doing everything from buying the wife's underwear to booking the mistress's spa reservations.

Carolyn, one of my instructors at NNI, had assured me that job satisfaction depended upon a good match. So I dreamed up my ideal situation. I wanted a live-in family in Southern California with at least two children, preferably three, and I wanted one of them to be a newborn because I loved caring for infants. Religion and ethnic background didn't matter much. My plan was to be on duty during the day and available for extra duty over weekends and evenings. I would have two days off a week, and when the parents were home, I would be free to come and go.

Rookie.

What I couldn't have known was that many wealthy folks are *never* without hired help for their kids. They arrange their lives so there is a paid caregiver available to them twenty-four hours a day, seven days a week. It had simply never occurred to me that there were people who really *didn't* want to spend as much time as possible with their children. That there were parents who did not hurry home after work so they could tuck Janie and Jack into bed. That there were, in fact, plenty of little Janies and Jacks in LA whose first words were uttered in Spanish, because they spent virtually all of their time with the Hispanic staff. "Isn't that cute—he's bilingual!" the mothers would brag to one another at charity events.

I would soon find out that LA is one big ladder. Nannies are the people who sit on the bottom rung, entertaining the kids, while the parents climb.

That night, after dinner at the International House of Pancakes, I spent two hours trying to decide what to wear for my interview the next morning. As it was late December, and I had come from the rain capital of the world, my suitcase held only clothing that would be appropriate for winter in Oregon. Mostly black, thick, and warm. And Friday was forecast to be one of the decade's hottest December days in Southern California. I was guaranteed to sweat rivers in my heavy black dress. But who cared about my discomfort—I feared I would look like a moron. Not that I had many options. I comforted myself with the thought that my black dress looked professional: It had clean simple lines, no distracting patterns, and an appropriate hemline. I decided to top it off with small gold hoop earrings and equally conservative black shoes with two-inch heels.

I didn't realize until much later how ridiculous I must have looked. *I don't fit in here!* my wardrobe shrieked. It only took one glance at my sandalfoot nylons to see that.

Finding an address in Los Angeles was more difficult than fishing the letter *Z* out of a bowl of Campbell's alphabet soup. For one thing, everything was in Spanish. For another, you couldn't tell if you were actually in Los Angeles, Studio City, Hollywood, or half a dozen other cities. Everything ran together, and unlike Cottage Grove, there were no signs that read YOU ARE ENTERING THE COVERED BRIDGE CAPITAL OF AMERICA, POPULATION 7,143. To make matters worse, street names were duplicated in every city. So, you might have been on Sepulveda in Westchester, or you might have been on Sepulveda in Van Nuys, which was in the Valley (what did that mean?) and technically part of LA.

Another problem was the division of cities into their eastern, western, northern, and southern parts. There was a North Hollywood, a West Hollywood, and just plain Hollywood. Where was the sign? Why no East Hollywood to round out the compass points? But more important, where was the Hollywood where all the stars lived? Where was Tom Cruise's house? No one told me that only a small number of famous people actually live in Hollywood. The real celebrity action is in Beverly Hills, Bel Air, or Malibu. And why didn't anyone mention that, besides Paramount Studios on Melrose Avenue, not much moviemaking actually takes place in Hollywood, either?

The placement agency did inform me that my first interview was with one of the top ten chefs in LA. Apparently his restaurant was so popular that it took three months to get a table. I didn't recognize his name. My mom steered the rental car high into the Hollywood Hills, on narrow, twisting old canyon roads. There were many lovely and stately homes in that area; some were beautifully restored to their original 1920s architecture. The address I'd been given matched a small but elegant Mediterranean-style house with a deep green front lawn. I hadn't been in California long enough yet to realize that this unassuming home cost as much as a mansion on ten acres (with a swimming pool and tennis courts) would cost in Oregon.

Before going up to the front door, I looked at my mother and said, "Wish me luck. How do I look?"

"Honey, just beautiful," she said proudly. "Don't be nervous. I know you'll be able to explain to the family how much you love taking care of children."

She was right. I wasn't there to interview as a deep-space physicist; I was there as a prospective *nanny*. I loved kids. And I knew how to take care of them. I even had a certificate to prove it.

A tall woman, about thirty-five and quite attractive, answered the door. She appeared to be about seven months pregnant. She introduced herself and showed me into the immaculate living room. The minute I sat down, a rat dog (the small, Chihuahua-esque kind that yip nonstop) came bounding into the room, yapping. I've never really been a dog person, and the little fleabags always seem to know it. Before I could say anything, the rodent ran over and fastened her small but powerful jaws around my ankle as if I were a fresh ham bone. Her teeth tore through my stockings and punctured my skin.

I winced and grabbed the little devil by the neck. Would strangling her cost me the job?

"Oh, Mimi, leave the poor girl alone," the woman said languidly. Why was she just sitting there, motionless? Her dog's teeth were embedded in my leg!

I squeezed harder on the pooch's neck. She finally let go, and I kind of flung her backward, head over heels onto the carpet.

This, of course, caused convulsions of near-epileptic proportions in her owner.

She jumped up, grabbed the little rat, and hugged it so close to her chest I thought she would suffocate the thing.

This was clearly not the job for me. I had been there a scant three minutes, but I actually stood to leave.

Suddenly the woman became apologetic. "I'm so sorry. Mimi can get a little aggressive with strangers."

As the dog trotted toward me again, she patted her hand at the air as if making a feeble effort to shoo it away.

"Are you all right?" she said in a half-sincere way. Was she talking to the dog or to me?

"Um, yes, I'm fine. There's only a little bit of blood. I'll be okay," I offered, blotting the wound with a Kleenex I found in my purse. But it hurt. A lot. I bit my lip. The rodent snarled incessantly.

"My husband is Jacques LaRivière. I'm sure you've heard of him," she began, rolling her eyes and looking heavenward. "He's one of the top ten chefs in Los Angeles."

*Yeah, sure, of course. Who hasn't heard of Jacques?* I feigned a knowing nod. It wouldn't have mattered what culinary celebrity she was married to; at the time, I didn't even know who Wolfgang Puck was. I did know this top-ten stuff sounded a bit dubious. I doubted the contest was anything like our annual chili cook-off, where blue ribbons were awarded by the Cottage Grove mayor after he tasted everyone's homemade entries.

"As you can see"—she patted her stomach lovingly—"I'm expecting, so I will need you to take care of little Dominic, our three-year-old. I'm due in March, so of course then I will also expect you to handle Zachary."

Handle? Like a prize Pomeranian?

"And of course I will need you to do the cooking as well." Probably seeing the look of shock on my face, she added, "Don't worry about pleasing my husband. He's never satisfied with any meal he ever eats."

She wanted *me* to cook for one of the foremost chefs in Los Angeles? This woman must be out of her hormone-saturated mind. I couldn't figure out what would possess her to think that a teenager could please one of the most discriminating palates in all of LA. Did she know that my previous cooking experience mostly consisted of making bologna boats?

I thought it best to sidestep that whole cooking topic, feebly starting to talk about my love for kids. Mrs. LaRivière seemed to be dutifully recording my comments, and possibly even her own observations, on a notepad. Or maybe she was composing a letter to her doggie psychiatrist about Mimi's recent trauma. I couldn't tell.

When she was through, she stood up as the dog continued to jump and yip. "Can you let yourself out?" she said, looking at her watch. "I must make a phone call. I didn't realize how late it was."

"Yes, Mrs. LaRivière, of course," I answered.

The house wasn't particularly large. The living area we had been sitting in was just down the hall from the front door. I gracefully got up to make my exit, the dog still nipping at my heels. I kicked at her in a mildly threatening manner.

By this time, it was noon and stifling outside. As I was about to close the door behind me, the little ankle-biter came bounding out across the front lawn, darting like an escaped convict who hadn't seen the light of day in forty years. Oh, great. Mrs. Famous Chef was undoubtedly engrossed in her phone conversation. What if the dog got away, never to be found again? What if she threw her skittering little self in front of an approaching car? Mrs. LaRivière would be beside herself with grief and would have her famous husband roast my head slowly over hot coals. I would *never* get a job in this town.

My ever-resourceful mother, seeing the panic on my face and immediately sensing the gravity of the situation, jumped out of the car and joined me in the chase. But sensible heels weren't meant for sprinting, and it took us quite a while to catch up with the four-legged inmate and herd her, in a manner of speaking, back down the street.

As I began to scurry across the lawn, stooping, cajoling, and shooing at the dog, Mrs. LaRivière ran out the front door, screaming in a high, frantic voice, "Mimi! Mimi! Where is my Mimi?" Her arms were whirling and flailing in the air, and her head spun around. I was sure she was going to go into premature labor on her porch right then and there.

Thank God that upon seeing the woman, the dog immediately charged back into the house. As Mrs. LaRivière glared at me, about to say something, the automatic sprinklers burst to life. The yard was quite large, and when I swiveled to look at the rental car parked nearly fifty feet away, I knew that not even a bolt to the street would save us from getting drenched. I turned, just as the powerful jets soaked me from head to toe, and calmly put my arm around my mother's shoulder. We held our heads high all the way to the car.

I had two more interviews that day. A quick blow-dry of my hair and a change of winter wear left us just enough time to make the next one. We headed off to Studio City. (Was it actually a city? Or just part of LA? Who was in charge of this naming thing?) I was to meet with a wealthy businessman and his wife. The agency hadn't told me what his business was; I just knew that the husband was a prominent executive, that the wife's family came from famous money, and that they had one child. As we parked in the driveway, I was surprised at the size of the house. The information sheet I had on the family referred to it as a bungalow, and the agency had specified that this was a live-in position. But it couldn't have been bigger than a double-wide trailer.

As I rang the doorbell, I could hear a woman yelling from inside. "Jonathan, stop jumping on the couch. Do you hear me? *Stop jumping on the couch!*"

The door quickly opened to reveal a haggard-looking woman in her early thirties. "Hello, I'm Julie Foshay. Won't you come in?" she said as the boy continued to bob up and down behind her. Jonathan looked about four. He was using the sofa as a trampoline, bouncing and yelling incoherently, oblivious to his mother.

"My, what a . . . uh . . . cozy home you have, Mrs. Foshay." I wanted to start out with a compliment.

"Jonathan"—she turned to yell at the boy again—"I told you to stop jumping on the couch." I followed her into a dining room just off the living area that was the size of a walk-in closet. We sat.

"So, Susan—it is Susan, isn't it?" she asked, but didn't wait for me to answer. "Tell me all about yourself." I didn't bother to correct her about my name. Still, I told her about NNI, how I'd scored the highest of my class on my certification tests, how I'd always loved kids, how I'd babysat for many families while growing up but that I wanted to live in a larger city, yada yada, yada, expecting her to break in at any moment when she'd had enough. But she just kept staring at me, smiling. Every so often she would yell out to Jonathan again, who by now had been bouncing nonstop for nearly twenty minutes.

When she finally did interrupt me, her first question was, "How much?"

I couldn't figure out why the agency wouldn't have told her the going rate for a nanny, but oh well. "Since I'm going to be a live-in nanny, I would like to make two hundred and fifty dollars a week," I said with as much confidence as I could muster.

She seemed stunned by this figure. "Oh no, we can't afford that! We're already mortgaged to the hilt with our recent remodel. Besides, I'm not sure where I would put you." As if I were going to be the third car and they only had a two-car garage.

Little Jonathan continued to wail like a banshee and do his jumping jacks. I wanted to wail, too. *Then why are you interviewing me? Why did you call the agency asking for a live-in nanny, for God's sake?*

On my way out the door, I took a peek at the stack of library books Jumpin' Johnny had knocked off the end table:

*The Hyperactive Child: A Handbook for Parents*

*Living with Our Hyperactive Children*

*The Myth of the ADD Child*

*Nature's Ritalin*

Okay.

I told the agency that this was definitely not the family for me—or for any other live-in nanny unless they planned to bring their own RV with them to work each day. I won't bore you with the details of my third and final interview that day. Let's just say, "toddler twins, a pregnant mother, lots of housework, bedroom shared with a parakeet, and a salary that was below minimum wage" and move on. I would later hear some true stories that made that sound like a luxury vacation. Many nannies had no time off, and did all the cooking, cleaning, childcare, laundry, shopping, gardening, message-taking, and errand-running for far less money than that. But then I still had stars in my eyes.

Zero-for-three. Needless to say, I didn't take the job as handler and chef, though it was offered to me, surprisingly enough. It had been quite a day in la-la land. As I lay in bed with traffic rushing by, horns honking, and people shouting, I could only hope that one of my two interviews the next day might bring something a little more . . . glamorous. After all, wasn't I in Hollywood? Was it all just makeup and camera angles?

So I feel like I can be a good role model as a mother because I love being a mom and I have great advice for everybody when it comes to mothering.

—Pamela Anderson

# the king and I

Not being a follower of the life and loves of Hugh Hefner, I was unacquainted with the claim to fame of Barbi Benton, the name the nanny agency gave me when they called bright and early the next morning. But with a name like Barbi, I could guess what she looked like.

"Oh yes. Yes, of course. You are the one from Oregon," said the house manager, Ms. Chambers, when I called. "When would you like to come up?"

"I'm available today, if that's all right."

"Good. How about elevenish."

"Uh . . . elevenish would be great," I replied. "Could I please have your address?"

"Just come to the block of Welby in Pasadena, near the Rose Bowl," Ms. Chambers said.

Okay, but what was the address? It sounded like she lived in a shopping center. The block of Welby. I didn't get it.

"Uh, Ms. Chambers, could you give me the street number? Is it Welby Street?"

"Yes. It's the block of Welby," she replied, sounding a little agitated. I didn't want to push it. I wasn't worried; I'd figure it out.

As we wheeled through the streets of Pasadena, it all began to make sense. The Barbi dollhouse took up an entire city block. There was no need for a number because there were *no other homes*. An ornate wrought-iron fence nearly fifteen feet tall surrounded the vast estate, with an entry gate straight out of Buckingham Palace. I half-expected to see a fur-hatted guard standing in the small brick house near the gate, but there was only an intercom. When I pushed the button, a woman's voice said, "Hello. Who's there?"

Entry granted. The heavy gates creaked and magically opened. The mansion in front of me was larger than any building in Cottage Grove, by far—bigger even than the Rainbow Motel. I hoped I wouldn't get lost. A uniformed maid ushered me through a lovely rose garden, past the house, and up the stairs of a small outbuilding—Ms. Benton's husband's office, as it turned out. Ms. Chambers was waiting. Only if she thought I had potential would I meet the family.

Before the interview began, we were interrupted by a pinch-faced, sack-bosomed woman with teeth like rows of Chiclets. She was probably sixty-five years old, her face seamed with wrinkles like an old soccer ball. She walked into the office, complaining under her breath about the swelling in her ankles. Without acknowledging me, she retrieved a white envelope from Ms. Chambers and then hobbled out. Ms. Chambers, noticing the confused look on my face, informed me that she was the current nanny and would be leaving in a couple of weeks.

"You're attractive. That will bother her," Ms. Chambers began. So Barbi was indeed a doll. I wondered what *Mr.* Benton looked like. Ms. Chambers sat looking at some papers on the desk in front of her. I assumed she was waiting for me to respond.

I paused a moment, then said, "Thank you. I hope that won't be a problem." If I lived here, I could ugly myself up a little. Maybe not wear any makeup; just wash my hair once a week. I guessed she hadn't had to cover this part of the interview process with the current Grandma Moses.

After I had given this woman the short version of the story I'd told Mrs. Foshay the day before, she began to rattle off a litany of rules and quirks that I would have to deal with. Standard-issue stuff. Except it wasn't.

For one, there was the refrigerator. It had a lock on it. All the goodies that Barbi and Ken did not have the willpower to resist were locked safely inside the colossal chrome Sub-Zero.

"Who has the key?" I inquired. Two intelligent adults kept their own food in solitary confinement?

"The chef does," she explained helpfully. "The only time he opens it is to prepare their meals. They are both very strict about their diet."

"Does she ever beg the staff to open it in the middle of the night?" I had to know.

The question got me a stern dip of her eyebrows.

"Of course not. What kind of people do you think they are?"

The kind of people WHO LOCK THEIR REFRIGERATOR! Why not just stock up on lettuce and bottled water and forget about security?

"Now, back to the issue of your looks," she continued. "You will, of course, be required to wear a uniform. Actually, it's quite lovely," she added, as if forestalling my protest that I would not be caught dead in a nanny habit. She pulled out a dress that looked like it belonged to Mary Poppins and displayed it to me proudly. Apparently, every member of the household was expected to work in costume.

With that out of the way, she proceeded to tell me about the family. I would potentially be caring for one baby boy, their first child. "She will rely on you a great deal," Ms. Chambers said delicately. "The month after Barbi had the baby, she and her husband left for a long vacation. You've had a lot of experience with infants, I'm sure?" I was still digesting the news of the parents' sabbatical when I heard a man's voice over the intercom. "I am done with my coffee," he announced abruptly. Ms. Chambers immediately buzzed the staff to remove the offending coffee cup. She rang into several rooms of the mansion, broadcasting the urgent situation until she found someone to take care of it.

*A little more background on this family would have been helpful.*

"Now, when you travel with the family in the convertible Rolls-Royce, you will always ride in the front seat with the driver and be in uniform. It is very important to them that when they are out for a drive, it is clear to onlookers that you are *the help*. Are there any questions so far?" she asked.

"Not yet."

"Good. By the way, how is your health?" she asked.

*What?* I was not even nineteen years old, for God's sake. How bad off could I be? Did she want to know about my menstrual cramps once a month and the fact that I dislocated my knee trying out for the track team in the eighth grade? The current nanny looked like she just emerged from an all-night bingo parlor with her portable oxygen in tow, and she managed to work here. How hard could it be?

We wrapped up the interview, and I was politely escorted out past the huge mansion. I never did see the inside, or Barbi or Ken for that matter. Clearly I was not going to be Skipper.

My second interview that day was with "a family in the entertainment industry." The Ovitzes. I didn't have a clue who Michael Ovitz was. I was actually a little disappointed when I didn't recognize the name—I'd imagined someone like John Travolta. The nanny placement agency told me only his last name and that he was president of a big talent agency. I just heard a bunch of initials.

Had I known that Creative Artists Agency (CAA) represented nearly every major Hollywood actor and actress I'd ever heard of, I would have had more time to get nervous before I arrived at his office. Instead, it all hit me at once. I stared in transfixed awe at the receptionists, who, all blasé as you please, confidently threw around some of the biggest names in entertainment. Cher. Sally Field. Michael Jackson. The two women behind the desk mesmerized me. Both answered a never-ending stream of calls from the ridiculously famous while simultaneously sign-ing for packages and greeting guests. Both of them were extremely pretty, poised, and professional. They were not wearing winter-weight dark dresses.

My first interview in this intimidating office was with Mrs. Ovitz. An assistant ushered me into a dramatic conference room with floor-to-ceiling glass windows where a woman sat quietly at a marble table. I was stunned at how blond and beautiful she was. She wore a butter-colored silk outfit and diamond stud earrings the size of small grapes. Her style and demeanor seemed that of a queen.

"Hello, I'm Judy Ovitz. It's nice to meet you," she said, smiling warmly and extending her hand to welcome me.

I gave my standard speech, and she told me about their three children. If I made the cut, I would next meet Mr. Ovitz. Michael was clearly the king, though I wasn't sure of what. But I did know who all the movie stars were.

I must have made it through the first round, because after a brief meeting with the CAA human resources manager, I was back watching those receptionists deftly field calls from Academy Award–winning actors. A beautiful woman dressed in three different shades of beige appeared in front of me and said, "Ms. Hansen, please step this way. Mr. Ovitz will see you now."

Just like the receptionists and everyone else in the office, the assistant was dressed in an expensive designer outfit. I, on the other hand, stood up in my blue dress and white patent leather pumps, humiliated that I was violating the Labor Day white shoe rule by more than three months. My mom and I had realized in the motel that I looked quite tacky, but it was this or the sprinkler-ruined black dress. Looking down at my fashion faux pas whites, I became even more nervous. I couldn't have felt more out of place if I'd been wearing athletic socks and Birkenstocks. I felt all the blood drain out of my face and into my hopelessly dowdy feet. The room began to turn slowly, then more quickly, in circles. Grabbing the backs of the chairs and then the receptionists' counter, I steadied myself and focused on not fainting.

We walked down the busy corridor, people bustling by in both directions. At the end of the hallway, I could see into a spacious office where an attractive man was seated behind a desk the size of two formal dining tables. He wore a telephone headset and reclined back at an angle that must have strained the limits of his ergonomically correct leather chair. He had short, light brown hair, bright eyes, and a white shirt that was meticulously pressed and starched. His conservative plum-colored tie matched the colors in a painting on the wall behind him.

My escort paused silently in the doorway, and I stood motionless. As the man said good-bye to his caller, he pulled the headset off and gave me a warm smile. In a very officious manner befitting the introduction of a visiting diplomat, the woman announced: "Mr. Ovitz, this is Ms. Hansen to see you. Your ten-twenty. She has already interviewed with Judy."

On the one hand, I was honored to receive such an introduction. On the other hand, how jam-packed was this guy's calendar? Did he have a ten-twenty-five?

"I need some uninterrupted time here," he told my escort. "I don't want to take any calls for fifteen minutes." She nodded and turned away, and I stepped into the inner sanctum.

The man gestured to a seating arrangement that was like one you might find in an issue of *Architectural Digest*—a leather couch and several low-slung chairs arranged around a modern coffee table at the other end of his huge office. An immense contemporary painting dominated the wall. I had never been in a place quite so intimidating, with perhaps the exception of the principal's office when I was grilled over my possible involvement in some prom-night shenanigans. I was petrified and sat silent and wide-eyed. Mr. Ovitz laughed and said, "You look scared to death, white as chalk. Just relax."

*Right. Every one of your employees whom I have spoken with says that you're the "most powerful man in Hollywood." It's just a wee bit intimidating.*

For thirty minutes he asked questions in the verbal equivalent of italics and exclamation marks. He did not seem much interested in my answers. My heart sank when he asked about my driving record and my ability to drive in the snow (apparently, the family frequently found itself in Aspen). For now let's just say that driving is not my strong suit. I stumbled a bit over that answer, but he didn't seem to care that my reply was not what you would want to hear from a prospective employee, especially one who would be entrusted with the safe transport of your precious children. He seemed most interested in his next question. We talked for several minutes about nanny school, as he had never heard of such a thing. He seemed to find the whole idea amusing. "What exactly do they teach you in nanny school?" he asked, becoming even more amused when I attempted to answer him. Once more I fumbled for words while he watched, grinning slightly. Later I came to believe that Michael was most comfortable when others were not. He seemed to enjoy seeing people crumble into nervous wrecks in his presence. So my terror during the interview must have just made his day.

Of course, when he invited me for a follow-up interview at his home, he made mine.

I would soon learn that CAA was one of the largest talent agencies in Hollywood. I didn't really know what agents did, but I quickly discovered that they negotiated with the studios in exchange for a percentage of their clients' earnings. As I had glimpsed at the office, their clients were the most well-known actors, directors, screenwriters, musicians, and authors in the industry. Martin Scorsese. Demi Moore. Julia Roberts. It was widely known that CAA had enough pull to get clients the most lucrative contracts.

Cofounder and president of the agency, Michael had the most pull of all. He had invented an entirely new kind of agency, one that relied on packaging—putting together stars, writers, and directors into one bundle and offering it to a studio as a whole take-it-or-leave-it proposition. He had enough leverage that most studios were forced to take it.

He was also credited with pioneering a new way of doing business. Poaching, or stealing other agencies' clients, had been rare before he came upon the scene, but Michael made it commonplace. (Legend has it that Michael had lured Dustin Hoffman over to CAA by offering to work for free.) He and his black-suited cohorts, who worked tirelessly and tended to be business school graduates and lawyers, were both dedicated to their clients and quite ruthless in getting what they wanted. I would later hear that one of his prized clients, screenwriter Joe Eszterhas—who earned millions for screenplays like *Flashdance* and *Basic Instinct*—claimed that when he was moving to a rival agency (ICM), Michael told him, "You're not going anywhere. You're not leaving this agency. If you do, my foot soldiers who go up and down Wilshire Boulevard each day will blow your brains out."

Probably best that I didn't know about his legendary vindictiveness when I was considering moving into his home.

When I pulled up to the curb near the Ovitz driveway, I saw four luxury vehicles sitting alongside a very exotic-looking black sports car. A man walked out of the house, who I'd later learn was Ron Meyer, Michael's partner at CAA. He would eventually run Universal Pictures.

He waved from the entryway, saying, "I'll be at Stallone's house if Michael needs me."

*Sylvester?* And I might be working here?

My hand began to shake as I reached for the intercom next to the twelve-foot-high wrought-iron fence. It hit me that I might actually live in a residence where you had to ask permission to enter—a far cry from even the most expensive home in our small logging community. No one there had intercoms or gates. Come to think of it, most people in my town never even locked their back doors.

The house, situated on nearly an acre of land, was a two-story Southern Colonial made of brick and wood, with three majestic white columns across the front and two massive black lacquer front doors with shiny brass handles. In the brick-inlaid driveway a man busily washed a pristine SUV; three other cars were lined up behind it. I would soon see this as routine: the same man came every Saturday morning and performed a full detail on all the family's vehicles.

Judy greeted me at the side door. She seemed friendly but a bit aloof. She was dressed in a coordinated casual outfit and looked even more perfect than she had before, if that was possible.

"Technically, this is our side front door," she told me as we walked into a family room with an informal dining area. Then she led me to the main entry with the tall black doors and said, "This is our *main* front door."

*Huh?* I'd been inside the home for all of two minutes and was already confused.

Judy glanced back and gestured for me to follow her. "Come on. I'll show you around."

Passing from the kitchen through the formal dining room toward the living room, I stopped dead in my tracks. *My God, my mother would die if she saw this.* The photos hanging behind the elaborate wet bar looked like a spread in *People* magazine. Barbra Streisand, posing with Michael. There was Michael with Michael Caine, Michael and Judy with Tom Hanks, and Michael with Jane Fonda on the set of a movie. My mouth hung open as if I was a tourist.

I remembered that the personnel director at CAA had warned me that celebrities, such as Paul Newman, came over to the house frequently. She had asked me if I thought I could maintain my composure, and I had assured her I could. I closed my mouth. I vowed to stay silent, almost stoic, during my tour. I hoped I was projecting casually, *I, too, live in a home where it is commonplace for Charlie Sheen to stop by for dinner.*

"Susan, you can follow me this way," she said, her voice snapping me back into the moment.

"Um, Mrs. Ovitz," I said, gently touching her arm, "uh, it's Suzy."

So much for trying to be mature and use my full name, Suzanne. I thought I would be taken more seriously if my name didn't conjure up the image of a ditzy cheerleader, but at least Suzy was *my actual name.*

As I followed her, I noticed that there was art on practically every wall. Perhaps not in the bathrooms or in the kitchen, but we moved so fast it was hard to tell. I had never seen so much art. She told me that there was even a gallery on the second floor above the family room. I didn't recognize any of the artists, except one. It looked like a real Picasso.

The country bumpkin inside me was screaming, *I have never been in a house like this!* My friends lived in homes with fake fur covering the toilet seats and blue water in the toilet bowl. A nice kitchen boasted plenty of frozen pizzas, Kool-Aid, and Cheetos. The only art collection I had seen up to that point in my life belonged to my friend Missy's dad. His John Wayne memorabilia filled their entire family room. I think his spittoon even had the Duke's picture on it.

"As you can probably see, Michael is one of the foremost art collectors in the country," Judy said, picking up one of the small animal ceramics and holding it up to the light. "Michael got this in Africa. Have you ever been on a safari, Suzy?"

*Oh, sure. Two of my friends can't even get cable television because their houses are on gravel roads too far away from the main highway. But we frequently jet off to the African savannah.*

It wasn't until much later that I would see this question as an early warning sign I hadn't heeded. It was the first evidence that the wealthy and famous, at least this wealthy and famous, didn't have a clue about how the rest of the world lives.

As the guided tour continued, we passed a young Hispanic woman in a starched white uniform. She and I exchanged smiles, but there was no introduction. Judy rattled off the schedules of the entire staff and added that I would have Saturdays and Sundays off. How many people did it take to manage this house? I'd seen at least six so far.

She took me upstairs to show me the room I'd be staying in. Located between the children's rooms, it was spacious and neat, with twin beds covered in matching peach-colored bedspreads. The cream-colored carpet had suffered quite a bit of wear and tear from live-in employees, but the room had its own TV. Even better, its own bath! At home, my two sisters and I had shared one bathroom. This was heaven.

In the midst of my glee, Judy asked me to come back to the living room for a talk. She began asking questions about my family and, in particular, about my mother, since Judy knew she had flown into town with me.

Then she insisted upon meeting my mother.

I stared at her, perplexed. Was that necessary? I was almost nineteen years old. I was grown-up enough to pick a job on my own. Did she want to gauge me better by viewing my mom? I felt a little like a foal that was being purchased—and the buyer wanted to check the teeth of the mare.

After a stilted exchange in which I explained that I *wasn't* going to get my mommy and bring her back for this job interview, she ushered me into the room of Brandon, her newborn baby. As we walked in, Michael was telling his son Joshua to leave the baby alone. Apparently, the six-year-old was trying to pick his baby brother up out of the crib. Next to Michael stood three-year-old Amanda. These children could have modeled on magazine covers. They were gorgeous, just like their mother. Josh was very blond, almost a towhead, and Amanda had long beautiful hair, a perfect natural mix of blond and brown—the color women all over LA paid hundreds of dollars trying to duplicate.

"Joshua, I'm not going to tell you again," Mr. Ovitz said. "Put the baby down and meet Suzy." Joshua turned, shot me a disinterested look, and once again started to reach into the crib.

"Amanda, this is Suzy," Judy said. "We think she's going to be your new nanny." *She's still thinking about it?* I guessed my final test was to win the approval of the kids.

"Hi, Amanda," I offered. She smiled shyly as she hid halfway behind her mother. "Hello, Amanda," I said again, peeking around Judy. "It's very nice to meet you."

Okay, on a scale of one to ten, I just scored a 5.5. Maybe. My last chance would be with the baby. I walked up to the crib.

He was the most adorable human being I'd ever seen. Despite the fact that his brother had been antagonizing him, he was attempting a grin and was gurgling happily. I reached down, picked him up, and cradled him in my arms. He fit perfectly. Bliss.

This was clearly my ideal family; a newborn baby to care for, a busy household with three children, and a full-time housekeeper.

"He's absolutely adorable," I said as I turned and faced Joshua. "Here, Joshua, sit in the rocking chair. This is how to hold your brother." I gently placed the baby in his arms. "Make sure you always cradle his head like this." I tucked a pillow under the arm that propped up Brandon.

Michael and Judy stood back, watching. They seemed pleased. Finally, Judy said, "Do you have any questions?"

My mind went blank. Blank. Blank.

"How do you feel about spanking?" I finally blurted out. *What did I just say?*

There was an awkward moment of silence, and then Michael said in a loud voice, "Oh yeah, I beat them all regularly." Then he let out a quick laugh.

Oh God. I'd meant to say something like, *It's just that I don't want to work for a family that uses spanking as a punishment. I don't agree with it.*

But I didn't say that. I didn't ask about what discipline strategies they *did* use with the children. If any.

And I certainly didn't ask about a contract, how many hours I would work each day, what I would be responsible for, or how I would be compensated for overtime. I didn't even ask if I would be offered health insurance.

I didn't ask anything.

Looking back, they must have thought I was more than a little naive when that was the only question I could come up with. But it probably wasn't an oversight that they didn't mention a contract, either. I fit the part that they were casting perfectly. I was a trusting, small-town girl whose only concern was for the well-being of their children. Money, working conditions, who cared? After all, when you have servants, it's nice to believe that they work for you mainly out of a desire to devote themselves to your comfort. It removes any pressure for equality or respect.

Michael said they would like to hire me right away. He wanted to know how long I planned on staying with them, and I told them I could commit to two years. They seemed happy with that. Michael told me he didn't like turnover because of the impact on the kids. Their cook had been with them for seven years, and he hoped she would stay forever. I was really glad that he realized how hard it must be on his children to have people come in and out of their lives. I didn't stop to think that there might be a bit more to the story of the cook's tenure. Judy mentioned that their last nanny was a young girl who decided after two months that she just wasn't cut out for the job, but I didn't let that bother me, either.

Michael told me to call his office when I got home, and they would make arrangements for my flight back. What a nice offer. I was so pleased with the position I had found. Going to Northwest Nannies Institute was such a great idea—all of the classes had really assisted me in becoming a "professional."

I had so much to learn.

I don't think many people really have an understanding of what it's like to be a working mother and not have the money to pay for the child care you want. I'm not a role model. I'm a very, very rich woman who has the luxury of endless supplies of help.

—Rosie O'Donnell

## chapter 3
# small town girl

Perhaps I need to back up a bit. Just a year earlier, I'd had no post–high school plans. My entire existence had transpired quite peacefully and uneventfully in Cottage Grove, a town tucked away in a remote corner of Oregon where the highlight of a typical resident's week was bingo at the Elks Lodge with a $250 pot. The best way to picture Cottage Grove is to imagine a cross between Dodge City in the 1800s and Mayberry from the *Andy Griffith Show*. It was a place where almost every young boy dreamed of owning a four-wheel-drive truck with a rifle in the gun rack, and most of the girls hoped for a boyfriend who fit that description. When we finally got our first fast-food restaurant, there was so much excitement that six hundred residents showed up at the school gymnasium to compete for a position that would have them saying, "Would you like to supersize your meal today?"

I didn't want to pursue that line of work, but what to do? Where to go?

Graduation day was looming. Some of my friends had busily applied to various colleges over the past year. I had been at my best friend Kristi's house when she filled out the paperwork for her father's alma mater, Stanford. I had just hoped to God her parents wouldn't ask me where I was going, because I hadn't applied to *any* colleges, much less "the Harvard of the West." Fortunately, they didn't ask me about my plans. I think it was just understood that it was a topic better left untouched, given my pretty much total lack of interest in academics. You might say I had pursued a degree in *social* studies.

My high school experience had, unfortunately, pinnacled with my election as homecoming princess of the sophomore class. My grades were always fine (that wasn't so difficult) and the times I lugged any homework home were few and far between. But keeping up on who was dating whom was my greatest motivation to go to school every morning. I was considered *the* go-to girl for any and all dish at Cottage Grove High. Great fun, but not exactly a college prep course load.

I began to rack my brain for career ideas. Nothing. My guidance counselor, luckily, noticed that I hadn't signed up to take any college entrance exams and handed me an application to a nanny-training program in Portland, the big city, almost 150 miles away. Nanny school sounded like the perfect plan—why hadn't I thought of it? I had been babysitting since the age of nine and had worked for several families for years. I loved being with children. I'd be like Mary Poppins. Northwest Nannies Institute, my counselor explained, had just opened and was one of only a handful of nanny-training schools in the country. I took it as a good omen that it was located so close to me.

Along with the application and a small processing fee, NNI asked for three letters of recommendation, which I easily provided from families for whom I'd been working for half my life. They also requested an essay entitled "Why I Want to Be a Nanny." That was a breeze—suddenly I was bursting with lofty aspirations, eager to provide the privileged toddlers of the world with the most devoted and loving attention. Besides, the tuition was reasonable, and my parents were more than happy to pay for my four months of "higher education."

A fat letter arrived in our family mailbox in April. The envelope bore a rich gold logo embossed in the upper left corner. NNI. I stared at it for a moment. I sounded out the initials in my best upper-class British accent—"ehn, ehn, eye."

"Congratulations," the enclosed letter began. "Your application has been accepted. You have been selected to attend the Northwest Nannies Institute as a fall enrollee."

I breathed a huge sigh of relief. I'd been a bit worried about the criminal background check. No, no felonies, just a dismal driving record, which they were fortunately willing to overlook. My rap sheet included four speeding tickets in the two short years I'd been licensed to drive. Okay, it was actually five citations, but they removed one from my record because I attended an all-day driver's safety course. That had been quite an eye-opener. As the members of my class of multiple offenders introduced themselves, I realized that I was the only student in the room who didn't have a prison record. After class, the teacher reviewed my poor driving history. She said she had never before counseled a teenage girl who had good grades and was on the rally squad. Unlike the other lead-foots there, she told me gravely, my chances for eventual life success were as high as fifty-fifty.

Surely she was kidding, but if she had known about the institute, I knew she'd have rated my chances a lot higher.

Just the thought of attending a school that looked like Harvard or Yale intrigued me. The elite training would certainly launch me into a different life, working for a well-to-do family with adorable children. My ever-positive mom caught my feeling of excitement and put her Cottage Grove spin on it. "Just think, Suzy, you'll probably live in a mansion, just like Pamela Ewing on *Dallas!*" She was sure that my down-to-earth influence would even spare my future employers some of the grief that had so fascinated her during the show's run.

On the last day of school, Kristi and I passed by a large piece of butcher paper posted in the hallway:

## SENIORS

### WHAT ARE YOUR PLANS AFTER GRADUATION?

| | |
|---|---|
| BEN BANGS | Colorado State |
| CRAIG JENKINS | Drink beer all summer, then go to Southern Oregon State College |
| DREW BIRDSEYE | Play drums for a heavy metal band |
| SHAUNNA GRIGGS | Pacific University |
| SCOTT CATES | Go water-skiing |
| ALAN GATES | Drive the boat that Scott is skiing behind |
| TAMI THOMPSON | Move as far away from this town as possible |
| JENNY HECKMAN | Beauty college |
| MISSY CHAMBERS | Work at the Hard Rock Cafe |
| AMY MCCARTY | Follow Ozzy around on tour |
| KRISTI KEMP | University of Oregon (Go Ducks!) |
| SUZY HANSEN | NNI |

NNI. That sounded dignified and respectable. I prayed no one would ask me what the letters stood for. I hoped they would think it was a small college in Northern Nebraska. Or maybe the National Neuropathy Institute? I'm not sure why I cared about what other people thought, since my hometown had a low percentage of college-bound seniors, anyway. I just didn't want my career plans to seem like a joke to my fellow classmates, sophisticated bunch that we were.

At the end of the summer, I packed my bags and bid my parents a tearful good-bye as I waved from my little Toyota. Roots ran deep here, and many of the kids in my graduating class had attended nursery school with me. I had never been away from home for any extended period of time. A hundred and fifty miles was beginning to feel like fifteen hundred.

I followed my directions to the home of the family that NNI had arranged for me to stay with. They were welcoming, but that first night I barely slept; skittish butterflies danced in my stomach. It felt just like my first day of school in fourth grade when I had carefully laid out my new school supplies alongside my Wonder Woman lunch pail.

The drive to the institute early the next morning took less than twenty minutes. First I passed through the heart of the financial district with all of its imposing, shiny new buildings, then through a part of town with shorter and older buildings, and finally to an area that looked decidedly underwhelming. Maybe I was lost. Perhaps I had to go through this area to get to where the stately institute lorded over the lush countryside. I unfolded the map again, checked the address on the letterhead, and continued to scour the numbers on the sides of the buildings. There must be some mistake. Where in the middle of all this concrete was my beloved institute?

I reached the cross street that appeared in my directions, slowing down to peer at a strip mall that resembled prison barracks. In the middle of the block stood a two-story stucco building, which I can best describe in architectural terms as one long beige box stacked on top of another. It was surrounded by a 7-Eleven (which looked like it might have been the very first one in the franchise), a "beauty" parlor, a shabby dry cleaner, and a low-rent Chinese takeout place.

Clearly I must have mixed up the directions. Maybe I'd read the address wrong? A hundred thoughts raced through my mind as I pulled NNI's letter out of my purse one more time. Aha! Maybe I was on the northeast side of Portland by mistake, not the northwest. But no. To my dismay, I read the address, 2332 Northwest Broadway, on the letterhead, then turned to the identical tarnished brass numbers on the side of the building.

I desperately wanted to turn my car around and drive straight back to Cottage Grove. (Well within the speed limit, of course.)

But I had come this far; the least I could do was investigate a little further. After all, I told myself, I could always go home and enroll in dental hygiene school. I had considered this once, until my mother commented that she thought it would be gross to look in peoples' mouths all day. If she couldn't see the good in it, I reasoned it must be terrible. Yet, suddenly, a career in dental decay was looking more appealing—and there would always be plenty of business in my home-town, because most of the men never left the house without a big wad of chewing tobacco and a chew cup.

I began to climb the concrete steps to the second story, and all my earlier excitement drained away. At that moment I could not possibly have imagined that in four short months I would be flying to Los Ange-les, going on interviews with some of the wealthiest people in the coun-try, and becoming the highest-paid nanny to graduate from NNI.

But right then my place was at an old-fashioned desk. The seat was attached to a wooden tabletop, the kind I remembered from third grade with hearts and initials carved all over. Fourteen other girls and women sat all around me in the neat rows. At the front of the room stood the teacher, a middle-aged woman who introduced herself as Carolyn. I stared at an enormous blackboard next to her desk, where the following was written:

## A Professionally Trained Nanny Is:

- Not a maid
- Prepared for the unexpected
- Always conducting herself in a professional manner
- Truly committed to the profession

Underneath there was an outline of some of the course material:

## Today's Subjects:

- Etiquette—Table Manners
- Grooming—Hygiene
- Family Dynamics—Husband and Wife as Parents
- First Aid/CPR

I was pleasantly surprised at the scope of material we would be covering. I would later learn that there are very few programs offering official training or certification as a professional nanny. NNI was one of the first of its kind. Carolyn and her partner, Linda, had started the nanny school just a year earlier, and, as with many start-up businesses, they did it all. Sometimes during our lessons they would have to interrupt class to take phone calls.

"NNI. May I help you?" they would say brightly.

"Yes. Uh, yes."

"No, we don't do pet-sitting."

"Well, uh, yes, sometimes our nannies do work for families that have pets."

"Uh, no, we don't offer a dog-walking service."

"Yes, I realize there are similarities between babies and puppies."

"Perhaps your vet would have a referral?"

"No, once again, sir, just human beings, not schnauzers . . ."

Nannies were still a new concept in Oregon.

I studied the other nannies-in-training. Most of the others were fresh out of high school, just like me. I found out that one girl had just graduated at the top of a class of fifteen, and several others were from tiny towns in rural areas. There were also a few older women in the class, divorced with grown children, who had never worked outside the home but were quite practiced in raising kids.

For the rest of the morning we went over our syllabus. In the months ahead, we would also be covering household management, health and safety, the physical and cognitive development of children, résumés and interviewing techniques, career planning, and employment contracts. But it wasn't all textbook work. We were also given a practicum family—literally a practice family—that we would work for during our training. And Carolyn explained that a mother would be bringing in a newborn to show us how to give an infant a bath.

I had a lot of questions. And I asked them all. First, why would we be discussing personal hygiene? Second, exactly what kind of grooming did she mean? And finally, isn't it probably best not to go into the child-care profession if you've never even given a baby a bath?

Carolyn asked me to stay after class to speak with her privately. Oops.

During our after-school meeting, she explained, "Not all of our students share your privileged background," as if my last name was Kennedy. But after peering at those around me more closely the next day, I realized that what Carolyn had said was true. I *was* judgmental—just like my mother had always been telling me.

Carolyn's words reminded me of my first babysitting job when I was in the fourth grade. I'll never know what possessed my mother to think that I was responsible enough to oversee a child only two years younger than me, but Mom had blithely promised my services to our Avon lady. She needed someone to watch her four children, ages one to seven, for an evening because she had an important date. I wondered who she was dating. And who was the father to the four she already had? But my mother had said I wasn't supposed to criticize people unless I'd walked a mile in their shoes, a concept she had explained to me more than once.

When I arrived, the Avon lady informed me that there had been recent reports of a prowler in the area and that I should call the police if anything suspicious happened. I turned on every light in the house and spent the entire night peeping out from behind the curtains. How could anyone let me, a nine-year-old who still played with Barbies and was scared of the witch in *The Wizard of* Oz, take care of her children in the face of such imminent danger? I wanted to call my mom. But the prospect of a paying job convinced me to tough it out.

At NNI I could now see that my very first adventure in babysitting had truly been an early indication of things to come. My talent as a busybody, my propensity to psychoanalyze people and their relationships, my alternating confidence and self-doubt, and my willingness to face the unknown, be it possible prowlers or shady strip malls. I was ready. Bring on the kids!

But there was more school. We were taught the definition of a nanny, to wit: "A nanny's role is to provide support to the family by serving as a loving, nurturing, and trustworthy companion to the children. A nanny has special childcare skills and a deep love for and understanding of children. A nanny offers the family convenient, high-quality care to meet each child's physical, emotional, social, and intellectual needs."

Our teachers urged us to remember that a nanny isn't a maid or a cook. Carolyn and Linda were experienced enough to know that there would indeed be families that were looking for a nanny to perform housework, such as doing laundry, washing dishes, or making dinner. They told of one family that even required their nanny to shovel snow from their Chicago sidewalk each morning; apparently the dad had a bad back. I learned that a lot of nannies were taken advantage of. But I thought I had the perfect plan. I would work for a family that had a maid and a cook, and then I wouldn't have to worry about scrubbing the floor and whipping up dinner. Why were all these other girls such pushovers? That wasn't going to be me.

Carolyn laid out a few more basic rules:

- Don't wear suggestive clothing.

- When you're out to dinner with the family, don't order the most expensive item on the menu.

- Maintain a professional decorum. Don't make your employers your friends.

- Do not be the wife's confidante about her troubles with her husband.

Or, in some instances,

- Don't be the mistress's confidante.

(And of course)

- Don't become the mistress.

(Was this rule really necessary? Wasn't it just assumed that you shouldn't sleep with your boss? Had this actually been a problem in the past?)

And right there on the board in big letters was written the cardinal rule, staring us in the face every day and stated and restated as often as possible:

- Get a signed contract detailing pay, hours, and rate for overtime, and any other expectations before agreeing to the position.

Another student named Mandie and I became close friends. She was only two years older than me, and she had silky black shoulder-length hair and a warm smile that made her approachable. I grew very fond of her. It might have been my mothering instinct that drew me to her—I felt the urge to take her under my wing. She seemed so alone, having driven all the way from Montana by herself. Her father, a lawyer and a man of few words himself, had given her only one piece of advice as she started her journey: "Count to ten before you speak." I didn't know it at the time, but soon Mandie would become one of the only friends I would have in a very foreign land. She would, one day, save my sanity.

Sitting in that classroom on the dingy side of Portland, I didn't fully grasp the possibility of nightmarish nanny scenarios. Sure, I listened to stories like that of a British nanny who went to work for the royal family in Saudi Arabia. The girls she watched grew obese from being force-fed—to get them "strong" for childbearing. One seven-year-old child weighed 165 pounds. The nanny was freaked out by such strange practices and was scared by the police who stopped her for some wayward blond hair poking out of her headscarf. She eventually ran to the British embassy to get escorted out of the country. It sounded awful, but awfully different from how I pictured my job. Surely in the United States everyone had the same sort of basic ideas about raising kids. Didn't they?

A few weeks into class, Mary, the family dynamics teacher, asked me to help take care of her own two girls and the special-needs foster children she cared for. She told me that, after careful consideration, she had chosen me from all the girls in class because of my maturity. I'd always felt I was the most responsible among my peers. As Jeff Foxworthy says, I was usually elected as the "spokesperson" to answer the door at our high school parties when the cops showed up. And what else could explain the fact that I had been chosen as the head of the fire-drill exercises in second grade and as the attendance-taker in the third grade?

I wasn't, however, nominated for a home-ec medal. Though we weren't expected to cook as nannies, Carolyn and Linda knew there would be exceptions. So we were required to prepare a meal, a personal favorite, for one of our practicum families to see if we could buy the groceries and make a dinner while caring for the kids at the same time. My personal favorite at the time was also the *only one* I knew how to make, unless you counted bologna boats. It was a casserole, with broccoli, cheddar cheese, a can of Campbell's cream of chicken soup, mashed potatoes, two cubes of butter, and a pint of half-and-half. This was all layered over a couple of pounds of fried hamburger. My grandmother used to make it for me every Sunday night. But somehow I had never noticed how long she slaved in the kitchen. I felt great nanny guilt for sticking my practicum children in front of the TV (educational programming, of course) while I stood over the stove. It took hours to assemble, but I thought it turned out great.

The six-year-old refused to eat it. He said it looked like throw up.

My four months of schooling went quickly, and by December I had graduated. I'd logged more than four hundred hours in classroom and practicum training and had passed my certification test with flying colors. I was now a highly trained and qualified childcare professional. I figured I could do that anywhere in the world—children are children, after all. So I set my sights on Southern California, the land of milk, honey, sunshine, and money. To my surprise, within a week I had several interviews lined up through a domestic placement agency in Santa Monica.

There was no doubt in my mind that it was time to leave the northwest. I knew that I'd miss my parents, my two sisters, and all my friends, but I had adjusted to life in a big city—well, Portland. It was time for bigger things. And there was no romance anchoring me in Oregon, anyway. Okay, there was my first love, Ryan, and our intense on-again, off-again relationship, but it was off now, and I suspected he probably couldn't wait for me to disappear so he could start dating the homecoming queen. I had never before made it three entire months without running back to Ryan. But now I felt strong and confident. I was ready for a new life.

Good-bye, covered-bridge capital of America.

I was off to the film capital of the world.

My friends who are actresses and who have babies are with them every day. You can work and still be totally involved with your baby.

—Jennifer Garner

# hollywood or bust

Going from NNI to my marathon interviews in LA to my new job happened quite quickly, almost like one of those movie scenes in which a child grows up in the space of one well-chosen song. I returned to LA less than a week after the Ovitz family offered me the position. Josh Evans, who worked in the CAA mailroom, picked me up from the airport. He was a cute guy, just about my age. He seemed really nice, and we laughed a lot on the drive to my new home. Maybe we could date? I knew it was time to move beyond Ryan. I later learned that Josh was Ali MacGraw's son with Robert Evans, who had once run Paramount Pictures and was now a notorious producer. It seemed strange that a celebrity child like Josh had to start in the mailroom at Michael's company; I didn't yet know that it was a time-honored tradition. Everyone in Hollywood, apparently, started in the mailroom—even Michael, who had started his career at the William Morris Agency before decamping to found CAA.

No mailroom for me, though. Just the playroom. But it didn't take long to see that they were very similar.

You first had to realize who was boss.

My real bosses were less than three feet tall. And they had lungs of steel. Right away I learned that when charming, dimpled, three-year-old Amanda didn't get her way, there would be hell to pay. Her temper tantrums were daily and lengthy. Her shrill screams reverberated like air-raid sirens. She would stomp and flail her arms as fat crocodile tears rolled down her cheeks, and the veins in her little neck would become engorged from shrieking. She carried on like a crazed Energizer bunny until she ran out of juice, which took a *long, long* time—up to two excruciating hours. Everyone had given up trying to stop her toddler fits.

I figured that with my institute-certified expertise, I could snap her out of it pretty quickly. But in all my experiences as a babysitter, I had never seen a child with such determination—or tonsil power. I had read every child development and parenting book that I could get my hands on, always wanting to be one step ahead of the kids. Sure, sometimes I had to hunt around for the solution—maybe a stern talk, a time-out, or chocolate ice cream. But in the end, *something* would work. This child, however, appeared immune to all of my maneuvers.

This was not the way I had planned to kick off my first job. But then again, I had planned to have all my stuff with me, too. Two days before I left Cottage Grove, I shipped my clothes and other belongings down to the house. I had the correct street address, but I assumed that my new home was in Brentwood, not Los Angeles. That naming nonsense again. Evidently, Brentwood was not its own city. As a result, all my earthly possessions ended up who knows where in California. It wasn't until two weeks later that they finally arrived.

Looking back, that may have been an omen.

Yet I blithely carried on. As I tried to take a wiggling Amanda to her room for a time-out, I saw Judy watching, looking aghast and a little dazed. She walked away, shaking her head.

I was mystified. I thought disciplining the kids was part of my job. But I didn't say anything.

Why didn't I ask how she wanted me to handle problems? I didn't have the nerve. Asking probably would have gotten me some answers, but at a price. Already I felt like a bull in a china shop. By the end of my first day I had come to dread Judy's silent but oh-so-obvious disapproval when I did something she considered foolish, like walking out to fetch the mail in my socks. Or when I returned what I thought was a garage door opener to her car. (How did I not have the sense to know that the "opener" was a buzzer that belonged in the dining room—so the family could summon the staff when they had minor emergencies, like needing more pepper?) And after I chatted about Ryan and how I missed him, she explained in no uncertain terms that she thought it was ridiculous to even think about having a long-distance relationship. In her opinion, they *never* worked out.

I quickly sized up the household as tense and tight, not the happy, laughing, rough-and-tumble place I'd been picturing. (How had I not noticed this during my interview?) Judy expected me to know all the answers already, and fielding more queries exasperated her. I figured the only way to operate was to forge ahead and ask for forgiveness later. Well, not that I planned to do much of that. I vowed to be the perfect employee. If that meant reading the minds of my forbidding Hollywood bosses, then bring me the crystal ball.

I never did discover any rules regarding the children's behavior. Apparently, they didn't use time-outs, parenting with love and logic, attachment parenting, or any of the other concepts I had studied. So I tried to make up my own rules. But Judy didn't seem pleased with any of them. She certainly hadn't liked my giving a time-out, and candy or other food bribes were forbidden in this house (more on that shortly). I wasn't sure what *would* please them; I didn't see one parenting book in the entire house. But this family did have rules about other things. Lots of them.

Even in the bathroom. On my second day, when I went to turn on the tap for Joshua's nighttime bath, I noticed that the spout was covered with what looked like a giant condom. Now, why in the world would someone want to protect their faucet? No idea. I pulled it off. How else was I going to run the water?

As with most things in the house, there was a reason—it just wasn't evident to me. After the tub was half-filled, I told Joshua to get in while I helped Amanda get undressed in the connecting bedroom. Within seconds there was a wailing that nearly rivaled Amanda's shrieking hissy fits. Heart pounding, I turned to see Joshua sitting in the tub, clutching his head and screaming, "You idiot! You're so stupid! I hate you!"

I realized that the cover had been placed there to protect the *children*, not the spout. Fortunately, the incident didn't require stitches, but in Joshua's six-year-old mind, I had committed an unpardonable sin.

Would I ever get the hang of this?

I decided to approach it like school. After all, I was getting tested constantly, so I might as well study. I began carrying a well-worn notebook, hastily scribbling every time I learned something new about their preferences, propensities, and peculiarities. I was *not* about to get caught without a smile on my face and a helpful attitude. I was determined to win their approval.

During the first week of my tour of duty, I added several major rules to my list:

• **DON'T TOUCH THE ARTWORK.** This one had me truly rattled because artwork was *everywhere*. It seemed there were few places safe to touch. I was petrified. What if the kids fell into a million-dollar painting? Would I be held responsible? Oops! Liability — yet another thing I had forgotten to clarify during my interview.

• **KEEP THE FRONT/SIDE DOOR UNLOCKED.** I assumed this was because they had so many employees coming in and out, including a never-ending fleet of construction workers conducting some kind of renovation. It might have seemed less than security-conscious, but there *was* a fence and a gate.

• **NEVER ACTIVATE ALARMS.** Under no circumstances was I to set off the security alarm or motion detectors. I wasn't exactly sure what would set them off, so I just decided to tread with caution. But there was a tiny problem with that plan. I was a sleepwalker. Throughout my childhood and into my teens, my mother would regularly find me wandering about the house in the middle of the night. I had once been discovered thoroughly washing my Ken and Barbie in the bathroom sink at 3 A.M. When I was a teenager, I would plug in my curling iron and get in the shower at 2 A.M. to get ready for school. So I was completely paranoid that one night I'd cruise around the Ovitz mansion in my pajamas and somehow set off a three-alarm fire bell. I thought I had a solution, though. I would lock myself in my room. Hopefully my sleepwalking self wasn't alert enough to figure out how to unlock the door. Years later I would hear Kathie Lee Gifford tell the story of how her husband, Frank, had mistakenly wandered—totally in the buff—into their nanny's room in the middle of the night, but at the time I mercifully didn't know of that possibility. Could anything be more excruciatingly embarrassing, at least for the nanny?

• **DO NOT FEED THE KIDS FAST FOOD.** The family followed a strict low-fat, low-salt diet that did not include French fries or Happy Meals. I assumed the cook got very creative with baby carrots and bananas.

• **ALWAYS CHECK WITH JUDY BEFORE GIVING BRANDON A BOTTLE.** She said she liked to feed him when she was home.

• **NEVER INTERRUPT MORNING WORKOUTS.** Michael was put through his paces every day by an ancient Japanese aikido master, or, once in a while, by Steven Seagal.

• **MICHAEL WILL ALWAYS TAKE CALLS FROM THE KIDS.** Ah. Exactly. See, this *was* the kind of family I wanted to work for: a family where the emotional well-being of the kids was the overriding concern.

These, of course, were just the *stated* rules. There were many, many other unwritten rules, but I'd stumble across those later. Meanwhile, I consoled myself with the thought that other people had it worse. I'd heard at school about a nanny whose boss had a tremendous irrational fear of dirt and made her don plastic booties and gloves each day when she arrived. No Saran-Wrap wellies for me! Just oodles of rules.

I was also trying to follow the guidelines I'd learned at NNI. I struggled from the very beginning to keep in mind one of the foremost principles that I had learned there: a nanny should not make her employers her friends. As a former teen social queen from a small friendly town, I found such a distinction difficult to make. When Judy left a couple of fashion magazines by my bedroom door, I thanked her several times. I was so touched that I studied the magazines thoroughly, wondering if she was trying to subtly pass on some beauty tips. Maybe this was her way of taking me, a young, unsophisticated girl, under her gilded wing. But apparently not. She smiled each time I thanked her but didn't follow up on my attempts to be friendly.

I couldn't figure her out. Cool and distant, yes, but high-maintenance socialite, no. She didn't seem to shop much on Rodeo Drive or "do lunch" with the girls like I'd expected. She didn't generally give her itinerary to the staff (I was getting used to the fact that I was part of the *staff*), but she flitted in and out most days, perpetually busy with something. I assumed it must be charity work. Routinely the two of us ate dinner with the kids, but the conversation always felt strained, like I was meeting my potential in-laws for the first time, over and over again. I kept trying not to say anything stupid. I kept failing. She would wave her hand dismissively, saying, "That's not at all what I meant, Suzy," when I ventured an opinion that didn't suit her. To add to the tension, I found it odd to sit at your own dinner table and buzz the kitchen to have someone bring you ketchup in a shiny silver boat.

I should have expected all this. Not a friend, and not family. As the experts at NNI had said, "The nanny is taking care of part of the family, but she is not a *member* of the family." Sure, I understood it intellectually. But it was a hard concept to remember when I was with these people twenty-four hours a day. We shared a roof; shouldn't we share more? I wanted to be treated as both a professional *and* as a part of the family. I knew I wasn't supposed to feel that way, but being so far away from my own family for the first time made me want to cling to this new one.

And yet there was so little to cling to. Judy was often gone, and when she was home she seemed distracted, busy, or generally unavailable. And I hardly ever saw Michael. He usually left early in the morning and returned about ten or eleven most nights. He didn't walk, he darted; he gave the impression of being a mover and a shaker. He spoke to me cordially but it was always quickly, in passing.

There was no time for me to bond with them; but there was plenty of time for me to try to bond with the kids. So much for my expectation of clocking out at six or seven P.M. Actually, I was learning that I would rarely clock out at all. I had naively assumed my job would end in the evenings. But Judy's idea of a nanny was a twenty-four-hour-a-day on-call presence. Eager not to be seen as a slacker, I didn't have the nerve to question her assumption.

I soon learned other employees didn't ask questions, either. It took nearly a village to support this household. Besides me, there was Carmen (the live-in cook), Delma (the live-in housekeeper, relief cook, and weekend nanny), Gloria and Rosa (the weekday housekeepers), a weekly gardener, and the guy who detailed the cars. Various other people passed through for extra gardening and little household fix-it jobs.

Carmen, the seven-year veteran, immediately became my friend and gradually, as time went on, a kind of mother figure. In her early forties, Carmen was short and pleasantly plump, with jet black hair and thick glasses. She usually wore white nurse shoes and a blue-and-white-striped shirt that hung over her white pants. I also grew close to Delma, who was only twenty-four, fairly close to my own age. Straight black bobbed hair framed Delma's round, full face, which usually had a sweet expression. She had already worked for the family for three years.

The support staff at Michael's office—including his assistant Sarah, who handled Michael's personal matters; a second assistant, who took care of his clients' needs; and Jay, who was Michael's assistant/agent-in-training—soon became other members of my little family. They were my sounding boards, my confidants, and they occasionally offered a shoulder or two to cry on.

They understood. We all had to meet the family's expectations. And Michael held *high* expectations. When Gloria began wearing rollers in her hair to do her work in the morning, Michael had his wife speak with her. Even though no one outside the house saw the maid who cleaned his bathroom and emptied his trash, Michael wanted her to look professional. Look professional, and perform like a perfectionist. The brass door knocker and the black lacquer doors it adorned had to gleam. The Plexiglas child-safety guards on the stairway must be wiped clean of children's fingerprints (a totally impossible job, as most anyone with kids can attest). The marble floors had to be kept as smooth and clean as poured cream. Each morning Rosa's first job was to remove all the lint off the dark emerald green carpeting on the stairs. As far as she was concerned, the handheld vacuum that was used on the stairs was not good enough. So she stooped down and snatched any errant specks of fuzz with her fingers.

But Carmen had the most status with Michael. Our nightly three-course dinners stood up to anything you'd find at Jacques LaRivière's restaurant. Twice a week she restocked the Sub-Zero refrigerator with fresh food bought at an upscale market, which she whipped into sophisticated and artful menus. The food was low-fat but truly delicious, and health-conscious Michael prized her culinary ability. Carmen was not shy about using his allegiance to her advantage. The rest of the staff grumbled a little when Carmen sat reading *Gourmet* in the kitchen while they scurried around the house, but she wouldn't budge. Why should she? She knew her job was secure.

Michael paid her a generous salary, but I learned that every couple of years she got fed up with her resident status and asked to live off the property. Carmen owned a home, she had a boyfriend, and she wanted to spend time with her family. In short, she wanted a life. But Michael wouldn't hear of it. He only allowed her to stay at her own house two nights a week, on her days off. Her high salary kept her in golden handcuffs. Carmen told me she would never be paid as well anywhere else, and she said that Michael's vindictiveness was well-known. She was convinced that if she left, she would be sent on her way without a reference and would have a hard time finding another job. I figured she was exaggerating. She had to be. They had stolen her right out of Neil Diamond's kitchen, hadn't they?

I felt pretty homesick by the end of my first week. One night I opened the drawer beside my bed and pulled out the journal that Kristi's parents had given me as a graduation present. "Wishes and Dreams" was scrawled across the cover in flowery script. I opened it up and reread the inscription:

*Suzy—*

*May all your thoughts be happy ones, and all your experiences mile-stones. We love you.*

—*George and MaryAnn*

I was suddenly aware of the enormous distance between me and the people who loved me and had watched me grow up. Here in Hollywood, I was an unknown. Sure, I was making some friends—Carmen, Delma, Sarah—but I was still lonely. It seemed the perfect time to christen my present and start recording my new life. Over the course of my stay in Hollywood, I would turn to this book almost nightly to pour out my decidedly mixed bag of thoughts and experiences.

I've been here a week now, and I'm just getting to know everyone, but it's kinda lonely. I miss my friends, my sisters, my mom and dad. I still really miss Ryan. Trying not to. Trying not to. Every day is the same basic routine. Well, not exactly. In order to have a beginning you have to have an end. I don't think my day has an end. Here's how it usually goes:

- Rise before 7:00 with Brandon, feed him, help Carmen or Delma fix the kids breakfast.

- Help get Amanda and Joshua dressed for school.

- Carmen packs lunches; intervene in the inevitable debate over its contents with Joshua.

- Help get the kids ready for Judy to take to school.

- Care for and entertain Brandon until Amanda comes home at 12:30 from preschool, and Josh at 3:30 from kindergarten.

- Read with all the kids, play with toys, or succumb to the lure of the VCR. God bless *Cinderella*.

- Eat dinner with Judy and the kids.

- Get Brandon ready for bed, help the other two with a bath and pajamas.

- Read to them. (Sometimes Judy reads to them.)

- Feed Brandon his bottle, rock him, and put him in his crib.

- Fill two bottles for Brandon, put them on ice, and bring them to my room. Take infant monitor to my room and listen for him to wake up.

- When he cries, traipse down the hall where there is not, thank God, a red beam of light from the elaborate alarm. Rock him while warming the bottle. At the precise moment he sucks down the last drop, remove the bottle and simultaneously slip the pacifier into his mouth.

- Repeat the bottle ritual a couple of hours later.

- Then it's morning, and I start all over again.

And I did not know that getting up with the baby in the middle of the night was part of my job description. I should have asked about that, instead of my idiotic spanking question! Nanny school never covered how to handle sleep deprivation on the job—I could sure use some pointers on how to get by with less than six hours of shut-eye.

In fact, I was probably wasting precious beauty sleep writing.

When you have children you have to step outside yourself.

—Madonna

# dazed and confused

It wasn't long before I started to feel more at ease, thanks to Carmen and Delma and the rest of the staff. They clued me in to the complex workings of the house, and showed me which goofs you could laugh about and which mistakes were cause for alarm. As I grew closer to them, they told me often what a great job I was doing. When I was beside myself with worry about Amanda's tantrums, they would assure me that it had always been that way. When I was depressed because Judy was hard to please and quick to criticize—"What's that car doing parked in front of our house?" "Why is there no lettuce in the refrigerator?"—they would teach me that whatever our answer was ("I'm driving my brother's car today"; "The lettuce is in the crisper") wouldn't ever be quite good enough, and I had to let it go. I appreciated their kindness; and they, in turn, loved the fact that I treated them kindly. I gathered that the previous nanny had felt somewhat "above" the other staff. I didn't feel that way at all—friends were friends.

The atmosphere in the house was generally much less stressful when we had it all to ourselves, which was after Judy took the kids to school and stayed out for the rest of the day. The heavy feeling of being watched and critiqued lifted for a bit, and we didn't have to be on our toes every single second. As the days slid into weeks, it got easier, but I was still dismayed at how awkward and stressful it was. Sure, I'd heard horror stories from NNI and from nannies I'd met in the local Brentwood Park. I listened to tales of nannies drawn into bitter custody battles, courted by both sides to testify on each parent's behalf when, in reality, both were neglectful and spent far too little time at home. I'd brushed off such difficulties as rare exceptions. But other issues—like feeling comfortable, welcome, and wanted—never entered my mind.

Not that I had much time to think. Brandon kept me busy all day long, as infants do, with constant feeding, burping, and changing. I didn't mind, really. I loved snuggling with him. And Brandon was still so little that I usually just carried him around the house all day long. Judy really seemed to enjoy doing things with the older children, and they hungered for her company. But she told me that taking Brandon along with the other two was too much for her, with the diaper bag, stroller, bottles, etc.

So I was in charge of Brandon nearly twenty-four hours a day. Like many other highly positioned Hollywood families, the Ovitzes had hired a baby nurse for the first few weeks of Brandon's life. She fed him, changed him, rocked him, and cuddled him, basically everything you'd think a new mom would do. She had left just days earlier, and I eagerly slid into her role.

We explored Brentwood together, often beelining for Brentwood Park and taking long walks through the neighborhood, which was charming and full of gorgeous homes that screamed "old money." Most were set far back from the road, many behind forbidding high hedges. A gate and an intercom system protected almost every one, and at least one house on every street was under construction. I learned that people in LA were fond of buying teardowns: multimillion-dollar mansions they razed and replaced with even bigger palaces that stretched right to the edge of the property lines. Countless fleets of construction vehicles passed through, prompting an array of "roach coaches"—a derogatory term for vans that served hot food and drinks—that parked on every block to attract the mainly Hispanic service people. It was on one of these strolls that I realized I now lived only a block from the O.J. Simpson estate on North Rockingham.

Despite my difficulties adjusting to the job, I was thoroughly enjoying my sneak peek into the lives of the rich and famous.

During one of my first weeks on the job, Michael's protégé, Jay Maloney, called me at the house. Michael had given Jay his seats for a Lakers game that evening, but Jay was unable to use them and casually suggested that I take them. When I gathered up my courage and asked Michael if it would be okay, he said, "Sure. Why don't you take a friend?"

I couldn't believe his generosity. Finally, a chance to get out and see the city. I had never been to an NBA game before. Since I had no friends within a thousand-mile radius, I asked if I could take Delma. Michael looked perplexed, but he agreed. He gave me the tickets and a VIP parking pass.

Ecstatic, Delma and I headed off on our adventure in her old car. When we arrived at the arena, a parking valet appeared at the door, ready to whisk away our carriage. I didn't have a clue how to handle the protocols of power, LA-style. So, did this guy need a tip? How much? Now or later? My last experience at a big venue had been when Ozzy Osbourne played in Portland. My friend Amy and I had hiked the North 40 between the parking space and the coliseum because we didn't have enough money to pay for stadium parking. I had certainly never encountered a valet at a sporting event.

Delma giggled, getting right into the spirit of being a big shot. I'd found a friend. I'd fine-tune parking protocol later; for now I gave him a whopping $2.

It got even better inside. Our seats were directly behind the visiting team—the Seattle Super Sonics were sweating on their bench not a foot from our faces. I didn't even care that I didn't know any of the players. Delma spotted the TV cameras right away and spent the rest of the evening checking out who the crews were filming—Jack Nicholson, as usual. We were only ten chairs away! I peered at the camera every time it pulled back for a crowd shot. Was I making a splash in Cottage Grove?

Our seats came with our own server, who came by several times to ask if there was anything we wanted. I was overwhelmed with all the questions running through my head: If I'm holding the ticket, does he think *I'm* someone important? Or can he spot an imposter?

We never did order anything because we were too embarrassed to ask if it was complimentary, and we only had $8 between us. Oh well. It was fun to have the perks of power, even if they were just borrowed for the evening. And my short-lived ascension into status that night at the Lakers game turned out to have a lasting benefit. From that day on, I knew the exact location of Michael's seats. Years later I would be very grateful that I could tune in to Lakers games and try to catch a glimpse of the children. But for now I was happy just sitting in the front row.

My lessons on the ways of the wealthy continued.

Next up, art.

As Michael was leaving for the office one Friday morning, he told me that some deliverymen would be arriving that afternoon with a large painting from his friend's art gallery in New York. The dealer, who sold Michael a great deal of art, was always treated as an honored guest when he came for overnight visits, sleeping in the luxurious guest suite just off the upstairs gallery.

All I had to do was show the deliverymen into the sitting room and tell them to hang the painting on a particular wall. Judy was going to be gone all day, and it was Carmen's day off, so Michael made it clear that it was my sole responsibility to handle this important matter carefully. I had no idea how much the painting was worth. My only frame of reference was one of the small paintings in the family room. Carmen had told me it was worth $750,000. This definitely required my full attention. The thing was probably worth more than most people in Cottage Grove would make in a lifetime.

Since I grew up in a place where it was customary for most men over the age of fifty to start almost every sentence with "Well, I reckon . . ." it is not surprising that my father's idea of art was the bowling trophy he won back in '69 for bowling a perfect three-hundred game. It also doubled as our living room clock. My mother's art collection consisted of a snowman that my sisters and I had made for her from one of those yarn things you hook—the kind that's on the square burlap, and you match the yarn with the painted pattern. My personal art collection included a framed picture of Jon Bon Jovi that I special-ordered through *Teen* magazine and kept on my dresser.

Michael must have called six times that day, nearly every half hour, wanting to know if the painting had arrived. No, it had not. I didn't even go outside the house for fear I'd miss the delivery. Finally, a truck appeared at four in the afternoon, and I buzzed it in the front gate. Two men approached the front door carrying a wooden crate that was about six feet long. I could see the package through the wooden slats, covered in butcher paper. I immediately led the men into the sitting room, where they began tearing the crate apart with claw hammers. When they finally pulled all the butcher paper off, there was yet another piece of solid black paper wrapped tightly around the painting.

"Where do you want it, miss?" one of them asked.

"Over here. See, those two hooks are all ready for it."

At that point, I expected the men to tear off the final cover, but they just lifted the art up by the sides and carefully and slowly hung it on the wall. Why hadn't they uncovered it? Had they been told to leave it that way? Perhaps Michael wanted it to be a surprise at an upcoming dinner party. He must be planning a grand unveiling. He would make a big to-do about pulling off the black cover, at which point he would expound on the virtues of his newest acquisition.

Four nights passed and still no grand event. The suspense was killing me—why didn't they unwrap the damn thing? To add to the mystery, Michael had a railing installed in front of the masterpiece, protruding out about three feet. I'd heard him telling Carmen not to let the girls (referring to all adult women in the house) touch it, dust it, or breathe on it. Right, I got it. But why keep it wrapped up? I couldn't figure it out for anything. Of course, I didn't want to appear the country bumpkin that I was by asking anyone.

Finally, one night I overheard a discussion about the painting. But how could they talk about it without seeing it?

*Ohhhhh.*

The art wasn't covered by *anything*. It was just a large black painting! No scene, no contrasting colors, no nothing. Just a canvas of black. I inspected it more closely and discovered that there were three separations, with black fabric wrapped around each panel. Could there possibly be three different "shades" of black? I know, ridiculous. It made no sense to me. I glanced at it from time to time during my stay, hoping something would click in my brain, but it never did.

I figured the "artist/fabric wrapper" who put this piece together must have had some phenomenal talent, imperceptible to all but the very wealthy.

By March I felt like I had a handle on some things. Although Amanda didn't consider me her new best friend, at least she wasn't chucking stuffed animals at me anymore during her tantrums. And Brandon's contagious smiles were constantly puffing out his model-perfect chubby cheeks. No colicky screamer for me, thank goodness, unlike one of the poor nannies I befriended at the park. She always had dark circles under her eyes and looked haggard, though she was near my age. The only way she could calm the colicky baby she cared for was to strap her into the car seat and perch the whole thing on top of the running clothes dryer. She was always afraid the baby would overheat, but the parents were grateful that anything worked and refused to look for any other solutions. She spent a lot of time in the laundry room.

But I was still struggling with other things. I could handle the long hours, but I realized what was really bothering me: how seriously my employers took everything. Sure, Delma and I would giggle over the panic that ensued when we couldn't find one shoe from a Barbie that Amanda hadn't played with in weeks. But the family seemed sincerely riled up over such matters. I got the distinct impression that to them, life was a chore. They seldom cracked smiles. A far cry from the Hansen household, with parents who had often led three girls in pretending they were the Jackson Five in concert. Complete with spoons for microphones. I had a hard time imagining my new employers rocking out with their kids.

And I kept flubbing up Judy's orders. They seemed impossible to follow. For example, the kids ate dinner at six sharp. On the rare occasions Michael made it home in time, they wanted the staff to be as invisible as possible while the five of them shared some much-needed family time. Invisible, of course, except that someone had to feed and take care of Brandon. Which I wasn't sure how to do without being seen.

And as much as I told myself not to, I missed Ryan. Blond, with a na-turally muscular build, Ryan looked a little like Matthew McConaughey. He was a year younger than me, still a senior in high school. I was always the more mature one, the overprotective, overly responsible adult, and Ryan played the part of wild bad boy. I think he had a hard time seeing beyond his family's legacy as timber fallers—I wondered if in some ways he didn't have many dreams for himself beyond graduation. We were clearly heading in different directions and emphatically not together. But I really didn't want him to date anyone else. Did I want to date anyone else? No one had really caught my eye since Josh Evans dropped me off.

It probably didn't matter; I had no free time, anyway. Maybe a story I'd heard from a British nanny who lived five doors up the street said it best: her five-year-old charge went to sit on Santa's lap and promptly told him that all he wanted for Christmas was a date for his beloved nanny. He thought she needed a boyfriend and Santa might be able to help.

I could see, though, that Joshua wouldn't be such a matchmaker. He hadn't warmed up to me at all. And it was only getting worse.

Michael's parents, David and Sylvia, came in from the Valley to stay at the house for a couple of days while Michael and Judy were out of town. I was feeling much more confident about my duties, but I was happy to have them there nonetheless. I liked Grandma and Grandpa Ovitz the minute I met them. Grandpa Ovitz was quiet, with a small potbelly, but you could tell the wheels in his brain were always turning. (Carmen told me he had some sort of job in the wine business.) Sylvia Ovitz was the caricature of a Jewish mother, and she had a heart of gold. She wore sweatshirts with rhinestones and sequins sewn all over them. She talked constantly, which drove Grandpa to his silences. The only time he really seemed to respond to her was when they argued. They would get caught up in an exchange that was like an old-time comedy routine. "Don't start. I'm telling you, don't start with me." It was clear they couldn't live without each other.

The night after Judy and Michael left, I walked into the kitchen after dinnertime to see what Joshua was doing. I found him sitting atop the center island all alone, playing with an entire stick of butter, which was beginning to get very soft. He had dropped the messy wrapper on the floor. I picked it up.

"Joshua, don't eat that," I scolded him. "You can't eat butter all by itself."

"Yes, I can!" he said loudly.

"No, you can't!" I responded just as loudly, breaking one of my own rules: *Don't engage in a shouting match with a child.*

"Yes, I can."

"No, you can't!"

"Yes, I can." His voice was getting louder and more imperious.

This was crazy. I was acting like a six-year-old myself. I had to do something.

I put my hand around his wrist and began to wrestle the stick from his hand, forgetting my other rule: *Always be smarter than the child.* When he jerked his hand away, yelling, "Let go of me, you idiot!" a big dollop of the greasy stuff flew through the air and stuck to the side of his face.

"I hate you. You gooooot b-b-b-b-uuuttter on me!" he screamed as he started crying. Then he threw what was left of the yellow mass at me. A huge chunk lodged in my hair.

I had somehow started a food fight with a six-year-old. I had to get control here.

I didn't do it quickly enough. Grandpa Ovitz heard the commotion and came in to inquire about the ruckus. I told him I had discovered Joshua eating a stick of butter and that he had thrown it at me, to which Joshua piped up, "But, Grandpa, she threw it at me first."

Right. Grandpa Ovitz looked at the butter on Joshua's face, then turned to see the clump in my hair. How to explain my way out of this one? Though Grandpa Ovitz had a gruff exterior at times, he was a very kind and caring man. Still, I was mortified when he gave me a you-should-know-better look as he wiped Joshua's face with a dishcloth.

Foolish didn't even begin to describe how I felt. I just couldn't find the words to explain that I had not purposely splattered his grandson with fat.

To make matters worse, Grandpa Ovitz said, "Perhaps you should take a time-out, Suzy. I'll talk with Joshua."

*Take a time-out?*

My face flushed. Could you ever reprimand a nanny in a more demeaning manner? And yet part of me was glad to get away from such a frustrating child. Perhaps it wasn't such bad advice.

By then it was past eight o'clock at night. I had already put Brandon to bed, and I knew that Grandma Ovitz would take care of Joshua and Amanda. Maybe I could use the time to really relax. I went to my room and put on my bathing suit, wrapped myself in a robe, and went outside to the pool. A simple rectangle set far away from the house next to a cabana and the workout room, the pool seemed like a shining oasis right then. I had never had the time to get in it before, and I thought a little exercise would be a good antidote to my anger. I'd swim a little, float in the eighty-five-degree water, and rinse the last of the butter out of my hair.

The pool wasn't huge, but a great slide made up for it. I decided to take the plunge on my stomach headfirst. *Aaaaagh!* The slide was slicker than I had anticipated, and I zoomed off the end, hurtling through the short length of the pool like a torpedo launched from a nuclear submarine. I hit the bricks on the other side of the pool deck at about fifty miles per hour, or so it seemed, and immediately began to sink like a big hunk of concrete.

It's strange what goes through your mind when you think you're dying. Most people would think about their loved ones, maybe an unfulfilled dream. I thought this: *I'm going to die in their swimming pool. My God, what an idiot they'll think I am. They'll be convinced that the last act of a dying woman was to throw butter at a six-year-old.*

What an embarrassing demise.

Of course, I wasn't dying. But this was pretty bad, anyway. I should never have come down to swim alone. Now I had compounded the trouble with Joshua a thousandfold. I shook my head a little to get my bearings, and then pulled myself out of the pool. A knot the size of a Ping-Pong ball was forming on my forehead. It started to throb. I held my hand to it and then looked at my fingers. The blood ran down my wrist and onto my arm.

So. I wouldn't drown. I would just bleed to death. I could just picture the headline tomorrow in the *Los Angeles Times:*

## NANNY ACCUSED OF THROWING BUTTER AT
## SIX-YEAR-OLD—APPARENTLY COMMITS SUICIDE
## TO AVOID THE WRATH OF SUPERAGENT OVITZ

The last thing I needed was for Grandma and Grandpa Ovitz to see me in this condition, so I slithered quietly up to my room and peered at the gash on my head. It wasn't long, only about half an inch, but it was very deep. And the blood would not stop running down between my eyes.

"Suzy, are you all right?" I heard Grandpa calling out. He must have seen the trail of blood I'd left on the marble entry.

"Uh, Mr. Ovitz, I'm up here, in my room. I bumped my head in the pool," I called back, not wanting him to climb the stairs. Too late. David Ovitz was in his midsixties, but in a flash he dashed up the stairs and was in my room.

"Let me see that," he said as he pulled my hand and the towel away from my face. "Oh my God, that is a nasty one; pretty deep. You'll have to get stitches."

Good grief. The situation grew more convoluted by the minute. Grandpa insisted on driving me to the emergency room to have the cut stitched. I should have just let Joshua eat the butter. Maybe he wouldn't have gotten sick. Then I wouldn't have gone swimming, and I wouldn't have had to explain this whole ridiculous mess. Adding to my embarrassment, poor Grandpa Ovitz was deeply concerned. He held my hand the entire time the doctor was suturing my gash.

I was hoping that I could remove the huge gauze bandage protecting the eight stitches in my forehead before Michael and Judy got home. I dreaded having them find out about this little incident. I just knew Judy would shake her head in disbelief, like she did when she overheard me reminding the kids to use their manners when speaking to the rest of the staff. Or she would clearly share her disappointment in me, like she did one day when I returned from shopping. She had asked me to pick up some clothes for Brandon at Fred Segal. When I brought back three baby outfits, she looked through the bag in disgust and said, "*Obviously*, Suzy, you and I have *very* different taste." I already felt awful enough about this incident and hoped she wouldn't rub it in.

Oddly enough, they both reacted quite differently than I expected. When Grandpa Ovitz related the tale over the phone that night, they seemed to find the whole thing funny. No trace of anger. "Sounds like Suzy and Josh got in a food fight," Judy said, laughing.

It wasn't *funny!* I was mortified. When I got on the phone and tried to explain what really happened, she didn't seem much interested.

> I feel like such a klutz about the whole incident. I'm so embarrassed, but Judy doesn't seem to care. The weird part is that she cares about other stuff that seems really unimportant to me. Yesterday I was walking downstairs carrying Brandon and his laundry basket when I met Judy. She shook her head like I was some kind of bothersome mosquito. She asked me why I was carrying all that stuff. I told her I was going to give him a bath. How else was I supposed to get the towels, washcloths, baby soap, and sponge downstairs? What was wrong with carrying it all in the laundry basket? She just gave me a huge sigh and kept walking up the stairs. The way she looks at me makes me feel like I am a thorn in her side. She never seems happy. Carmen says not to worry about things like this and that Judy has never been happy with any nanny. Carmen must be right, because Judy has already told me twice how much she couldn't stand "that nanny" Leticia, who was apparently Amanda's favorite nanny.
>
> I suppose this is one of those situations where you're not supposed to take it personally. But how do you not take it personally when you think someone doesn't like anything you do?

"Suzy, you must have hit those bricks pretty hard. I think that you should go see my acupuncturist, just in case," Michael suggested two days later upon his return home.

*Huh?*

"You probably jammed your neck pretty good," he explained. "Better safe than sorry. Have it looked at now so you won't have any back or neck problems later."

Oh. How kind. I told him I appreciated his concern. He had Sarah make an appointment for me the next Saturday.

I'd heard of acupuncture before, but I didn't know the details—Cottage Grove wasn't exactly the mecca of alternative health, after all. Upon arriving at the office, I was ushered into a small room with a table that looked like a cross between the medieval rack and a barber's chair. The doctor entered, asked me a few questions about how I'd sustained my injuries, and then told me to lie facedown on this odd padded apparatus. After he cranked a handle on one side and rotated a wheel on the other, I was elevated to the proper position.

"This won't hurt a bit," he said as he pulled on a surgical glove and reached into a drawer full of short, thin needles. I braced myself. Surprisingly, he was right; it didn't hurt. I was also surprised that he had inserted five of the needles into my lower back and the rest in various parts of my body, including my ears. None of them were anywhere near my neck.

Then came the disturbing news.

"Aha!" he said.

*I don't like it when doctors say "aha."*

"What?" I demanded.

"Oh, you have weak kidneys," he said matter-of-factly.

"How do you know that?" I asked.

He nodded sagely, ignoring the question. "It's probably the result of your parents being in conflict at the time of your conception."

*What?*

Don't get me wrong; I'm very open-minded. In fact, my grandmother worked for a chiropractor before most people even knew what one was. But the idea of conception conflict causing my compromised kidneys was a little hard to swallow. Did that mean problems with, um, incontinence? That would greatly decrease my chances of ever finding a husband, wouldn't it? I'd be a spinster forever.

The receptionist handed me the bill when I left, along with a self-addressed envelope for my convenience. The total was $75. It seemed a fair amount. But then it occurred to me that this was Michael's doctor and that he had suggested I come here. He'd even made the appointment. Maybe he was intending to cover the expense since health insurance was never discussed in the contract non-negotiation.

When I got back to the house that afternoon, I put the bill on the desk downstairs where the mail usually stacked up. I didn't give it another thought, except to thank Michael later and to tell him I felt fine and didn't think I'd have any problems. I didn't share with him the impending doom that I was sure lay ahead about me spending my life wearing Depends. That would be my own private torment.

The next night, as I was getting ready to lock myself in for the evening, I noticed a piece of paper on my dresser. It was the acupuncturist's bill. I thought it odd but figured that Rosa, seeing my name on it, had brought it up. The next morning I returned it to the desk. That evening, as I was getting ready for bed, I noticed it was back on my dresser. Again, I went downstairs and put the bill back and made a mental note to talk with Rosa. The next day the bill reappeared in my room. The bill went back and forth like that four times before I had a chance to tell Rosa to leave it on the desk.

"But, Miss Suzy, I didn't put anything on your dresser," she said in her Spanish accent.

Ohhhh. *Judy* was putting it in my room.

I paid the bill myself and, as with too many other subjects, never brought it up again.

I never thought I'd be one of those moms who would have trouble going back to work, but I did. I thought it was going to be easy to juggle everything, but half the time I run around with my hair on fire.

—Melissa Rivers

# working girl

I was trapped at the house every weekend.

Okay, maybe *trapped* was a strong word. But when you can't leave on a weeknight, sticking around for Saturday and Sunday essentially means that you're stuck at home *all the time*, and *trapped* pretty much summed it up. The awkward situation became apparent quite quickly. Monday through Friday I was on duty twenty-four hours a day. I couldn't go out on Friday nights because I had the night shift with the baby, and I had to be back on Monday morning when everyone woke up. That left me forty-eight hours of blissful freedom starting Saturday morning. Of course, if I left the premises, I'd have to be back by Sunday night—any arrival after everyone went to bed would set off alarms. But leaving the premises required a car. And I didn't have one.

Judy told me during my interview that I would be allowed to use the family's Jeep Cherokee on my days off. This arrangement sounded generous to me, because I didn't want to bring my less-than-reliable transportation to LA. Besides, the family also owned a Mercedes, a Jaguar, and a Porsche. Problem was, ever since I arrived, nearly every weekend they drove the Jeep to their beach house in Malibu. (Owning a second home just twenty miles away from the first seemed strange to me, but this wasn't the only other residence. The family also owned a New York apartment, which Judy spent a great deal of time decorating long-distance. They kept quiet about their place in New York, because, as I was told, if people knew they had it, they would ask to borrow it all the time, which would be a big pain in the neck. I thought the whole thing was weird. What kind of riffraff, exactly, would ask to borrow their apartment?) To top it off, I didn't even have a bicycle to get around in the city where the car was king. When I tried to explain the situation to Judy, she shrugged and said she was sorry she had forgotten about taking the Jeep to the beach house, but she didn't like other people driving her Mercedes.

In the beginning, it didn't really matter because I didn't know a soul in Los Angeles. My social life revolved around the household staff, and I didn't need to go anywhere to see them, anyway. And besides, I was *tired*. I retired to my room on my days off, where I'd read, catch up on my sleep, or write in my journal.

If the whole family was home and I wasn't on duty, I only ventured out of my room to grab a sandwich or some cookies. After all, it was my precious time off, and who wants to run into their boss on days off? Lord knows I stuck out in their family like a pig in a flower patch. My concept of family time was playing Monopoly and water-skiing at the lake, not riding in a limousine to Disneyland and being escorted by a guard through the gates to avoid the lines. So I hid. Michael made it a priority to spend weekends with family, and they fluttered in and out on the Saturdays and Sundays they were not at the beach house. I'd listen at my door until I heard the Jeep pull away, then I'd search out the other staff. But sometimes the family stayed put, roaming around the house, and I'd twiddle my thumbs in my room for hours, unable to work up the nerve to ask to borrow the Jeep.

I knew that I had to force myself to get some semblance of a life, no matter how I did it.

One day while reading the *LA Times*, I saw a notice for a game-show audition in Hollywood on the next Saturday. Maybe I could win some money . . . or even a new car. At the very least I'd get out and do something. I called the number and signed up. I'd find a way to get there somehow.

After throwing on my classy little black dress, I trundled over to the studio in the truck that I had convinced Rosa to lend me. I didn't have a clue how ludicrous I looked until I caught sight of myself in the security mirrors at the studio. The faded Chevy pickup lacked a front bumper but boasted a Baja Mexico license plate tied to the grill with bailing wire. And you couldn't miss the enormous camper shell slapped on top. I reached out the window and handed the guard my confirmation number, faux diamond bracelet dangling. My face was framed nicely by the ring of red dingle balls tacked all along the headliner and by the fuzzy dice hanging from the rearview mirror.

"Have a nice day, ma'am," he said, handing me back my piece of paper with a strange smile. "Just pull under this overhang and follow the arrows to the parking structure."

I struggled to put the truck into gear. This was no easy feat, since someone had creatively substituted an eight ball for the gearshift knob.

Looking down, I could see the pavement through the floorboard from which the shifter protruded. The transmission made a grinding noise as I tried to keep one of my dainty heels on the clutch, the other on the accelerator. As I let up slowly, the creaky old truck lunged and jerked and finally lurched forward, passing under the overpass that read MAXIMUM CLEARANCE 8 FEET 6 INCHES.

To be honest, I don't know that I even gave that measurement much thought until I was halfway through the garage and heard the awful sound of tin scraping against concrete. At first I thought it was just some machinery, and I continued on my merry way. I began to suspect there might be a problem when I glanced in my side mirror and saw sparks flying and then got a whiff of the burning steel. I pulled the hand brake and jumped out, only to see that the camper had been shaved down an entire inch. I looked around the parking structure suspiciously for the *Candid Camera* crew. No luck.

The actual tryouts didn't go any better. And, of course, I was overdressed. The Bob Barker wannabe host judged contestants on energy, enthusiasm, and whether we had a genuine laugh. My real giggle wasn't real enough, apparently. Suffice it to say, I wasn't chosen. I bolted from the studio audience like I'd been shot out of a cannon.

After I caught my breath and started the ignition, I remembered that the truck was jammed up into the rafters. But what to do? In a moment of sheer brilliance, relatively speaking, I took a ballpoint pen from the dash and let just enough air out of the tires to lower the truck another inch. Too bad I wasn't trying out for *MacGyver*.

Later, when Carmen and Delma asked about my new star status, I admitted I didn't even make it past the first cut. (But at least my auto shop teacher would have been proud of my ingenuity.) They all laughed and said that maybe I was a candidate for *The Gong Show*.

Maybe I should have stuck to the relatively unembarrassing confines of my room.

> Okay. What lessons did I learn today?
>
> 1. I need to think carefully about my wardrobe before I go out in public.
>
> 2. I'm not as gregarious as I thought.
>
> 3. Apparently, a Maytag washer is not in the stars for me.
>
> 4. I shouldn't drive other people's cars.
>
> P.S. How in the world did Tim Taylor's grandma win the showcase showdown? Call Mom and find out.
>
> P.P.S. Also have Mom ask Grandma Taylor if Ryan is really dating Tim's old girlfriend. I hope it's not true.

I had no need to hibernate in my room on weeknights, though. Michael stayed out with clients or attended meetings Monday through Thursday, with rare exceptions. And one or two nights a week he would send someone from the office to pick up Judy so the two of them could attend screenings, charity dinners, awards ceremonies, or parties with clients. The first night I observed this ritual, I assumed they had special plans because Judy sported a stunning black sequined dress. She seemed excited as she stood primping her hair in the hall mirror, waiting for a driver to pick her up. I was talking with her, telling her how great her dress looked, when the front gate buzzer went off. I figured the limo driver was at the intercom. But I peeked out the curtain to see a weather-beaten, dented old Volkswagen Bug idling in the driveway.

The driver, who was very young, stuck his head out of the window, waved, and honked the horn once. Seeing me at the window, he yelled, "I'm here to pick up Mrs. Ovitz. I can't shut the car off. Can you send her out?"

This was the first time since I arrived that I actually felt sorry for Judy. She had looked like an eager Cinderella going to the ball until she opened the door and saw her pumpkin sitting there spewing exhaust. I watched the old Bug as it chugged out of the driveway, sputtering and backfiring. I later found out that Michael had a habit of sending whoever was handy in the office, in whatever vehicle they happened to own, to pick up his wife. That particular driver had been hired to work in the mailroom only three days earlier. It seemed possible to me that Michael didn't know him from the Hillside Strangler. Yet, I had heard that when Michael started his agency, he had ordered new Jaguars for himself and for his partners. Apparently, in LA, you are what you drive!

And I drove a baby buggy.

When Judy was out with the Jeep during the day, I had to figure out an alternate way of fetching the kids from school. Joshua was in kindergarten at John Thomas Dye, an exclusive private school set high up on a hill, and Amanda attended half days with the three-year-old class. Carmen came to my rescue, offering to lend me her car. I was very grateful, but from the first time I took it, I was instantly aware of how out of place it was on the grounds of the private school. There I was, amid the Beemers, Bentleys, Jags, and occasional limos, pulling up in Carmen's rust-colored Corolla. The bumper hung off precariously, and the paint peeled off in chunks. When I followed the parade of new cars making their way to the waiting children, I had to constantly rev the engine to keep it running—I didn't know which would die first, the engine (of age) or me (of embarrassment).

I knew what they must have been thinking: *Who the hell is that? And why does she keep revving that engine? What an eyesore. It shouldn't even be allowed on school grounds. Can't they do something about that, that . . .*

*thing? I don't pay fifty thousand dollars a year for this! Someone ought to call the headmistress.*

I was sure Michael never gave a thought to his wife or children riding around in such heaps. He was known for his efficiency, after all, and they did get people from Point A to Point B. But was there logic to any of it? To these rules and regulations and rituals?

I still couldn't see it. I kept stumbling badly, trying to adhere to their sacrosanct social code, but I blindly crossed some invisible line more often than not.

Especially with information.

In Cottage Grove, everybody knew who your parents were, where you lived, what kind of car you drove, and whether you had smuggled Bud Light into the homecoming dance. But in LA, you could control what you revealed about yourself. You could keep unflattering details close to the vest, or you could even invent a whole new persona. There was no Aunt Madge to pipe up, asking if your hair didn't used to be more of a dishwater blond than platinum.

Michael valued such privacy immensely. He did not want his picture in the party pages of *People*. He did not want stories told about him. He had no desire to see his name in the gossip columns. But even more so, he didn't want certain details revealed to anyone. One day he was practicing aikido in the workout room when the phone rang. I answered, recognized Dustin Hoffman's voice, as a practiced staff member should, and said coolly (shrieking inside, though) that Michael was taking his martial arts lesson and would have to return the call. I relayed the message to Michael and got pursed lips and a slight shake of the head. He explained that no one had known about his aikido until a story had run just recently in a New York newspaper. He hated that and didn't want any more talk of his martial arts expertise. Clearly, I had disappointed him.

Michael expressed this kindly, in soothing tones, actually putting his arm around me. The effect was odd. I sensed that he did appreciate my work but that I'd have to zealously guard against making more mistakes. It would be years before I read this Paul Newman assessment of Michael, but I could certainly relate to the contradiction: "He's a cross between a barracuda and Mother Teresa."

I just never felt like I could relax around him. I knew I wasn't the only employee who felt that way though. Carmen had confided in me that after working there for seven years, she still never felt at ease.

> It's funny: even though he's not a tall man, Michael somehow has a presence of enormous stature. He doesn't need to raise his voice. His very being just demands respect. When he says jump, you not only say how far and how high, but how long would you like me to keep jumping, sir? Maybe it's because he's always so impeccably dressed. Even when he returns from working out, his plush robe looks starched. Maybe he makes Delma iron it.

I continued to figure out all kinds of things about my new home. One of them was why there was no answering machine or voice mail. I would have thought someone so powerful would surely screen his calls—no telling who could get hold of his home phone number, though it was certainly unlisted. Later I realized that there was no need for such electronic devices. There was always someone home, usually at least four or five people. Although many times Judy was frustrated with the messages she received, because—except for me—everyone on the staff was a native Spanish speaker. It was difficult for them to write in English, but Judy got upset when she couldn't tell who had called. So they started coming to me after they had taken a message, asking me to spell the names correctly. I was happy to help.

I certainly knew the names. Phone calls from the stars came in every single day.

The closest I'd come so far to meeting a celebrity in person was Michael's partner, Ron Meyer, who wasn't really a celebrity—though he did look a lot like Sylvester Stallone. But I spoke to many industry giants on the phone. I wasn't prepared, however, for the call that came one particular afternoon. Joshua picked up the phone to answer it, taking a break from watching *Top Gun* for the hundredth time. I couldn't believe my ears.

It was Tom Cruise.

I was so excited that I ran to the extension in the kitchen and quietly picked up the receiver to listen. I stopped breathing.

"Hi, Tom," Joshua said excitedly. "I'm just watching you in *Top Gun*, and my favorite part is when you go into the spin!"

I was about to go into a spin.

"Hi, kiddo," Cruise said cheerfully. "What part is on now?"

"Oh, the part where you say 'I have a speed for need,'" Joshua blurted.

I suppressed a laugh and covered the mouthpiece, but I continued hanging on his every word.

"Uh, oh, that part," Cruise stuttered.

He was so sweet. He remained on the phone with Joshua for five minutes, answering all his questions about the movie. Although he had a vested interest in being polite, since he had been essentially discovered and was represented by Michael, I think he really got a kick out of talking to his little fan. I could hear that he was at a loud party, but he never rushed the conversation.

Finally, he asked if Michael was home, and Joshua yelled out, "Daaaaaddddddyyy! The Maaaaverick is on the phone."

It took everything I had to hang up and not stay on to listen to that wonderful voice, but my sense of propriety and self-preservation finally kicked in. I placed the receiver back on the hook very delicately.

A couple days later, Delma and Gloria came to me, all dimpled up with smiles. They said they had a love message for me from a Thomas Cruz, and they wondered if they had the spelling right. They loved teasing me about my little crush, which was only growing since I heard his voice live. Maybe he'd visit someday? Imagine. They'd have a field day with that one.

My friendship with the other girls in the house grew deeper, and I gradually found out more about the recent history of the family. Carmen had also been close to a previous nanny, Leticia, who had worked there when Amanda was a baby. Between Leticia and me had been the other young nanny I was told about when I interviewed. She had lasted only two months. Carmen told me more about the girl, who had apparently been very snobbish. I couldn't imagine how lonely she must have been—the conversations and laughs with Delma and Carmen were a large part of what was sustaining me. They were much more of a family to me than my Hollywood hosts. I was, however, beginning to understand why my predecessor decided she wasn't cut out for the nannying life.

Carmen also told me that when Leticia left, there had been an unpleasant scene between her and Judy and that Judy had said she could no longer come in the house. A few weeks after that, Leticia had called Carmen asking to come back to visit Amanda. Carmen had to coordinate it carefully. Joshua couldn't be there—he would tattle—and she was too scared to let Leticia in, so the meeting had to be on the sidewalk. I sympathized, but I told Carmen that I thought asking Amanda to keep Leticia's visits a secret from her parents was too much pressure to put on a three-year-old.

Then I saw one of the reunions. When Carmen told Amanda that Leticia was at the gate, she dashed out the front door and pumped her little legs all the way down the driveway. There, as if outside prison walls, stood Leticia, a plump Hispanic woman grasping the black iron bars and pressing her face into the space between. My heart sank. Her smile lit up the street. It was clear Amanda adored Leticia. Little did I know that would be me someday, just another in a long line of departed souls.

I've been trying to follow the rules, so each morning I've asked Judy if she wants to feed Brandon. She says she doesn't have time right then. I've checked with her the last five mornings and she has always said she doesn't have time. Maybe I'm making her feel bad that she isn't able to give him a bottle. Maybe I should stop asking her.

I often found myself gravitating toward my friend in the kitchen and frequently chatted with Carmen as she concocted meals. On one afternoon, I watched idly as she stirred a large pot of cream of leek soup. She smiled, hummed, and happily dumped salt into the pot.

Shocked, I glanced up sharply. Michael prided himself on staying in excellent shape. He didn't just dabble in aikido; he held a black belt, and he religiously followed a very strict diet. He absolutely forbade any salt, butter, additives, or fatty foods in his meals. Michael and Judy watched the children's diets, too, especially monitoring them for fats. Skim milk and tiny pats of butter for flavor, no fried chicken, no Big Macs, no chocolate milk shakes. Their Happy Meals consisted of grilled swordfish and yellow squash.

"Carmen!" I exclaimed. "I thought he didn't eat any salt."

Carmen didn't respond. She just kept humming and smiling as the salt gushed into the vat.

"Little Soo-zita, Miguel"—what she called him when he wasn't around; it was "Mr. Ovitz" to his face—"would not eat half the dishes he asks me to make if I did not put in a little flavor," she said, laughing. "He loves all of my cooking; I put everything in that I need to make it *muy bien*. Then I just tell him it tastes so good because I am such a good cook."

"Carmen, I can't believe you put salt in his meals," I cried, pushing her on the shoulder. "He thinks he's on such a strict diet."

What if he found out? She'd be fired for sure. I didn't think I'd ever have the courage to do something like that. But Carmen wasn't worried. She often said that his low-fat diet was more important to him than Judy.

Carmen may have been a great cook, but when it came to the dinner parties, professional caterers ran the show. I had heard so much about Michael's love of entertaining that I was very curious about my first gala. Carmen showed me the guest list. As I read the names, I made some guesses about who they were.

**MICHAEL AND JANE EISNER** (I'd met them before and knew they were very good friends and had something big to do with Disney.)

**IRWIN AND MARGO WINKLER** (I made a note to call home to let my family know that Mr. Arthur Fonzarelli himself was coming to dinner. My sisters and I had been big *Happy Days* fans as kids. This Irwin guy must really be Henry Winkler.)

**STEVE MARTIN AND HIS WIFE, VICTORIA** (Carmen said she thought she was an actress, but I had never heard of her.)

**SEAN AND MICHELINE CONNERY** (Mrs. Connery had called that day and refused to believe that Judy wasn't home. She told me over and over exactly *who* she was, demanding to be put through, as if I was the social secretary who had been told to hold all calls. I must have told her five times that Mrs. Ovitz was *really* not in. Finally she just hung up on me in disgust.)

**BARRY DILLER** (I had never heard of him. Maybe he was Phyllis Diller's husband?)

**DIANE VON FURSTENBERG** (I was pretty sure she was the clothing designer.)

**AARON AND CANDY SPELLING** (Now, I did know who he was. I had loved *Charlie's Angels* as a little girl.)

**BARBARA WALTERS** (Last, but certainly not least.)

"Oh God, I hope Michael doesn't seat me next to Barbara Walters," Judy had said to me several days before the party. "He can seat her next to Jane. She's much more well-read than I am." I was shocked. Judy struck me as both intelligent and beautiful, and she was certainly accustomed to interacting with celebrities. Why would she be insecure?

In the dining room stood two square marble tables placed a few feet apart. Each table sat eight people, and generally anywhere from eight to sixteen people attended the dinner parties. Michael was known for getting up and rearranging everyone and their food about halfway through each meal, regardless of whether they had finished eating. I guessed he didn't want anyone spending all his or her time with just one person; he enjoyed mixing the personalities and conversations. I figured that was why Judy was nervous. She knew the chances were good that she would eventually sit next to the famous and well-read Ms. Walters. She didn't seem to have a choice where she sat at her own party. Apparently Michael decided that.

Right before the guests started arriving, Judy asked me if I would take her picture with Michael. He stopped briefly to pose while I struggled to figure out how to operate the camera. I heard Michael say, "Don't stand so close to me."

Judy had on a beautiful white angora sweater that was finding its way onto his black suit.

"What am I supposed to do? Not go near you all night?" she inquired with all sincerity.

He shot her a look that said, *Yes! If that's what it takes to keep my suit lint free.*

"SMILE!"

Luckily, my role during a dinner party was not to be a photographer. I was supposed to sit in the family room with the children until the guests had been seated for dinner. Joshua ran back and forth from the family room to the dining room to talk to the guests during the cocktail hour—a pint-sized comedian. Throughout the arrival and predinner time, waiters dropped in to the family room to bring us hors d'oeuvres. Intermittently, the celebrities paraded through to see the children. I didn't know whether I was supposed to dress up or wear my usual nanny attire, a T-shirt and shorts. I thought I would look stupid sitting in the family room with the kids wearing an evening gown (not that I owned an evening gown), so I just stayed in my shorts. Just before the guests sat for dinner, I took the kids in to say a final good night and then swept them all off to bed, just like Maria in *The Sound of Music.* I was slightly embarrassed as I carried Brandon into the dining room. I felt like a mutt entering a stuffy dog show filled with purebreds.

The night of this first party, I practiced my blasé and nonchalant attitude toward celebrities. I talked to Steve Martin briefly, until his wife interrupted him because he was eating cashews. She scolded him for eating something so full of fat. "Oh, are these not healthy?" he asked her, as if he was a child and she was the mother. He kept such a straight face that I couldn't tell if he was putting her on, and I'm not sure she could, either. She looked at him in disgust and turned around on her skinny heels to leave the room. By the looks of her nearly transparent body, she took a passionate interest in the pursuit of caloric restriction.

It turned out that the Winkler guy hadn't ever been on *Happy Days.* He was the producer of a whole lot of major hits, starting with the

*Rocky* movies. And Barry Diller, the CEO of an entertainment company, wasn't Phyllis's husband. This was a good thing, since his date was the fashionable Ms. von Furstenberg. Barbara Walters cancelled the day before the event. The hostess was relieved, but I was very disappointed that I only got to talk to her on the phone. I had been a huge fan of *20/20* since I was a child. In fact, my mother blamed that show for my overzealous interest in other people's business.

Not long after my first dinner party, I was introduced to the family movie-screening tradition. They had a monthly ritual of showing prere-leased movies to the family and a few close friends. One of the living rooms featured a giant screen that could be pulled down from the ceil-ing, and a CAA employee would come from the office to run the huge projector from a small room in the back wall. It was like a miniature movie theater. They were always kind enough to invite me to join them. It was a nice perk, but I could never really relax. Sitting on a couch halfway between the projector and the wall, I spent the whole time scrunching in my seat, afraid my head would be in someone's way or would project upon the screen.

One evening, Michael invited Dustin and Lisa Hoffman to join us. Almost immediately after the movie began to roll, Mr. Hoffman began to kibitz, either to himself or to his wife, I wasn't sure which. "The char-acters are crying before we are," he spit out. I gathered this was not good. He rose up and jabbed toward the screen, like he wanted to start a fight with anyone who would disagree.

This went on and on. It was like sitting close to the inconsiderate clod in a movie theater who has either seen the film before and now wants to narrate it for the rest of us or who's seeing it for the first time and offers a stream of constant criticism. Perhaps he was just in a bad mood? Finally, after commenting extensively on just about every scene, he stood up, said, "Bad movie," and walked out of the room to get his coat. Michael and Judy exchanged shocked glances.

I had never heard someone talk to Michael like that. It was so far removed from my perspective—worried every second that I wasn't doing things properly or that he thought I wasn't measuring up.

But then I got a sudden welcome surprise. Late one evening as I headed downstairs to get Brandon's bottles, I heard Judy talking to Michael in the family room. When I heard my name, I leaned over the banister as far as I could. I put my hair behind my ears as if I were the bionic woman, straining to catch any of the words. If I tilted any farther, I'd catapult down the stairs.

"How is Suzy doing?" Michael asked.

"She's night and day different from that last girl," Judy said. "She's great."

Did I really hear that right? I was thrilled. I had taken the lack of communication and warmth to mean that she just didn't like me. Maybe I had been misreading her. Maybe I had it all wrong. Maybe she really hadn't been judging me all this time.

Then the kids started screaming, and I couldn't hear the rest.

I'm hoping my children will save me from my vanity. It sucks to have to grow older. We all have to accept it.

—Gwen Stefani

# chapter 7
# crimes and misdemeanors

The next day, while the kids and I played Candyland in the family room, Judy came in and said that Michael had offered to pay for my nails to be done. If I wanted nails like hers, she would send me to her "girl."

She had impeccable acrylics. It was so kind of her to offer. I didn't give a thought to how I would maintain my own set. I supposed I would eventually need to remove them, but I'd worry about it later. And maybe I could stop my lifelong habit of biting my nails.

"I'd love to," I eagerly responded. "Thank you, Mrs. Ovitz."

"We're not going to the beach house, so you can take my Jeep this weekend," she volunteered. I was stunned. So I must have overheard that conversation between them correctly. Judy liked me after all. Things were definitely looking up.

The following day, Judy handed me the keys along with the address of the salon. I hadn't traveled more than four blocks from the house when the short blips of a police siren went off. I turned to see red lights swirling in the rearview mirror.

Oh my God, what had I done?

I couldn't have been driving more than twenty miles an hour down the residential streets of Brentwood, but with my infamous record, I couldn't afford another citation. Shoot! I suddenly remembered that I hadn't changed my Oregon license with the DMV. There was some sort of a time limit to change it to a California license. Would I be fined? I couldn't afford a fine. My pulse quickened as I pictured myself in hand-cuffs, being stuffed into the back of the police cruiser. I next pictured being let out of my cell to make my one phone call. Would I call my mother or Carmen? My heart began to do butterfly kicks in my chest as I pictured the Jeep being pulled onto a tow truck and whisked away to some lot in the bowels of Los Angeles.

"Driver's license and registration, ma'am?" the officer said, jolting me out of my nightmare.

"Uh, yes, I've got it here somewhere, sir. Let me look in the jockey box," I replied as I began to dig around.

"The *what?*" he said.

"Oh, sorry, the glove compartment." I made a mental note to ask my father if that was just a family term. Was *everything* here different from Cottage Grove?

My first thought was to tell the officer I'd left my license at home. I could give him the Ovitz address as if I was a California resident and perhaps he'd just give me a ticket using my name and that address. I fig-ured that if I gave him the Oregon license, he'd be able to pull up my citations, and I'd soon be wearing a striped uniform.

But then he said, "Did you know that your plates are expired?"

"Uh, no, Officer, I didn't. This isn't my car. It belongs to my boss," I said. "My boss, Michael Ovitz." I made sure I stressed the last name. Would it work? I crossed my fingers.

"*The* Michael Ovitz?" the officer asked, surprised, as if there were sev-eral Michael Ovitzes in town.

"Yes."

*Please, please, please.*

"Okay," the officer said. "I'm giving you a verbal warning."

*Thank you! Thank you! Thank you!*

"Tell Mr. Ovitz to get his plates renewed. Have a nice day." He tipped his hat and walked back to his car. My heart began to slow to normal again as I put the car in gear and pulled out into traffic. Was this how the name-dropping thing worked? It was the first time in my entire life that I had been pulled over and *not* received a citation.

On my way to the salon on Hillman Avenue, I drove—mostly in circles—through Brentwood, Santa Monica, and then Pacific Palisades. When I finally located the address, I was in a very seedy section of LA I didn't yet know. Just as when I'd finally found the nanny institute in a less-than-upscale section of Portland, I was dismayed to see that I'd arrived at the right place. The address I had was an old run-down apartment building with paint chipping off the walls. Did Judy really come here to get her beautiful nails done? I just couldn't picture it. But there was no mistaking the numbers.

I climbed the two flights of stairs to apartment number 223 and knocked. The door opened with a burst of stale, hot air. A strong odor of heavy perfume and polish remover nearly knocked me over. In the tiny confines of what looked like a one-bedroom apartment, I would be lucky not to choke to death.

"You must be Suzy," said the woman who answered the door. My prayers that I was in the wrong place vaporized. "Come on, darlin'. Come on in. You're lettin' all the hot air in," she said as I stepped cautiously inside.

I glanced at one of the windows, which was covered with cardboard and taped shut. About five foot six and 250 pounds, the woman was immense. She wore a black tank top from which her meaty arms protruded. Her buttocks and thighs were screaming to be released from their sausagelike encasements—a pair of shiny black spandex pants that had obviously been stretched far beyond their intended limits.

"Come here, sweetie. Sit down. Let's have a look at your nails," she said as she wheeled her tray of supplies between us.

Nearly two hours later, when she was all done, I had to admit my new nails looked terrific. But the whole thing hadn't quite met my lofty dreams of a leisurely day at the salon. I tried to visualize Judy driving into this run-down neighborhood and sitting on the orange and green plaid couch amid the pungent odors of solvents just to save a few bucks on her acrylics.

But Michael had offered to pay for my nails, and I appreciated it. I did not want to look this small gift pony in the mouth.

Two of my nails had broken by the time I returned two weeks later for a fill, and the woman in black spandex promptly repaired them. Grateful that the cost would be put on Judy's tab, I thanked her and left without paying. By the following visit, I had broken several other nails. Only this time, after the woman fixed them she said, "You owe me four bucks."

"Huh?" I said. "Judy said she was paying for it."

"Sorry, girl, Mrs. Ovitz didn't pay me for last week. So you owe me two bucks from then and two bucks for today. She said she wasn't going to pay for broken nails, only for your fill. I guess Mrs. Ovitz thinks if you break them, you pay for them."

I gave her the four dollars and a generous tip, and gave up on having my nails done. It wasn't very practical, anyway.

> I don't get it. The whole thing with the nails is weird. I wonder why Judy made sure I paid $2. She seems like she's afraid I'll take advantage of her. I bet she and Michael didn't talk about it, because he was the one who offered to give me the nails as a little extra gift, and I know he wouldn't care about two bucks. I think he wanted to show me that he appreciates my work. I think Judy must be like Oprah, who still buys her false eyelashes at Walgreens. I know she wasn't as poor as Oprah was as a child, but I know she didn't grow up with the kind of money she's surrounded with now. It seems like money is Michael's domain. So maybe one area she feels like she can control is how much she gives the hired help? Carmen says it has always been like this, so not to take it personally. The whole thing seems kinda sad to me.

A few weeks later, Judy and Michael called from the Mediterranean, where they had gone on a week-long private cruise with a group of friends.

"Hello, the Ovitz residence. This is Suzanne."

"Hello, this is the overseas operator. Mr. and Mrs. Ovitz are calling."

"Okay."

"Go ahead, sir. The charges will be $3.52 a minute," the operator said.

Michael came on the line first, and the connection was awful. "Suzy, we're calling you from somewhere in the Mediterranean. Is my art okay?" he asked.

*Did he really just say what I think he said?*

"Yes, Mr. Ovitz. Everything is fine. Brandon's taking his nap, and Amanda and Joshua are outside," I told him as the connection broke up again.

"I couldn't hear you, Suzy, bad connection. Is everything okay?"

"Yes, sir, everything is fine."

"Can we talk to Joshua?" he asked.

"Yes, of course. He's outside. Hold on a minute." I put the phone down, ran outside, and called to Joshua. It took two or three minutes to get him to the phone.

"Hello. Are you there, Mr. Ovitz?"

"No, Suzy. This is Judy," she snapped. "For God's sake, where is Joshua? This call is costing us a fortune."

She said a quick hello to Joshua, and then he handed the phone back to me.

"Hello, Mrs. Ovitz. Amanda . . ." Buzzzzzzzzzz. The line was dead. She'd hung up.

I tried to analyze what had just happened.

- $20,000 private cruise. Parents don't give it a second thought.

- $15.00 phone call to check on the kids. Parents think this is way too spendy.

It baffled me.

I just could not understand the household's money rationale. On one hand, Judy made Delma scrub stains out of a cheap T-shirt of Brandon's instead of buying him new clothes. At other times they would spend money on oddball things as if they minted it in the attic. Catering for a dinner party could run more than $12,000 and no one would bat an eye. How did they decide what was important and what wasn't?

A few days later, while they were still on the cruise, I walked into the laundry room and spotted Rosa using an iron with a frayed cord. It was so old that I could see a flash of the copper wire through the cloth insulation, a definite health hazard, not to mention a fire just waiting to destroy the house. Never mind the inhabitants—think of the risk to the art collection!

"For God's sake, Rosa, we need a new iron," I said. "They must not know that this one is in such bad shape."

"You know how Miss Judy is 'bout money," called Carmen from the other side of the kitchen.

"I know, but I am sure they don't know how bad the iron is. I'm going to the store where they have an account and charge a new one. I'm sure it will be fine," I said with great authority.

The next time I was out, I bought a new iron with a coated electrical cord. Then I wrapped the frayed cord around the old one and put it in the garbage.

Two days later, when they'd returned, I overheard Judy talking to her friend Jane in the foyer.

"They sure love to spend all my money," she complained.

"Mrs. Ovitz, I was the one who bought the new iron," I interrupted, rushing in.

No answer.

"I insisted that we needed a new one," I continued. *So my friends don't get electrocuted and the artwork doesn't go up in smoke.*

"We could have put a new cord on the old iron," she explained. "Do you have the receipt, Suzy?"

Fortunately, Carmen had retrieved the old iron before the trash went out.

She knew Judy far better than I did.

Luckily, I was only a few days away from a much-needed reality check. My best friend, Kristi, called me from Eugene, where she was in her freshman year at the University of Oregon. She asked whether she could come visit me during her spring break. Finally, some company! I was ecstatic. Judy even agreed to let Kristi stay at the house. When Kristi arrived, she was wowed by her first up-close-and-personal look inside a Hollywood home. She thumbed through a book by Danielle Steel, her favorite author at the time. She was pretty surprised that it had a long personal message to my employers.

I gave her a tour of the house, the art gallery, and the grounds, where the gardeners were pruning the shrubs. We waved to them, and they smiled and waved back. I brought Kristi into the four-car garage to show off the car collection: the black Jaguar, the black Mercedes, and my own personal favorite, the Porsche. I waved my arm over it like Vanna White on *Wheel of Fortune*. I was trying to be smooth.

Then I set off the car alarm.

WAAAAA! WAAAA! WAAAA! WOOOP! WOOOP! WOOOP! WOOOP! WAAAA!

"Damn it! I can't believe I set off the alarm!" I wailed.

"Are the police gonna come?" she asked.

"I hope not! Ohhh! I can't believe I just did that!"

The gardeners came rushing up, pruning shears in hand. Then Carmen and Delma dashed out from the house.

"Soo-zita, was that you again?" Delma asked. (Okay, okay. I had set off alarms a couple of times before.)

"Yes! Michael and Judy are going to kill me."

The alarm was still ripping through the air—WAAAA! WAAAA! WAAAA! WOOOP! WOOOP! WOOOP! And it seemed to be getting louder. Or was that my imagination? What was I thinking when I went near that car?

"I feel like such a dork!" I yelled over the noise.

"You're not a dork," Carmen said. "I've done it, too. There are a lot of alarms 'round here. But don't worry, you'll get the hang of it."

"I know the routine!" Delma shouted. "Come on out of the garage. I'll call Sarah and ask how to shut it off and reset it. Michael does not have to know you did it."

Everybody left the garage, and we shut the door behind us. Thank God it muffled the horrible wailing.

She put her arm around my shoulder. "Anyway, Soo-zita, we're like a family here. A *familia* within *la familia*, you know? We look out for one another."

But even my friends couldn't bail me out every time. On the third day of Kristi's visit, we took the kids on a walk. Little Brandon was sprawled out in his giant, fuddy-duddy English pram—a baby accessory that was all the rage with movie-star moms—and Joshua and Amanda were walking alongside it. At one point, Joshua insisted on pushing the pram. I hesitated, but he was being so bratty and demanding that I finally gave in to avoid a scene.

"Only for a minute," I said. "This baby carriage is very big and heavy. It's not really meant to be pushed by little boys."

"I'm not a little boy!"

Great. I had just committed the cardinal sin of all sins in nannyhood. Always call a little boy a big boy, or don't say anything at all. "I know you're not, honey; I forgot. You're a big boy," I said, praying that groveling would work.

"I'm not a little boy!"

"Okay, Joshua, I said I'm sorry. Now here you go." I stepped out of the way and let him get in front of me. Then he started to push the pram a bit too fast. I picked up my pace to keep up. "Joshua, not so fast; be careful."

"I don't have to be careful," he whined. "You can't tell me what to do."

"Yes, I can, honey. And you *do* have to be careful."

"I know how to do it!" he yelled. The next thing I knew, he was popping a wheelie. It all happened in one frightening flash: the top-heavy pram started to tip over and the baby slipped forward, feetfirst, heading straight for the pavement. My heart jumped in my throat. I rushed in and scooped up Brandon before he fell. Then the pram went crashing over sideways, its wheels spinning in the air. I was so scared that I didn't even reprimand Joshua. As we walked back to the house, stunned, my arms shook so much that Kristi offered to carry Brandon for me. I didn't dare put him back in that pretentious—and dangerous—pram. When we reached the gate to the house, my heart was kicking against my chest like in *Alien* before the creature popped out. *My God, I can't control these kids,* I thought. *I can't take them anywhere and keep them safe because they won't listen to me.*

Inside the house I told Judy about the incident. Furious, she immediately shouted, "Go to your room, mister!"

"I won't go to my room!" Joshua yelled back. "Don't tell me what to do!"

"You don't tell me what to do! I've had enough of this disrespect from you," Judy shouted.

"You don't know anything," Josh spit out.

"How can you say that to me? You're so incredibly condescending!"

"No, Mommy, you're credibly sending!"

"Oh God, I can't believe you act like this. Forget it!" Judy stormed off and slammed the side front door.

Joshua just stood there grinning, knowing he'd won the battle.

The scene felt familiar. Day after day, Joshua would do something that just begged for discipline, his mother would give him a time-out, he'd refuse to go, and then she wouldn't follow through. I don't think she knew what to do, so his behavior just got worse. How was I supposed to get anywhere with a child whose own mother didn't know how to claim her authority over him? She fought with Joshua the same way he fought with his sister. Amanda often witnessed these scenes, and she was climbing on board the bratty train, too. I could see that sweet little Brandon would probably model his older brother's behavior once he got old enough to understand how things worked in the household.

Having inadvertently shown Kristi some of the trickier aspects of my job, I wanted to also show her the bright side of living in Hollywood. We decided to splurge on a fancy dinner, so I called Sarah and asked her where we should go. She offered to make a reservation at Spago, a trendy place where we were sure to have some star spottings. Fantastic. We were both excited since neither of us had ever been to a place like Spago. Kristi had been wearing nothing but jeans and sweatshirts most of the time at college, and I spent most of my days in shorts and T-shirts, so we dolled ourselves up as if we had been invited to the Oscars. I didn't think much of it until we got to the restaurant. Almost everyone in there wore jeans, T-shirts, and khakis. And there we were, me in my fits-all-occasions black cocktail dress and Kristi in a similar dark blue number with a strand of pearls around her neck.

At least we weren't wearing pantyhose.

Sarah had listed the reservation under Hansen/Ovitz so that they would give us special attention. As for star sightings, we picked a dismal night; lesser luminaries, such as Sally Struthers and Ricardo Montalban, were the only ones on view. The meal, however, was excellent. I had free-range rosemary chicken; Kristi tried one of Wolfgang's famous goat-cheese pizzas. Then they brought us a great dessert and made a point of telling us that Michael had paid for it. How nice. I took out my checkbook and paid the rest of the bill. I had planned on thanking him the next day, but I didn't see him until the day after that, and then only briefly. By the time I did express my gratitude for the desserts, he seemed a little confused.

"They were supposed to put the entire meal on my tab. So you paid for it with your own money?" he asked.

"Yes, of course."

"Hmm. I told them to pick up the whole thing. Here . . ." And with that, he pulled out his checkbook, asked me how much it had been, and wrote me a check. I thanked him profusely. Maybe this was Michael's way of showing his appreciation for all the care and love I gave the children.

I can't believe that Michael got us reservations at Spago and paid for our dinner. Not just anyone can get reservations. Sarah said if a "no name" calls, it can take over a month to get in. Wolfgang Puck himself made a point of asking if everything was all right with our meal. It's so weird. It's getting routine to see the likes of Martin Scorsese dropping by, and no one in the house acknowledges how surreal it is. I've already gotten used to living in a place where answering the phone might mean talking to Cher or Chevy Chase or discussing diaper rash with Cristina Ferrare. The other day I took a message from John Travolta, and he seemed really nice, like an average kind of guy.

Maybe it's like Oprah always says: you're still the same person you were before you became famous; it's just that millions of people know you.

I don't like children being spoiled materially, and he won't be—I'm not megarich. I've got plenty of money, but I can't afford private planes. Gucci shoes . . . never happen in a million years. If he gets them as a present, fabulous. But it won't be from me.

—Elizabeth Hurley

chapter 8

# doc hollywood

I let a few more weeks fly by before I worked up the courage to ask Judy if I could use the Jeep again. Even though I knew they weren't going to the beach house that weekend, I still didn't know if I could pull it off. But she said yes. Freedom! But what to do? Since I had no off-duty friends to spend time with, I decided to cheer myself up a different way. I'd spotted a nice little spa when I was buying shoes for the kids at the local Brentwood shopping mall. The nail salon experience had been disappointing, to say the least, but I hadn't given up on my spa fantasy. All I could think of that morning was my noon facial appointment and how I would luxuriate in all the little attentions they would provide. Soothing music, herbal teas, and a zen atmosphere. The package even included a neck and foot massage, which sounded heavenly. I had earned some relaxation time in Eden. I was going to live it up, LA-style; I even thought I'd treat myself to lunch at a bistro after.

The sign in the window read SALON FLEUR DE LIS. HAIRSTYLING, FACIALS, AND PEDICURES. The girl at the desk immediately whisked me to a back room and told me to change into the white bathrobe that hung on the back of the door. Then I was to have a seat in a large Naugahyde chair.

Within minutes, a small woman wearing a starched white lab coat began circling me. She was stroking her chin, poking at my face, and saying, "Uh-huh. Uh-huh," under her breath, as if I were an antique piece she was appraising. I didn't know her ethnicity, but her heavy accent and very dark eyes intrigued me. You don't get a lot of cultural diversity where I'm from, and it sounded exotic to my ears. She introduced herself as "Sa-meen-a."

"Hi, young lady," she said. "Weee must give you a peeeel."

I blanched. Did I really look so bad that she had to comment on my need for improvement? I was so embarrassed. I had no appeal. I knew I should have put on makeup before I went to the appointment.

"No, no, my deeear. A peel," she shot back after seeing my shocked expression. "You need an acid facial peeeel. The sun has caused your skeeeen great damage. And you have had act-nee in your life."

No kidding. I was still a teenager.

"Weee must go far beyond a simple facial. Something that penetrates much deeper. You must be from the country," she added.

"Uh, yes. I guess I'm from the country." This woman must think I'm in the blazing hot sun out on the prairie each day, with no sunscreen. Just like Laura Ingalls. Now I know why Nellie Olsen always had such pale skin. She was from "the city" of Walnut Grove. "You can actually tell where I lived from looking at my skin?" I asked.

"Oh yes, most definitely. Wait, you will see. When I am done your skin will look and feel like silk. Like a little bambino's behind. I suggest our most powerful peel. It is exactly one hundred and ninety dollars," she said.

So much for my lunch at a bistro; it looked like it was going to be Carl's Jr. instead.

Simina began to dance around like she was possessed, draping me in a large plastic apron from my neck to my ankles. Next she worked a healthy lather of cleansing cream over my face and then wiped that off with a scalding hot towel. I felt as if I'd been instantly sunburned. With my face still glowing, she slipped on a pair of twelve-gauge rubber gloves that ran past her elbows. The kind firemen wear. Then she draped a heavy flame-retardant apron over her neck. She opened a large jar and began to dip a small paintbrush into it. Taking great care not to spill the toxin onto herself, she spread the chemical jelly over my entire face, skipping only my eyelids and lips. I tried not to think about why she was treating the stuff like Ebola.

Almost immediately I could feel a pleasant tingling sensation. Maybe this wouldn't be so bad.

"Do not move, Miss Sue-zah-na. It will take seven minutes to activate. I will come back to check on you," she said, backing out of the room.

But the tingling changed to a stinging sensation, and my worry flared up full force. Agonizing over the unknown is part of my DNA. Had she said it would take seven minutes to activate? What if my body made it kick in early for some reason? A full seven minutes would land me in a burn unit. As the minutes ticked away ever so slowly, the stinging intensified. Could my face actually be disintegrating? Impossible. This was a spa in LA, for Pete's sake. On the right side of the tracks.

I leaned up, squinting, trying to read the ingredients label on the jar of gel. I saw a long word and then "acid" afterward, followed by "propylene glycol."

Oh God! I *was* in trouble. I may not have known any foreign languages, but I did get an A in auto shop, and I knew those words. She'd put antifreeze on my face! I tried to yell but remembered Simina's orders to remain motionless. Would my face crack in two if I moved my mouth? I had to try something. There was *antifreeze* on my *face*.

"Suh-meen-hah, Suh-meen-hah," I managed to mumble feebly.

No answer.

Suddenly an oven timer beeped, startling me. The seven minutes were up, and at that precise moment, Simina reappeared, checked her watch quickly, and then began applying scalding hot towels once again, this time to rinse off the nuclear residue.

I was afraid to touch my skin.

"It will be a little tender for a day or two, and then you shall see. You will have de skin of a baby. That will be one hundred ninety dollars, please," she said, and with that I was left to my own devices.

I was okay. I still had a face. And I had forty-three cents left to my name.

Simina was right. When I got home, I noticed my skin was tender but not as bad as I expected, given the burning sensation I'd experienced.

What I didn't know was that the chemical was supposed to penetrate the first two layers of skin. I might have rethought that $190 expenditure had I realized that little fact. I had been expecting moisturizing and toning, certainly not second-degree burns. She had given me a special lotion to use once in the morning and once at bedtime to ease the discomfort. It must've been pure Novocain, though, because after I smoothed it on, my entire head went numb, and I began slurring my speech. I decided to use it only at bedtime.

The next day, Grandma Ovitz happened to be visiting. She remarked on the nice pink glow I had, asking if I'd enjoyed my facial. I told her yes, it had been quite an experience and left it at that. On the second day when I woke up and faced the morning mirror, I jumped back in horror. My entire face was peeling more dramatically than the worst sunburn I'd ever had. I looked like I'd survived a fire. By that night, I was shedding complete layers of skin, like a rattlesnake in August.

I couldn't keep my hands from peeling it away in large sheets. Underneath lay yet another layer of hot red skin just waiting to dry out and scale away like the previous layer. I began to panic. It didn't help matters when Judy told me I looked like I'd just escaped from a leper colony. Terrified, that afternoon I drove back to the salon and approached Simina.

"Oh my God, Miss Sue-zah-na. You have touched your face, haven't you? You're not supposed to pick at it," she said, as if it was *my* fault that my entire face was molting. How could I not peel it? It itched terribly and for the most part fell away on its own, anyway. I just wanted to keep the flakes off my clothes and off the furniture. Simina had no further advice other than to keep using the lotion and keep my hands off my face. I slunk home feeling defeated. How did people in LA look so put together all the time?

Skin-peel fiasco!
   It's now the fourth day, and my skin is still very blotchy, something like a Guernsey cowhide. I had no idea it would take so long for all these layers to slough off. It seems like the lady could have given me just a tad more info on what to expect. I

know they say you have to suffer for beauty, but the ratio of torture to aesthetic enhancement is pretty steep here, not count-
ing the humiliation factor.

And to top it off, Judy informed me that she was considering
getting a facial, but now never plans to make an appointment
at that salon if there's any chance she'll turn out looking like me.

Note to self: Get more information before allowing anyone to
paint me with a chemical you can buy at a local auto-supply
store.

I'd had enough adventure for the time being, so I wasn't too sorry
when Michael and Judy decided to go away the next weekend.
Grandma and Grandpa Ovitz came to stay and help out as they generally did when the kids' parents left town, just in case of an emergency.
That Saturday evening, we had one.

Earlier in the day it became clear that Brandon felt sick, and by nine
o'clock that night his temperature had skyrocketed to 104.2 degrees. I
hadn't seen many fevers that high before, and Grandma Ovitz and I
decided we needed to call the pediatrician's office. The on-call doctor
told me to bring the baby straight to the emergency room, and he
would meet me there. Grandma stayed at home with Joshua and
Amanda while Grandpa drove Brandon and me to the hospital. (I wondered if Grandpa was remembering our last trip to the ER. Thank goodness my head had healed.) Brandon was burning up, but oddly enough,
he smiled and cooed at me. When we got to the ER, the doctor was just
arriving and was busy helping find a seat for a woman who appeared to
be straight off the cover of the *Sports Illustrated* swimsuit edition. He
looked about Doogie Howser's age, and I could hardly contain my irrational rage. *Focus, buddy! On the baby, not that Victoria's Secret model,
who I might add is probably just dating you because she thinks you're
worth big bucks.*

The doctor ushered us into a small examining room and took Brandon from me. He felt the glands in Brandon's neck and forehead, and
then felt the top of his head. "Here," he said, "feel this." He put my hand
on the top of Brandon's head, over the soft spot that every baby has.

"Is this normal?" he asked.

"No, no, of course not," I answered. Brandon's soft spot was bulging right out of his skull, though Brandon just kept smiling.

I was screaming inside. He was a doctor, and he was asking *me*? Did this clown just get out of medical school? We needed answers!

But then the doctor said that he was very concerned, and I started to get scared.

"He may have meningitis," he said.

I knew that was a serious infection that involved the brain. Grandpa Ovitz and I stared at each other in fear and disbelief.

*What should we do? What should we do?* I felt very shaky.

"I've got to make a call," the doctor said. I felt reassured that he was consulting with someone more experienced. He picked up the telephone, and Grandpa Ovitz and I listened intently. Apparently, this young doctor was just starting in the practice with the older pediatrician, the children's regular doctor, whom I had met previously.

"Yes, Brandon Ovitz," he replied. "No, you don't have to come down here; I can handle it. Okay, if you insist, all right, good-bye."

When the older doctor arrived, I began to relax a little. He must've seen cases like this before. But then right away he said, "This baby isn't sick. Look at how happy he is."

*What? No!*

The younger doctor disagreed with his mentor, and I felt my loyalties switch quickly back to him. *How long has this old guy been around? When's the last time he had a refresher course?*

"I want to do a spinal tap," the young doctor blurted out.

"Are you kidding? You know whose child this is, don't you?" the older doctor responded.

"Yes, that's why I want to call them right now and get permission."

"They're on vacation," I said. "But I've got an emergency number."

That's when Grandpa Ovitz stepped in. "I'll call Michael. Everyone just stand by." After Grandpa talked to Michael, he handed the phone to the young doctor.

"Yes, Mr. Ovitz," he said. "Yes, that's right. I want to do a spinal tap, and I need your permission." Silence for a second. Michael must have sensed how young the doctor was. "Well, uh, yes, Mr. Ovitz. Uh, me personally, I've done a hundred of them." Then he handed the phone to me. Michael asked me for my opinion. What did I know about meningitis? I just told Michael that it didn't look normal, that his soft spot was very swollen and that I'd never seen it like that.

"We'll be there as soon as we can. We'll try to get a plane out tonight," Michael said. With that, the young doctor took Brandon down the hall. He brought along an assistant, who would be holding Brandon down while they put a needle into his back.

"It's all in the holding down," Doogie Howser explained. I pictured little Brandon stretched out under glaring lights while a young girl pressed down his tiny arms and legs and the doctor plunged a needle into his spine. I wanted to be there to soothe him and hold him. I tried to follow along but the assistant turned me back. I felt so bad for Brandon that I was getting a little nauseous.

Grandpa Ovitz and I fretted in the waiting room together. After we had been there about twenty minutes, the assistant came out and advised me to check on the other two children. "Have them touch their chins to their chests," she warned. "If it's painful or stiff, they may have the same thing."

Worry threatened to overwhelm me. By then it was nearly 11 P.M. Carmen picked up the phone right away. "I can't wake them up," she said when I told her what to do. "It's the middle of the night. It will be terrible." She and I both knew that Amanda would scream for hours after being woken from a sound sleep in the middle of the night. "Please, Carmen, just do it. This is serious," I told her. I called back in ten minutes. Over Amanda's wailing in the background, I heard Carmen saying they could move their heads just fine, with no pain.

After another ten minutes, a nurse came out carrying Brandon, and my heart did a tilt-a-whirl. He wasn't smiling anymore and clearly had been crying a lot. He was stretching his arms out to me from all the way across the room. He needed me. He wanted me. I started to cry.

I crossed the room toward him and the nurse said, "No, no. We're not done yet. He was crying and I wanted to bring him out here to let him know you were still here. We have some more tests to do, and the doctor wants to admit him." And with that, she walked back through the swinging doors with Brandon's cries echoing behind her. I tried to pull myself together as I sat in a heap, my face in my hands and Grandpa Ovitz's arm around me.

I decided to call my old friend Mandie from nanny school. I'd probably be waking her up in Montana, but I really needed to hear a friendly voice. She did her best to reassure me that everything would turn out all right.

Grandpa Ovitz and I waited for what seemed like hours until another nurse came and escorted us to the children's ICU ward. When we walked in, Brandon's foot was all bandaged up with IV tubing, and he was lying in a horrible, cold, cagelike steel crib. The poor, sweet little guy. I asked if I could hold him, and they said yes, as long as I was careful with the IV line.

By then it was way past midnight, and I told Grandpa Ovitz to go home and wait for Michael and Judy; I would stay the night. I couldn't stand the thought of little Brandon being alone in that awful place, in that awful crib, even if he fell asleep, which he didn't do for another two hours. I held him on my lap with his chest on mine for the rest of the night.

I woke up at five in the morning, stiff from scrunching up in a chair like a cat curled on a small stool. I think I'd slept a couple of hours. Brandon was still sleeping on me when his parents arrived around eight o'clock. Judy rushed up to me and kneeled down in front of my chair, taking Brandon from my arms. I felt so bad for her because Brandon immediately squirmed around and began crying and reaching for me. Judy looked into my eyes with an expression I'd never seen on her face and gently handed him to me.

I wanted to cry all over again.

"Oh look, he wants Suzy," she said quietly to Michael. "Why don't you go home, Suzy. It's been a long night, and we can stay with him now." Her voice was gentle.

I rested my cheek on Brandon's soft hair and cradled him against me until he stopped whimpering. When I looked up, she was still looking at us with soft eyes. In that moment, a wave of genuine compassion and empathy filled the space between us. And it came from both directions.

Although I did not want to leave him, I knew I needed a break. I went home and slept most of the day. Judy said Carmen and Delma could watch the kids, and I was grateful. I had a new appreciation for being in my own bed. When I called the hospital and checked in around 5 P.M., Judy said they hadn't gotten the test results back yet and that she had hired a private duty nurse to come in and take care of Brandon. My heart sank when she said that he had been crying a lot because he wasn't used to the nurse.

The next morning when I returned to the hospital, I finally heard some good news: the test results showed that Brandon did not have viral meningitis, only a bacterial infection. His temperature had gone back down to 99 degrees, and they were getting ready to discharge him.

When I got home, there was a large bouquet of beautiful flowers sitting on the foyer table with a card addressed to me. I opened it immediately. It was from Mandie.

*Dear Suzy,*

*I am thinking of both of you. I know how much the children mean to you. I hope Brandon is okay, and I hope you're holding up.*

*Love, Mandie*

For about the fourth time in two days I broke down in tears. At about that moment, Michael came in and saw me sitting at the foot of the stairs, holding the flowers in my hands.

"Who are the flowers from?" he asked nonchalantly.

"From my friend Mandie." I sniffed.

"What for?" His face showed no emotion.

"Because I've been having a hard time about Brandon," I mumbled. I was actually a little embarrassed that I was so upset and he seemed to be taking it in stride.

Michael continued to look at me blankly.

*Hello! This was traumatic for me!* I wanted to shout. Didn't he get it? I loved his son. I couldn't believe he didn't know that this was difficult and that I had been very scared.

But he didn't seem to understand. He paid me to take care of his kids but not to fall in love with them.

I did that on my own.

I'm very hands-on. It's important to me that my kids know that I'm their mommy and the nanny isn't.

—Toni Braxton

chapter 9

# beauty shop

I'd been working for only a few days when Judy had commented, "I hate it when the baby wants to go to the nanny instead of me." In the ensuing months, though, I saw that she managed to let this go. It seemed so sad to me that Judy accepted such events as the price one had to pay for having a nanny. She must have believed she had to give up some of the joys of motherhood just because she had the resources to hire help.

But some things she didn't want to give up. One morning I was feeding Brandon rice cereal after the older kids had gone to school. Judy walked in, took one long glare, hands on hips, and said, "What are you doing?"

I attempted an answer. "Uh, I'm feeding—"

"Don't you think I should be informed that he is eating solid foods?"

I swallowed. "Um, when we were at the pediatrician's office the doctor said Brandon could start on rice cereal mixed with formula."

"Well, whatever. I am the one that should be feeding him his first bite."

"I'm sorry," I said, handing her the plastic bowl and baby spoon. I was scared to tell her that I'd been following the pediatrician's orders for the past two weeks. Didn't she already know that? But she was right, a mother should be the one to give her child the first bite. I left the kitchen silently, feeling incredibly awkward, and went upstairs to change Brandon's crib sheets.

When I came down the stairs with a basket of dirty laundry, I saw Judy's Mercedes leave the driveway. I walked into the kitchen and found Carmen wiping cereal from Brandon's face.

Did Judy feel left out of Brandon's daily schedule? I didn't know what to do. I knew she wanted to be involved in Brandon's life, but I had always been responsible for feeding him. Maybe I didn't see my job description the same way my employer did.

I sure could have used a Standard Operating Procedures manual.

I knew that Amanda and Joshua, like many other children with live-in nannies, had already experienced their fair share of caretakers before I arrived on the scene—the image of Leticia waiting in front of the gate flashed in my mind. By the time I joined the household, they had learned to protect their feelings: they didn't want to lose another friend, so they did their best not to make one. But I hadn't been prepared for them to treat the time they spent with me like a dentist visit. The kids I babysat in Oregon had seen it more like a trip to a toy store.

I knew Joshua and Amanda could be affectionate; I had seen their excitement when Kristi visited. Once I decided to kill two birds with one stone—I tried to emphasize the fun in making new friends like Kristi by getting the kids involved in an after-school activity. As a babysitter, games and art projects were my stock in trade, but I had found it hard to entice these kids away from the TV and the huge selection of videos. I set up the table in the family room with construction paper, glue, and glitter. They designed cards for Kristi while I wrote their words down in a letter. Despite a few skirmishes over the glitter, they had a great time. Josh loved to make rainbows, and Amanda lost herself in the glue sticks.

It wasn't unprecedented for Amanda to have such fun. Sometimes we got along famously, dressing up in costumes as Sleeping Beauty, Cinderella, or princesses and doing silly dances to Raffi tunes. We played "telephone" and "baby" and "guess what I think." She was an adorable moppet. But often, right in the midst of our fun, some tiny thing would set her off. She wanted the kind of crackers she'd had at school; she wanted to watch *Cinderella* instead of playing on the swings; she couldn't find her Malibu Barbie. She would then scream and wail and throw things, both hers and mine, long past the point of exhaustion.

One day Amanda spun out of control because her mommy was leaving. She flew out of the house after her mother, kicking and screaming. She was three; she knew what she wanted, and she wasn't getting it. There was no end to her frustration and fury. She screamed, she kicked, she cried huge gulping sobs. I started to carry her to her room, but she wiggled right out of my arms and almost fell down the stairs. I think she was scared that she wasn't able to control her angry little body, and neither could I. So we just stopped there on the steps, and she sobbed more quietly. I finally sat down below her and looked up at her sad, wet face.

"Amanda, I am so sorry you're upset and having such a hard time," I told her. "I love you."

"I love you, too," she said, for the very first time, and plopped her heaving body onto my lap.

A turning point? I hoped so. Amanda soon announced that she wished I was her mommy. I could have taken it as a sweet compliment if it hadn't been during dinner when her actual mother was sitting *next* to me. I was mortified, and I figured Judy was, too. It was bad enough that Judy thought Brandon preferred me, but Amanda had *actually said it out loud*. NNI hadn't provided a script for this situation. The best thing I could come up with was, "Oh, honey, I'm too young to be your mommy."

"Amanda, it probably makes Suzy feel good to have you say that," Judy said.

I almost fell off my chair.

This from the woman who treated me like an irritating pest. Her difficulty setting limits for the kids had led me to believe that she was simply lacking in parenting knowledge, but just when I stopped expecting anything from her, she would respond to her children or me in such a wise and caring way that I got my hopes up all over again.

But Joshua still wasn't taking kindly to me, and he continued to be suspicious of my ability to actually care for him. I wished he would let down his guard and see that I was on his side. There were flashes of hope; our best times seemed to happen each day just after he got out of kindergarten. We quickly worked out an understanding that I would not tolerate hearing him describe his classmates as stupid, mean, or ugly. Instead, we agreed to call them "characters," with much lifting of the eyebrows, as in, "Suzy, Chantel was a real character today. She broke the wheel in the hamster's cage." Or, "Tayla dropped my project. What a character!" The way he'd ham it up was hilarious, and he loved being in on a joke.

He was an extremely bright child and a tightly wound perfectionist, very much like his father. When we sat down together to go over his homework, which he undertook with great concentration, he would get extremely frustrated over little mistakes, rubbing holes through the paper with his eraser. It couldn't be easy living that way.

And Joshua was just old enough to begin emulating some of his father's behavior, something he was doing more and more. When Michael wasn't home, Joshua seemed to think he could control everyone in the house. I could see that his actions turned off all the employees— no wonder, considering that he threatened to have the staff fired, me included, on a weekly basis. It was hard to deal with his outwardly difficult and hostile behavior, even though I understood that he was just a six-year-old boy determined not to let anyone new into his life. Underneath the obnoxious protective layers, he was a loving child. That was obvious, given his devotion to Michael's mother, "Nana."

When we talked about her, Joshua corrected me regularly, telling me that I was not saying her name correctly. "It is 'Non-uh,' not 'Nann-uh,'" he would say, rolling his eyes, asking why I couldn't get it right. When this happened, I was more interested than irritated. At least he felt unreserved love for someone in his life other than his parents. I wished he would trust me, but I didn't know how to make that happen. I tried to show him that I cared about him every day, especially because I knew the rest of the staff just tolerated him.

More than once when he was going off on one of his tirades, calling everyone on the staff "morons," I remember Carmen saying to him in Spanish something that sounded like, *"Como say chingas."* When Judy asked Delma what that meant, Delma told her, "Go in peace, little one." The actual translation was, to put it mildly, a little harsher. But Judy was never the wiser, and Carmen used it often, always with a peaceful smile on her face. This was her private little act of revenge for all the times Josh said she was stupid and a moron or that he didn't have to listen to what she said.

He didn't like listening to any of us, really. One day, when I was helping Joshua get dressed, he threw a fit because he couldn't find his blue socks. He started his usual rant—calling Delma a stupid idiot moron and saying it was all her fault. I told him that it was *not* okay to call people names. Just then Judy walked into the bedroom, "Well, where are his socks? Those girls are always losing things and costing me money." So much for trying to give a lesson on being respectful of adults.

But *my* lessons continued.

One morning I stepped out the front door as Judy was getting ready to take him to school. He was peeing on a tree. *Peeing on a tree.* Waiting until he'd finished his business, I approached him and reprimanded him for his behavior. I didn't think twice about it. After all, he was in full public view in the front yard, which faced the street. "Mom said it's okay!" he yelled back at me while trying to wipe the stray drops of urine from his loafers.

"I doubt your mother would want to see you peeing in the front yard," I replied.

"Oh yeah, you don't know anything! My mom said I could, and my mom is in charge of you," he shrieked emphatically. "Annnnndddd-ddd . . . I can have my daddy fire you if I want to!" Again with the firing.

Judy entered the conversation as she glided toward us. "Oh yes, Suzy. I told him it was okay. We're in a hurry, and I didn't want him to go all the way back into the house."

Joshua silently stuck out his tongue at me and walked away.

I gave up. I would add this to my list of rules. Make this #42, article 12, section 6 of the house bylaws: it is okay for the children to relieve themselves in the front yard if we're running late.

After the peeing incident today, I doubt whether I'll ever fit in. One day I feel as though I'm doing a great job and the next, something like this happens. Me working here is like trying to mix Metamucil in water—I never fully blend. I can't get the kids

to trust or like me. Carmen says it's best to say, "Okay, Judy."
Maybe I should make that my new mantra. Okay, Judy.

I wish I had someone to talk to. I need some friends here!
Getting the mail is the high point of my long day. I love to get
funny cards with news on the latest happenings at home.

Cottage Grove updates:

- Football stadium condemned—finally!

- Got our second fast-food restaurant—Taco Time. In a grocery
  store parking lot, of all things.

- Amy's dad, Bob, won a new barbeque at Bi-Mart's lucky number
  Tuesday. No more lighter fluid and briquettes for him.

    Note to self: You're living in the entertainment capital of the
world, and the highlight of your week is hearing about your
friend's dad's new grill. Get a social life. Actually, a life of any
kind would be an improvement.

A couple of nights later, Mandie called and announced that she
wanted to come and work in Los Angeles. It had become quite clear
that most people in her home state of Montana didn't have nannies. I
was thrilled. Finally, a way out of this loneliness. I told Judy about her,
giving a glowing account of her abilities and personality and asking her
to think about recommending Mandie the next time someone she knew
needed a nanny. Of course, I didn't mention the "count to ten before
you speak" rule of conduct Mandie's father had offered her.

Judy said that their good friends the Goldbergs happened to be looking for a nanny. Leo Goldberg was the head of a studio, a real bigwig. I
called Mandie about the job, and within two weeks she came to LA
with her mother, just as I had, to interview with them and with a few
other families the local placement agency had found for her.

After she completed her interviews, Mandie called me for advice. She
had just returned from the San Fernando Valley, where she met a very
nice woman with sweet children who said her husband was an actor. By
this time, however, I thought I knew how Hollywood worked. I clued
Mandie in to a basic principle: a lot of people say they're actors when, in
reality, they're just trying to break into the business. I told her the

woman was probably exaggerating about her husband's "film career." For all we knew, he could have been a caterer on the set. This seemed plausible, especially since Mandie reported that the family was remodeling their home and currently had only one bathroom.

Exactly my point! What big Hollywood star could get by with only one bathroom? Or would consider sharing a bathroom with the nanny? And besides, I was confident that no one who's *really important* lived in the Valley.

Mandie kept insisting that she clicked with the mom and kids, and she really wanted to take the position, but in my infinite wisdom I convinced her to take the job with the Goldbergs so we could live close together. "Just call the placement agency and tell them you decline the offer from this Costner guy, whoever he is."

(Yes, Mandie and I are still friends. Years later we still laugh about that, but she stopped asking for my advice on her career choices a long time ago.)

The Goldbergs lived in Bel Air, not far from Brentwood. I was already planning how often we could see each other. The best part was that Ellie, the youngest child she would be caring for, was only a couple of months older than Brandon. Their moms had commented on how great it would be if we got the babies together for playdates. Yippee! Adult conversation! With a friend who understood the challenges of the job.

From the very first day Mandie moved to LA, we started sharing nanny tales almost nightly over the phone. The first time she called, she was in dire straits. She'd only been with the Goldbergs for three days. "Suzy, can I ask you something?" She sounded so hesitant.

"Sure. What's going on?"

"How do you eat at your house?"

"Huh?"

"I mean, where do you do it? Can you just do it when you want? Can you just take what you want?"

*Was this another family that put a padlock on the Frigidaire?*

"Don't they let you eat? You sound like a starving refugee. When did you last eat?"

"Well, actually, it's really been three days," Mandie confessed. "Nobody's said anything about it. They have a maid who also does the cooking, but I haven't really talked to her. So far, they've just eaten out all the time. It's not like your house, where you have Carmen and Delma to talk to and eat with. It's more formal here. My first hint was when she told me not to call her Margaret; it was *Mrs. Goldberg* to me. I didn't exactly get the message that it would be okay to make myself at home in her kitchen after that."

I cut her off to give her a serious pep talk, which would become the template for most of our calls. "Stop right there! You haven't eaten in three days? March yourself into the kitchen, open the Sub-Zero, and make yourself a big fat sandwich!"

"Nobody's shown me around the kitchen. I feel so uncomfortable going in there. What if I take something they're saving for something special?"

"Right, better you just stay in your place, hiding in the servants' quarters. Maybe someone will take pity and throw you a crumb."

After I hung up, my brain started spinning. I had to sign that girl up for some take-charge-of-your-life classes. Then again, I've always been much better at giving advice about what people should do with their lives instead of minding my own. I was the one hiding out in my room for forty-eight straight hours each weekend.

In addition to baby Ellie, Mandie also cared for the Goldbergs' eight-year-old daughter, who we would soon learn had a mantra similar to Josh's "I hate you; you're an idiot." Lucky Mandie got to hear a more customized version with: "You're fat *and* ugly."

What could we do? Mandie and I laughed about how our daily predicaments would probably sound a bit odd to other people outside of our gated homes.

"Okay, here's one for you," I said the next night. "Judy came into the kitchen and saw me loading the leftovers from the children's plates into a green plastic trash bag, and she was aghast. I'm telling you, it actually took her a moment to catch her breath. I thought something was terribly wrong. I ask her if she is okay, and she says, 'Suzy, never, never use those bags for the trash can. They're heavy-duty and only to be used for the trash compactor. They're too expensive to put in the garbage can.' Then she walks into the pantry and comes back out with a box of *thinner* bags and puts those into my hand."

I started giggling, and then Mandie started in.

"That's nothing. The other night I was cooking my dinner with the housekeeper, and we got to talking, and before I knew it, the pan's burning. It really stunk up the place."

"Wait, stop," I interrupted. "Whoa, you're eating now?"

"Oh yeah, the housekeeper told me that Mrs. Goldberg asked her if she had ever seen me eat, so I got that straightened out. But the best part about being a spineless jellyfish is that I lost five pounds."

"Woo-hoo! That's great," I said, wondering if we could start the "nanny diet" craze. Living in a house where you feel like you're always just visiting does have its advantages. "Okay, go on with your story; sorry I interrupted."

"While I'm scrubbing to get the tar off the bottom of the old stained pan, Mrs. Goldberg comes in and goes ballistic. 'My God, what have you done?' she shrieks at me. Then she runs over and grabs the pan out of my hand and says, 'You've ruined this pan.' Then she tells me I have to buy her a new pan."

"Why didn't you just clean the one you burned?" I asked.

"I was trying to, but she had declared it legally dead, and that was that."

"So what happened?"

"Yesterday I had to go down to the May Company and buy a whole set of pans. It cost me half a week's paycheck."

"Why a whole set—I thought you only burned one of them?"

"I know, but she made me buy my own set to cook with. I can't use hers anymore. So now there are four pans in the pantry with Post-it notes on them that say 'Mandie's pots and pans.' It's like they have cooties. When I think about it, I shouldn't be surprised. I should have seen it right away."

"Seen what?" I asked.

"That she was tight. I didn't tell you what happened with the agency yet?"

"No. What happened?"

"Well, it was a mess, and of course I ended up paying for it—or at least half."

"Paying for what? Did you break something at the agency?"

"No, I didn't. But get this, since you recommended me, Mrs. Goldberg didn't use the agency she normally gets all her help from."

"Yeah, so . . ."

"Okay, so Mrs. Goldberg was thrilled that she wouldn't have to pay a fee to an agency. I didn't think much about it, because I just wanted to go to work here closer to you."

"So what was the problem?"

"The other nanny who was here before me told the agency the job was opening up because she was leaving. After I interviewed, the agency called. So when I was hired, I guess they figured they were entitled to the fee. Mrs. Goldberg was outraged that the agency had gotten her name. I ended up offering to pay half of the twelve-hundred-dollar placement fee because she was so upset about the mix-up."

"Oh my God, half; that's two weeks pay for you." I gasped. "I can't believe she let you pay half of the fee so she could save a few bucks."

"At least she isn't making me pay it all at once. She's going to take a hundred dollars out of each paycheck until my half is paid."

*Had I heard her right?*

"Unbelievable. Mandie, can you imagine what half a month's pay is to them? If you broke down Mr. Goldberg's earnings, he probably makes twelve hundred dollars an *hour*. Yet she thinks nothing of letting you give up two weeks of your income for something you had no responsibility for. Mandie, you have to get a backbone!"

I almost started to laugh again, but I could tell Mandie was taking it hard. So I offered my condolences.

"I gotta go," I said, ending our conversation abruptly. "Brandon's crying." I told her I'd call her later in the week and ran to the baby.

It's my usual ten o'clock lockdown time, and I double-checked the sleepwalk-proof door. But I can't sleep, thinking about Mandie and the Goldbergs. Maybe I was a little hard on her tonight. I can tell she's really frazzled and worn out. Can't believe she agreed to get up with the baby seven nights a week, even on her days off, because Margaret—oops, Mrs. Goldberg—has a sleeping issue, and if she wakes up in the middle of the night with the baby, she can't get back to sleep.

Maybe I ought to quit criticizing Mandie . . . Hello, Suzy, you're on call twenty-four hours a day, too. Let's see, that works out to about 99 cents an hour?

Man, we're both such wimps. At least I have two nights a
week that Delma covers for me. I'd better get to sleep. Brandon
will be awake soon. With the cold he has, he's been up every
two or so hours for the last few nights.

One night I couldn't wait to get Mandie on the phone so I could
relate my latest episode. Judy had been working out with her personal
trainer, Jennifer, a gorgeous aspiring actress who was determined to
make it on her own. Michael and Judy liked her and had offered to help,
but apparently she didn't believe in the adage "It's not what you know,
it's who you know." Even though the high point of her career thus far
had only been an antiperspirant commercial. Today they were talking
about hair. Jennifer mentioned her favorite salon in Westwood. I was
sitting nearby with Brandon, and out of nowhere, Jennifer offered me
the name of the salon and stylist who cuts her hair. I knew there were
only two reasons a woman would suggest a hairdresser to another
woman. One is if she was asked. Two, if she thought the woman needed
a little *help*.

I got the picture. I decided to try the unsolicited recommendation.
Judy agreed that I could take time off for an appointment the next Friday. I didn't realize that in LA things always take longer than they are
supposed to, and I certainly didn't comprehend that appointment times
are only made as starting points. In all the years that our family friend
Diane had cut my hair, she was never more than fifteen minutes late.
So I set aside precisely an hour and a half, for which I was given permission.

I had never been to a salon where so many different people attended
to me. First, the receptionist confirmed my appointment. Then a greeter
offered me a drink. Next I spent forty-five minutes reading *Glamour*
and *Vogue* cover to cover. After that, another person escorted me to the
sink, and then another attendant washed my hair. Then a girl put in my
perm rods. I was told that after I was finished processing, then and only
then, would I see the salon owner, Franck, who would actually cut my
hair. At least this was a little closer to my spa fantasy than my ghetto
nails and Scarface experiences.

But I was already starting to worry that I would be late getting back to the house. I was trying out a new thing called an air-dry perm, but after over an hour of sitting in a chair with my hair in curlers the size of sewer pipes, I realized it was going to be more than another hour before my perm would be "dried." Judy relied on my help at dinner-time. I knew that she wouldn't take it well if I got home late. I called the house with a report. Carmen answered, sounding frazzled. She said she couldn't talk and was busy with dinner. She hung up abruptly after I apologized and told her I would be on my way. There was a knot grip-ping my stomach. I really couldn't be late.

But I had a flash of sheer brilliance. I would just leave, and go home with the curlers intact. The prep girl said that would be fine. I could take the rollers out myself in the morning and bring them back the fol-lowing day. So much for getting my hair cut by Franck, but at least I would still have really cool new curls.

Right.

On the way out, I remembered that Carmen had asked me to pick up yogurt for the kids' lunches. It wasn't all that uncommon in Cottage Grove for women to do their grocery shopping in curlers, so it never occurred to me to consider how I looked. Forget my hair; I was worried about having to face Judy two hours late. There I was, running down the aisle of a crowded Ralph's grocery store, my hair in giant rollers with a long pink drinking straw through each, looking like I had just stepped out of an alien aircraft with all my antennae on high alert. I noticed a few shoppers who had nothing better to do than stare and point me out to their companions. I whirled through the aisles, disgusted with the shallowness of LA. What was the matter with these people, anyway? I suppose they've never found themselves in a similar situation. They've never had the desperate need to shop for yogurt and ignore their petty focus on their looks.

It wasn't until I got a look at my reflection in the glass cases of the frozen food section that I saw what they saw.

I wanted to melt away. Burying my head as best as I could in a copy of the *National Enquirer*, I shuffled through the checkout line. Why were other people able to negotiate the ins and outs of self-maintenance with such ease? I knew the reaction at home would be even more humiliating.

And indeed, Carmen and Delma greeted me by doubling over with laughter. Brandon took one look at me and started crying.

"Suzy, I want you to tell me what happened to your head," Josh said, like a stern, wary dad. He was so earnest and concerned that it made me feel better momentarily. I reassured him and gave him a big hug. I even started laughing along with the others.

But then Judy came into the kitchen. "I didn't see how you were going to be back by four o'clock if your appointment was at two-thirty," she said irritably.

*Thanks for mentioning that when I made the appointment.*

She glared at the curlers and spikes. "And *what* did you have done to your hair?"

Carmen and Delma had to leave the room because they couldn't stop laughing, and Judy's ears were beginning to steam. She sure wasn't seeing any humor in the situation. I set the grocery sack on the counter and let my heavy, oversized pink head hang. Why didn't she tell me how long these appointments take? Couldn't she have given me more time off? Did she *want* me to look foolish?

I decided that the best policy was to keep my mouth shut, given the black thoughts that were parading through my head. And despite all my efforts, I had missed dinner. When Judy left the kitchen, Delma got out a plate of food she saved for me. She heated it in the microwave while I went up and got Brandon ready for bed.

I felt very sad and alone.

Just when I feel like things are working out with Judy, this happens. Either she's under a lot of pressure or she doesn't like me. I just can't figure out which. I don't foresee winning her favor anytime soon.

I miss Ryan; I wish he was here. Or I was still there. When the slightest thing goes wrong, I want to call him and hear his voice (although who knows what he'd say about my hair fiasco). So much for moving on. Today I saw an ad in the newspaper for a support group for "Women Who Love Too Much." Must be an offshoot of that book I loved. I swear that author must have been spying on me. I am guilty of every stupid thing she mentions, including wanting to drive by his house a million times while his new girlfriend is visiting to see if I could see them through the curtains. It's only because I'm in another state that I haven't sunk to that all-time low. Maybe going to those meetings would help me get over Ryan.

You start living for your child and you stop living for yourself. I'm a regular person. I'm a hands-on mother.

—Whitney Houston

# it's a mad mad mad mad world

"Going on a recon, Sarah!"

A guy from the CAA mailroom popped in and out of Sarah's office practically before I could blink.

"Gotcha," Sarah replied.

"What's a recon?" I asked, watching the gofer dash down the hall.

Sarah leaned across her desk and lowered her voice. "It's shorthand for reconnoiter, like in the war movies," she said, glancing around. "You know, they send out a scout to recon the area to make sure there are no enemy soldiers around."

*Huh?* "So what's that guy doing, checking for other agents who might be hiding downstairs waiting to snag one of CAA's clients?"

"No. He's going out to scout the best route for Michael's next appointment."

"So he can avoid any land mines that might be in his path?" I laughed, bouncing Brandon on my lap.

"Yeah," Sarah said, nodding vigorously. "You know Michael can't stand to waste time or to be late; he'd rather die. So whenever he's going to an appointment across town or within about a twenty-mile radius, he sends a gofer to check the traffic and figure out which of the various routes are fastest. Then the gofer phones back and gives Michael the game plan. Sometimes I even draw up a map for Michael to take with him."

"Wow, that's crazy," I said. But it made sense. For heaven's sake, Michael had his hair cut right in his office every few weeks so he didn't have to waste time going to a salon.

Making frequent visits to CAA had really opened my eyes to Michael's world. At first I simply thought it would be good for Brandon to visit his dad, but then I realized the bonus was that I got to interact with someone older than six. In her midthirties, Sarah was plain but pretty. Unlike most LA women, she eschewed makeup and the latest fashions. And she was sweet. I had always appreciated her kindness and weekly phone chats (okay, I vented for most of the conversations).

But her perspective was the real treasure. Sarah knew, perhaps more than anyone, what life with Michael was like, because he spent most of his time at work instead of at home. Quiet and conservative, Sarah handled her many tasks with great calm and efficiency. She was Michael's right hand—her compact office even sat adjacent to Michael's huge one.

"Your job is intense," I proclaimed.

"Suzy, you're the one whose job is intense," Sarah said. "I couldn't imagine living in that house. Do you know that when Judy calls here she refers to you as 'the nanny'? I always say, 'You mean Suzy?' but it never seems to click with her. She acts like I don't know who you are or like you're not a real person."

"At least she admits to *having* a nanny," I replied. "I've met lots of girls in LA whose employers won't even do that."

Confidentiality agreements were just coming into vogue, and many girls were having to sign nondisclosures before working for a celebrity. Some employers were even requiring their household help to sign ironclad agreements promising they would never reveal *who* they worked for.

"One girl couldn't give her own mother her address at a star's home," I told Sarah. "She had to rent a post office box to receive any mail!"

Sarah gave me some more background on my boss. He was a master deal-maker, and after cofounding CAA, it had taken him a relatively short time to build a multimillion-dollar client list by acquiring all the big names in the industry. He did everything, from coddling his superstar clients to courting new talent to supervising his agents, who handled film, television, and book deals for the biggest names in the country. His reach was like that of an octopus with tentacles touching everything. Virtually everyone who interacted with him experienced his self-assured charm, and they were all just as aware of his reputation for ruthlessness toward people who got in his way. (I later learned that his favorite book was *The Art of War*.) He drove himself fiercely, and he drove his staff just as hard.

Despite the stress, the CAA staff was amazingly loyal. They were on a championship team; after all, they were the big guns in town. To outsiders, they were *all* intimidating. But there was a downside to the company's culture.

"Suzy, did I tell you about the time my childhood friend's dad died?" Sarah asked. "I got the news on a Thursday and asked Michael immediately if I could go to the funeral on Monday. I told him I would probably be back in the office by noon. I knew he wouldn't be pleased, though." She bit her lip. "After all, Monday is traditionally our busiest day."

"What? You're kidding. This was for a funeral, right?" Sometimes in Cottage Grove they would close businesses for the afternoon so the owners could attend memorial services.

"I know. But he said, with a look of grave disappointment, 'Sarah, I can't believe you'd leave me on a Monday.'"

"Really?"

"If you're surprised by that," she said, amused at my dismay, "wait until you hear about Karen's request for time off. She's one of the most important people in this building—she does the payroll for the entire company every two weeks. Three months ago, she was due to give birth. She asked for my advice on how she should approach Michael about her upcoming maternity leave—could she do payroll from her home? I joked, 'Leave time? You'll be lucky to get out of the office on the afternoon you deliver.' Only problem was, that prophecy turned out to be true."

"You're kidding! What happened?" I asked, switching Brandon to the other knee.

"Michael is very big on not wanting anyone to know how much money anyone else in the agency makes. It's a secret that's guarded as closely as the envelopes from Price Waterhouse on Oscar night. Karen is probably the only person besides the CFO who does know, and I'm sure Michael had her sign a forty-page nondisclosure agreement in blood.

"At any rate, as it turns out, she was going to be induced on a Saturday night, and with any luck, she hoped to deliver on Sunday. I told Michael that Karen was certainly not going to feel up to coming into the office on Monday, that she'd probably be out for at least three weeks, maybe more."

"So what did he do?"

"He had me send a computer, printer, and all the accounting ledgers to her house and said she could do the payroll from there."

I stared at Sarah.

"Oh, Karen was happy," Sarah assured me. "That way she got to spend more time with her baby."

It was easy to see why such an arrangement would be natural for Michael. After all, his own kids had a baby nurse and then a nanny—what would a mom need to do, anyway?

It got me thinking about what the children's lives would be like when they grew up. They'd probably live out their entire existence with people being paid to take care of all their needs. They would never learn how to do much on their own.

Then again, maybe this wouldn't be a problem.

I pictured Brandon, Amanda, and Joshua all grown up, trying to figure out how to work a broom and dustpan, wondering where you'd find such tools. I could see each of them getting their own set of wheels: a Porsche for Amanda, a Ferrari for Joshua, and a Hummer for Brandon. It would certainly be different from my high school experiences, which included helping my friend Christine shove her old Volkswagen down a hill to get it started. Amy and I would push from behind and Christine would steer. I would be wheezing and gasping from the exhaust, holding on to the bumper of the ancient Bug. Christine would yell out when we were going fast enough, and then Amy and I would both pull on the door handles and swing ourselves up into the passenger seat, landing on top of each other. Christine would simultaneously pop the clutch and off we would go. She could never afford to get that starter fixed. Some-times friends are a good substitute for money. But I didn't believe the reverse was true.

What would the kids do as teenagers if they ever had car problems? I had trouble picturing them doing anything more strenuous than dialing up their personal assistants on their cell phones. One night as Carmen and I were eating dinner, I brought up the subject. "What are these kids going to do when they grow up? They've never even been asked to put their own clothes in the laundry basket, and they'll never empty a dish-washer in their entire childhoods."

"Soo-zita, it doesn't matter," she said. "They will have so much money, they won't have to."

I couldn't help thinking about it for the next few days. How do chil-dren like this end up? How do they go to college and take care of them-selves, prepare meals, iron a shirt, know how to separate lights and darks for the laundry? For heaven's sake, Amanda wasn't aware there were people in the world who didn't have cars with automatic windows. The first time I took her to the store with me in Delma's car, she quizzically glanced back and forth between the roll-up window handle and me.

"Where's the window button?"

"Some cars don't have automatic windows, Amanda. Sometimes you've got to roll them up *yourself*," I said, putting the emphasis on the last word. "This is how you do it." I demonstrated the act with the driver's side door. She looked at me as if I had just given her a detailed description of the theory of relativity.

I didn't know it then, but many celebrity offspring lived this kind of sheltered life. Years later a fellow nanny told me a story about the four-and six-year-old sons of one of the most famous talk-show hosts in America. As they settled into first-class seats for a flight, the kids asked their nanny, "Who are all these people on our plane?" In their short lives, they had never flown commercial.

On the occasional weekends that Mandie and I were both off duty, we loved to shop. We wouldn't have dreamed of going to the fancy designer boutiques on Rodeo Drive; instead, we spent many afternoons at the Beverly Center in West Hollywood, a huge mall with a Hard

Rock Cafe on the street level. My work wardrobe still consisted mostly of shorts, jeans, T-shirts, and sweatshirts; clothes that could withstand barf, dirt, paint, and snot. It wasn't what most women would call a professional wardrobe, unless you were in my profession. But sometimes I longed for different attire. On one particular excursion, I was accosted by a very convincing saleswoman who brought half of her coworkers over to the three-sided mirror to rally support for the release of my credit card.

"Oh, my dear, that is *you*," one of the salesladies said.

"Do you travel? That would be great for traveling."

"Gorgeous, absolutely stunning; it makes you look so thin," said another.

Thin? I never thought I was fat, but anything that made me look skinnier was *fantastic*.

"I'll take it," I said. "Wrap it up." The saleslady lovingly folded the white cotton one-piece jumpsuit into a neat square and placed it in a bag. Mandie had eyed me warily during the fitting but kept her mouth shut. That was very unusual, but I was sailing so high on the compliments, I didn't even notice. Looking back, the entire store was made up of those clothes you see on infomercials—the kind that can be worn fifty-six different unflattering ways. But all I heard was the salesladies saying it was perfect for traveling, and I would soon be traveling.

That's right, we were going to Aspen with the Eisners. During my interview, Michael had asked if I skied and whether I could drive in the snow. Maybe I'd be helping the kids out on the bunny slopes? I pictured myself swishing gracefully downhill, a neat row of bundled-up tots in my wake. But as I started packing up the kids, nobody asked if I had ski clothes. I wasn't going to say anything; I stuck to my policy of trying to figure out what was going on instead of asking questions. So I just threw in a couple of Oregon sweaters for the chill, figuring I could rent skis if I needed to. And besides, I had a new outfit for the private plane.

When Saturday finally arrived, I took one hasty look in the mirror. Since it wasn't full-length, I could only see my new ensemble from the waist up. Pretty stylish, I thought. When I went downstairs, Joshua and Amanda were standing in the foyer with their suitcases. Their eyes grew large.

"You look like an astronaut," Joshua blurted out.

Amanda pointed to the magenta sash tied around my waist. "What *is* that?" she asked as disdainfully as a three-year-old in pigtails can.

"An accent," I explained feebly.

Michael appeared, looked me over from head to toe, and gave me an expression I can't describe, somewhere between disappointment and embarrassment.

I decided to go upstairs and change.

When I got to my room, I stood on a chair so I could see myself "full-length" in the mirror. Oh no. The kids were right; I looked like either a snowman in a children's school play or a member of NASA. When I turned around, I could clearly see the little red hearts on my underwear through the white material of the suit. Good God.

Humbled, I changed into my standard nanny uniform, substituting jeans for shorts with my T-shirt. I slunk downstairs and started loading luggage into the limo, trying to hide in the mountain of baggage we were bringing for six days in Colorado.

We met the Eisners at the airport. Their entourage consisted of Michael and Jane; the Eisners' male nanny, Paul, who was a few years older than me; and the Eisners' three sons, ages nine, twelve, and eighteen. We were going to meet Mr. Eisner's mother in Colorado, plus the oldest son's girlfriend was flying in from somewhere on the East Coast. The Eisners were good family friends, and Michael, Disney's CEO, had offered use of the Disney corporate jet. Once on the plane, you couldn't forget where you were. Everything on board had either Mickey Mouse or Goofy printed on it, from pencils to napkins and glasses. I couldn't help but giggle when a big Mickey smiled at me from each square of toilet paper.

I began to worry that I'd be staring at that toilet paper for the duration of the flight—my stomach was doing loops the whole time we were in the air. I wasn't feeling well, at all, but I managed to keep it together on the plane. After we landed, despite my nausea, I helped to load the more than twenty pieces of luggage back into the limo and then unload it at the Eisners' house. But then I started to feel clammy, and queasiness rolled over me like a tidal wave. I chalked it up to the flight and told myself it would go away shortly if I could just make it to a chair to sit down for a few minutes. But by the time everyone was inside the house, I knew there was something much worse going on. This was not going away. I realized that in addition to starting a menstrual meltdown of nuclear proportions, I must have picked up some sort of flu.

I stumbled into the bedroom that Brandon and I had been assigned, but it was only a minute before I heard my name being called. When I emerged, Mr. Eisner and his mother were standing in the hall, and they both did a double take when they saw me. My face shone white as a sheet, and I was sweating profusely.

"My goodness, Suzy, you look awful. Are you okay?" Mrs. Eisner asked.

"You should lie down," her son said. I started to answer them when I saw Judy standing in the hallway with a confused expression on her face that said, *What are you talking about? I didn't notice anything wrong with her.*

I quickly went into the bathroom and locked the door, and I overheard Judy complaining about the less-than-pristine conditions of their quarters. The place was a sprawling, indifferently decorated, semirustic vacation home. It was a relaxed place, for kids and dogs and skiing—the kind of environment that seemed to make this very controlled family ill at ease.

But even that couldn't distract me very much, and within seconds I was lying on the freezing tile floor in the fetal position. I knew Judy didn't have time for me to be sick, and I figured her denial autopilot was kicking in. She was just like her husband in that way; sometimes she didn't seem to have a lot of sympathy for her employees. I could just hear her: *We didn't come all the way to Aspen to have to adjust our fun to the physical limitations of the help.* I heard Michael in the hall loudly asking, "Where's Suzy? Where's Suzy? We've got to get going." I was in so much pain that I couldn't muster the strength to answer. I knew Brandon was asleep in his crib. If they'd just leave, I could go lie down in bed and I might recover. I was in too much pain to muster up a response. I just kept silently wishing they would go away: *Leave, leave, leave. Please, just let me recover in peace.*

"Where's Suzy?" I could still hear him shouting on the other side of the door with the kids answering in unison, "I don't know, Dad. Let's go!"

Finally, mercifully, I heard the front door open and close. The house grew empty and silent. When I did manage to grab the doorknob and pull myself to my feet, I found that everyone had left—except for Brandon, who was lying in his crib, quietly playing with his feet. Had they really all just left without knowing where I was? Why didn't they take the baby with them? What if I was seriously sick and couldn't watch him?

Then it hit me. They really didn't notice me enough to see that I might have my own needs. I felt very, very alone.

By the next night, whatever disease I had contracted had passed through me like a bad winter storm. The cramps kept me company for the next two days, but I could cope with that. Once I emerged from my room, I discovered that people were scattered all around the enormous house. The Eisners' oldest son was in the kitchen with his girlfriend. She was an heiress to some famous fortune and was more self-absorbed and aloof than anyone I'd ever met. I don't think she uttered more than a few words during the entire trip that didn't have some reference to her family's wealth. I had to give her credit for coming up with inventive ways to squeeze in references to her financial stature, regardless of the topic: the snowfall outside, her night's sleep, the way she salted her potatoes. Hers was a most unusual talent, honed to an impressive degree. All right, I couldn't stand her.

On our third evening in Aspen, the entourage traveled to Goldie Hawn's house for dinner. Brandon and I stayed home since they would be out late. The Eisners' nanny stayed home, too. He seemed like a nice enough guy, short and fairly quiet. But I had met very few male nannies—mannies?—and I was more than a little intrigued by him.

After making polite conversation for a short time, I sheepishly asked, "Uh, can I get your opinion on something?"

"What's that?" He looked curious. Maybe he was warming up.

"Judy suggested that I could date the oldest Eisner," I said, embarrassed as the words tumbled out.

Paul busted up laughing.

It wasn't *that* funny.

"Now wait a minute, Paul," I blurted in self-defense.

"No, no. I'm sorry," he said. "I wasn't laughing at you. It's just that we nannies are at the lowest level in the pecking order. In fact, I don't know if we're actually *in* the order. There is no way in the world that an Eisner would date a nanny. Just wouldn't happen. They don't mix with the hired help." Then he stood up and left the room, laughing to himself.

Obviously, I still had more to learn about the social ladder of the wealthy. But maybe Judy did, too. I thought she had actually been sincere in her suggestion, which she had mentioned to me twice. Maybe she meant it as a compliment to me? Or maybe it just seemed like he and I were close in age, and she hadn't even considered the other dimension. I had always thought Judy had an air of slight awkwardness about social status and wondered how comfortable she really was with her wealth. I'm sure she never thought, growing up, that she would be married to a man worth millions. Maybe she thought it was just a fluke, something that even a nobody like me could blunder into.

The conversation with Paul put voice to some feelings that had already been brewing. Being treated like I was invisible much of the time was beginning to take a toll. I was getting more and more attached to the children, but the way our relationship was structured made things confusing for both them and me. The subtle communication—the one that Joshua was already picking up—was that I cared for them because I was paid to. It didn't matter that my love and affection for them was authentic. I was beginning to see that the wealthy saw the position of nanny as one that was decidedly low status and easily replaceable.

Paul was right. I'm just the hired help. Even if I'm ten times more attractive and fun than Miss Prissy, it doesn't matter. I'm simply not in the same league. I'm not even playing the same sport to be able to join the league. My problem is that I don't like hearing the truth. Paul was just trying to tell me what my "place" was. He seems to have accepted his role in the Eisners' family. Something weird he shared was that Mrs. Eisner seemed to have the standard practice of asking every guy she interviewed

if he was gay. The nanny before Paul had warned him about
this and had suggested he "not take it personally." I've decided
to apply that logic to my situation. I just have to keep reminding
myself that my employers aren't my friends and that it's not
personal. Why am I complaining? I'm working in the job of my
choosing, and I'm being paid better than most nannies: Buck
up, Suzanne! And scrounge around for some Advil in the
medicine cabinet.

Michael was the only one who was actually going to ski the next day,
but we all traipsed out to the slopes and took the gondola ride to the
top. There at the summit stood a man taking family pictures of everyone in their colorful and expensive ski gear. Judy approached him and
discussed the price of a group photo. When she returned, she asked if I
could wait over on the side while they had their picture taken. She said
they wanted "just family" in the picture.

"Yes, of course," I answered, mentally rolling my eyes. *Yes, I understand that you do not want the nanny in your family photo album.*

Then they all started taking off their ski jackets and caps and piling
them on me to hold. "Suzy, I'm glad you're here," Judy said as she
walked toward the photographer. "You make a good coat rack."

The whole trip made me feel like the Griswolds' Aunt Edna in *Vaca-
tion,* strapped to the top of the family truckster on the way to Wally
World. When we finally got back home, I immediately talked to
Mandie, who had just returned from a trip to New York with the Goldbergs. She said some guy named David Geffen and his friend Carrie
Fisher had been with them on the plane. She recognized Fisher as
Princess Leia from *Star Wars* but didn't have a clue who the guy was.
She had him pegged as some sort of record producer. He spent time
chatting with her about the kids and turned out to be quite nice, so we
both surmised that he couldn't possibly have been anyone very important. Bigwigs don't waste their time visiting with nannies.

Leave it to the girls from the country to be wrong again. We didn't
recognize the name of Geffen, the biggest music mogul of our time.

Mandie's trips were always more eventful than mine. Her family was friends with Kurt and Goldie, too—she'd flown with them once back from New York. She described them as surprisingly normal. While they were flying, Kurt made sandwiches for the kids, and Goldie led sing-alongs for everyone. I tried to imagine Michael asking everyone on the plane, "Did you want mayonnaise (without hydrogenated oils, of course) on your sandwich?" and then Judy breaking into a round of "Ninety-Nine Bottles of Imported Beer on the Wall."

Somehow, I just couldn't see it.

I hope I'm not failing as a parent in order to be a professional woman. It's a very difficult balance, but it's something I am fighting for.

—Uma Thurman

# chapter 11

# LA confidential

I found it pathetic that Mandie and I never had a shortage of tales from the cribs.

"Wait. Before you start, I have a question," she said one night.

"Shoot. What is it?"

"You had to put in your own phone line in your bedroom, right?"

"Uh-huh; it's separate from the four lines on their phone," I reminded her.

"Well, when I moved in, Mrs. Goldberg said I didn't need to install my own phone, that I could just use hers. So now at the end of every month she goes through and marks all the calls that are mine so I can pay her back. The problem is, she makes these little comments when we settle up, like 'You talked to someone for an hour and a half.'"

"Why don't you tell her, 'Yes, I did. I *like* to have contact with the out-side world'"? I asked. "Are you saying that she goes through your bill and highlights all your calls? Bet those 5 minute calls to Missoula really set the missus back. What does she say? There's one for 43 cents. . . . Oops there is another one, Bozeman, Montana. . . . Oh, here's a real whopper: $6.28 to Helena. Glad I caught that one."

Mandie interrupted me. "I am not kidding."

I couldn't hold myself back. "All righty then, I'm glad your reimbursements to them are keeping them out of the welfare line. Have you guys had your government cheese delivered this week?"

It didn't help that her employer just had a tiny stained-glass window installed in one of the downstairs bathrooms. Price: $15,000. But poor Mandie got more personal payroll deductions than legitimate IRS withholdings.

I was happy to listen to the poor girl's woes—and even happier that I was doing so on a phone line I paid for myself.

Besides, I needed to talk to her, too. I was dying to tell someone about the thousands of dollars' worth of clothes that a personal shopper had brought to the house. I could not believe my eyes when the van pulled up and two men hustled in, rolling racks of couture creations for Judy's consideration. A beautifully dressed saleswoman, wearing a suit that cost more than I earned in a year, went through each dress with her, writing down her selections in a tiny notebook with a Montblanc pen (who knew a pen could cost $500?). No wonder Judy didn't shop much—the stores came to her!

By now I had spent so much time around the house that my world had narrowed, and these little scenes gained importance. I had no perspective. I was always on duty, and my workdays were endless. I knew I deserved at least half the blame, and that only made me angrier. I was furious at myself for never mentioning a contract and for never discussing how many hours I would work or what my responsibilities would be.

I'm learning that there is no "after work" for me. No dinner plans with friends, no movie nights. Isn't there some employment statute that says you get two fifteen-minute breaks and an hour lunch during an eight-hour day? I guess it doesn't apply to nannies. What is the rule for a 16-hour day? Maybe you get four fifteen-minute breaks and a two-hour lunch. Are there even any California labor laws for people who LIVE at their jobs?

Mandie and I thought we needed to end our pity party and expand our nanny world, so we signed the little ones up for a Gymboree class in Santa Monica. A little more interactive than the neighborhood park,

Gymboree brought together babies of a similar age to play, sing songs, and socialize. And then the parents—and nannies—could socialize, too.

Mandie and I listened, bemused, as one mother laughingly told a group of her friends how her nannies had to pass the "ugly" test.

"I go to Bob's office for the very first interview to check them out." She chortled. "The fatter and uglier, the better. You can't be too careful these days, you know."

I didn't know then, but I do now. Robin Williams ended up divorcing his wife and marrying his nanny. And Steven Seagal named his daughter after a nanny he later had another child with. Maybe the paranoid wife had a point.

"Suzy," Mandie said, keeping an eye on Ellie tumbling nearby, "you'll never believe this, I finally met Mel Gibson *in person!*"

I grinned. Mel was to Mandie what Tom Cruise was to me.

"And I was such a klutz, I can't believe it!" she moaned.

Oh no. "What happened?"

"Well, I peeked at the invitation list for the Goldbergs' anniversary party that was on Mrs. Goldberg's desk. Talk about a who's who. I mean, everybody was on it, from Dolly Parton to Quincy Jones, and right there in the middle was Mel Gibson. Oh boy, I thought, I'm finally going to meet him. So I volunteered to let people in, kind of like a doorman. You know, so I'd get to shake his hand or something."

"So did ya?"

"I'm getting there. So, I'm standing there, saying hello to Shirley MacLaine, Kelly LeBrock, Don Johnson—I could barely catch my breath. I was wearing that blue dress you like. Finally, after I'd let about forty people in, there he was. My God, he's good-looking, even better than in the movies."

"So, what did you do, try to hug him or something?"

"No, no. I started to say, 'Hello, Mr. Gibson,' but nothing would come out but air. Suddenly I was breathing like a Thoroughbred that had just crossed the finish line. I started to turn away, not wanting him to see me like that, and I fell head over heels across a chair and landed on my back with my feet in the air, minus one shoe."

"Oh my God." I laughed.

"I know, I almost died."

"Did he help you up?"

"Not exactly. He started to, but out of the corner of my eye I saw Mrs. Goldberg looking very irritated, so I just scrambled up by myself. I wondered what he thought—or do you think he gets that all the time?"

"I'm sure he's used to it, Mandie," I said consolingly. "Don't worry about it. You handled looking like a starstruck moron the best you could. Thank goodness you didn't inconvenience Mel. Margaret—oops, I mean Mrs. Goldberg—would have never forgiven you for that. And I hope you didn't break the chair, because you know you would have had to pay for it!"

"Oh, everything that goes wrong is usually my fault," Mandie said. "Mine or Graciella's." Graciella was their housekeeper.

"Yes, it's good to have help to blame for every last little thing that happens," I agreed. Mandie and I had already discussed many times the tendency within our respective families to blame the "help," especially when anything was missing. Such minidramas occurred practically every other day.

"You should have heard Judy going on about the car seat yesterday," I said. "No one could find it, and she was freaking out. Gloria and Rosa and I kept patiently asking her if she was sure it hadn't been left in one of the other cars, and she snapped, 'Of course I'm sure! I think the gardeners took it. These people are always stealing from me!' As if a gardener needs a car seat. Of course, an hour and fifteen minutes later it was found in Carmen's car. Imagine that, *in the car.* She had taken Amanda to the store with her."

"Don't get me started," Mandie replied. "Graciella and I spent an hour looking for one of Ellie's outfits the other day. Mrs. Goldberg was sure that *the construction workers* replacing the windows had taken it. 'Leave it to *them* to steal from a baby!' she told us. As if these guys would steal one little pink dress. It turned out to be in the diaper bag in the car."

We broke into a fit of giggles, the kind that release the built-up tension of weeks. We were still laughing as we left the Gymboree class with our charges in tow. Mission accomplished: kids tuckered out, nannies through with therapy.

\* \* \*

One day I overheard Judy saying my name over the phone. I listened as hard as I could. "Oh yes, you'll definitely need a nanny," she said agreeably. "Mine is a lifesaver. I don't know what we'd do without her. She's like my right arm."

*Her right arm???* My right arm about fell off.

"She does more than just take care of the kids. In fact, just the other day she saw I needed to make lunch reservations at the Ivy, and she took it upon herself to call for me since she knew I was busy."

It was the kindest thing she had ever said about me. Our rollercoaster relationship had hit a new high. Now if only I could freeze it there, at the plateau. Later that night, Judy told me she'd spoken to Sally Field. She asked if I knew another nanny I could recommend—Sally was on bed rest, due to give birth in a few months.

None of my NNI classmates seemed quite right. But what about Tammy Munroe? She was a year ahead of me in high school, and I had always admired her. I knew she would be perfect. In truth, I thought Tammy was perfect at everything—blond, beautiful, nice, smart, kind to small animals, and went to church every Sunday. About the only thing missing was a great job. She was still in Cottage Grove, working at the local frozen yogurt shop with my younger sister Traci.

With Judy's permission, I called Sally (addressing her as Mrs. Field, of course, just in case she had formality issues like Mrs. Goldberg) and told her all about Tammy. Her breezy manner made the conversation easy, and she sounded genuinely kind. Buzzing with excitement, I called Tammy and urged her to fly down and interview right away. She was on a plane to LA in less than a week to interview personally with Sally after a great phone call with her.

"Hurry, tell me, how did it go?" I demanded when she returned from Sally's house. Tammy was staying in my room while she was in LA, and I'd been waiting with my fingers crossed, hoping the stars would align to bring my friend to me.

"Well, you know I was nervous before I left," Tammy said, flopping onto a peach-colored bed, "and by the time I got there, it was so bad that I wanted to throw up. But I knew that I'd have to face you, so I forged ahead."

"You were too chicken to chicken out!" I teased her.

"I buzzed the gate, and this incredibly gorgeous man came out. Suzy, I thought I was going to faint he was so good-looking."

"Someone famous?" I smiled knowingly. She'd have to get used to the parade of celebrities.

"It was Sally's husband, Alan, a real sweetheart. Sally was, too. But I have a feeling they think I'm not very street-smart," Tammy said. "Alan asked me, 'With our lifestyle, we need someone who's going to be comfortable with us. How do you feel about that?' I told him that I felt okay about them. I was comfortable enough. But I asked how they felt, if they were comfortable with me. And then Alan doubled over laughing."

"Tammy, you're a teenager from Mayberry, USA. Why should they be uncomfortable with you?"

"I know!" Tammy cringed. "What an idiotic question. Alan said he was sure I'd fit in just fine."

The two of us spent most of that weekend holed up in my room, watching TV, reading magazines, and talking excitedly about Tammy's future. I encouraged her to enroll in NNI in the months before Sally gave birth, which she thought was a great idea. As the night wore on, our stomachs started rumbling. We were starving, but Michael and Judy were home, and I didn't want to go downstairs.

"I sure hope it won't be like this for me if I get the job with Sally," Tammy said uneasily. "I can't believe you feel so awkward in the house where you live."

Having Tammy visit made me realize how accustomed I've become to feeling uncomfortable most of the time. How could I have ignored the advice about contracts that I got at nanny school? I'm just kicking myself. It's my own fault. I used to consider myself fairly bright, but I gotta admit I was a nitwit not to be more assertive about the hours I was expected to work. I need to get up the nerve to tell my employers that I would like to have a talk. It would be so much easier in a professional office to go knock on my boss's door. But here, what can I do? Ask Judy if she could step into my bedroom so we could talk in private? I can see it now . . . Here, Judy, have a seat on my bed so I can go over some job satisfaction issues with you. Oops, hold that thought . . . Brandon is crying, and now he has a poopy diaper. Just as soon as I am done, we can continue with my employee evaluation.

I'm always so quick to criticize Mandie for not standing up for herself. But it's so much easier to berate her for being a doormat than to stop being walked on myself.

Note to self: Ask if I can meet Mandie next Friday night for dinner.

After Tammy left, I thought for at least the tenth time that I should call Carolyn or Linda for advice. But every time I came close, I realized I couldn't handle the embarrassment. I'd never even entered into a verbal agreement about my working hours and responsibilities, the very thing that they must have drilled into us a hundred times in school. I didn't have anyone to blame, and I didn't know how to fix things. Depressed, I decided to call it a night. Time to lock myself in and try to sleep. My brain, however, wouldn't cooperate; instead it frantically tried to find some sort of solace or solution. I picked up the monthly nanny newsletter I subscribed to. This issue featured a questionnaire that parents could use during a formal job evaluation. I decided to rate my own performance. Maybe I was overthinking everything and my situation was just fine. Better than average, even.

1. **Does nanny limit personal errands during work hours?**

   Doesn't own a car, bicycle, or pogo stick, so that hasn't been a big issue.

2. **Does nanny offer options for handling child's behaviors when appropriate?**

   Could casually mention that Dr. T. Berry Brazelton does not recommend parents reason with a three-year-old as though she's thirty. But what do I know? I am only nineteen and my entire net worth is less than $700.

3. **Does nanny take the initiative in planning activities for the children?**

   Yes. Then sits alone at the table with the art projects.

4.   **Does nanny support parents' discipline style?**

Hmm. No discernible discipline style. But will support whole-heartedly once aware of it.

5.   **Does nanny support parents' TV restrictions?**

Again, no discernible restrictions. Kids allowed to watch R-rated movies. But will implement restrictions posthaste once given them!

The next section left white space to evaluate the family on things like time off, supporting the nanny in discipline issues, and paying overtime as stated in the contract.

I closed my eyes.

I'd been trying to ignore my metastasizing dissatisfaction with my job, but it was becoming harder and harder to avoid. Would I be miserable the whole time I lived here? I had promised two years, and I had, oh, 578 days to go. The future stretched out in one never-ending loop of *Sesame Street*, dirty diapers, and squelched rage.

I rolled over to turn on the TV, just in time to watch Robin Leach profile yet another one of our recent dinner guests on *Lifestyles of the Rich and Famous*.

It reminded me of a story Mandie recently related.

A nanny named Sheila had a job similar to ours, and like us, she had a frequent need to blow off steam. Over coffee at Starbucks, Mandie had innocently asked what was troubling her, and Sheila was ranting about celebrities on TV talk shows. "Mandie, I just hate it when I see all those holier-than-thou stars lie in front of millions of people."

"What do you mean, lie?" Mandie asked. "Lie about what?"

"About everything; their children, their lifestyles, their political causes!"

"What exactly are you talking about, Sheila?" This didn't sound like a generic tirade. "Are you talking about someone in particular or all celebrities in general?"

"I don't know about all of them, but I know about one for sure."

"Who?" Mandie was on the edge of her seat now. "Which one? What did they do?"

"Mandie, I swear to you, I had to leave the house because the guy had such a huge cocaine problem," Sheila confessed. "Since I was doing some of the housework in addition to being the full-time nanny, I would occasionally help clean the bathrooms. More often than not, in the morning there would be a pile of white powder sitting on a hand mirror on the bathroom counter. When I realized what it was, I used a hand vac to suck it up."

Mandie suppressed a snicker at the thought of hundreds of dollars' worth of drugs being vacuumed up with a Dirt Devil.

"Oh my God—did he know you did it?"

"No, and I don't care if he did know; it serves him right," Sheila spat. "At least he never said anything, probably because he had so much of it all the time. What's one small pile?"

"So who was it?" Mandie asked.

And Sheila told her.

"No way!"

"Yes. He was my last employer."

"That squeaky-clean guy?" Mandie gasped. "At least that's his investigator image on TV."

"The very one," Sheila confirmed.

"But, Mandie, it wasn't just the cocaine snorting at home that got to me. It was watching him on a talk show. There he was, telling the understanding host about all the evils of drugs and how he was afraid it was going to influence his kids, living in LA, the drug capital of the U.S. Next he said he now had to move to the midwest to keep his kids from falling prey to its evil spell, blah, blah, blah. What a crock of shit!" Sheila cried angrily as she wiped her runny nose with a wad of napkin. "And to top it all off, they won't let me see the children since I quit; they said it wouldn't be good for the kids."

After I heard this from Mandie, I realized that I had met or knew the nannies for most of the celebrities I saw in television interviews. And the mothers' descriptions of their own homemaking and childrearing prowess were vastly different from what their nannies described. If any of their employees ever came forward with the truth about what the stars *really* did behind closed doors, they'd probably need to be placed in a Nanny Witness Protection Program—something Demi Moore's nanny may have considered after she filed a lurid lawsuit that basically charged Demi with intimidating her in order to keep her around.

Tales like these have kept coming over the years, although they no longer shock me like they did then. There was the story of the hugely successful movie-star couple who made a point of always talking about how devoted they were to their two children. I knew for a fact that both kids were so lonely and disturbed by the complete lack of attention paid to them by either parent that they peed on the floor to get noticed—which certainly worked, since they were way past the potty-training stage. And then there was the daughter of a famous dead rock star and a certifiably crazy mother whose nanny actually wanted to adopt her because she feared for her safety when her mother was on a drug binge.

One of the most pathetic stories a nanny shared with me was of her director boss who had some sick need to reveal every graphic detail of his romantic liaisons with the actresses he worked with. She finally had to quit, even though she loved the children, because she felt too uncomfortable hearing about his extramarital affairs.

No, things certainly weren't what they seemed on TV.

Stories like Sheila's, however, propped me up in some weird way. Other celebrity nannies had it much worse. I merely had to deal with issues that were poignant, not prison-worthy.

Like bedtime. One night Judy said that she'd like to put Brandon to sleep.

Usually on the nights she was home, she and I worked together to get the kids down, but Brandon's slumber fell to me. This division of labor was partly my own doing. Even when the two oldest and I had become violently ill with food poisoning a few weeks back, waking up the baby with our constant vomiting, I felt I had to persevere. Judy offered to put Brandon back to bed and get up with him when he woke up. She even said that I could get her out of bed if I needed her. I was taken aback by this unusual display of kindness. Maybe I shouldn't have been so scared of her after all.

Yet I didn't take her up on any of it. I was so afraid of being seen as a less-than-perfect employee that I said I was fine, that I could take care of it. And it also seemed like it would take more energy than I had to tell her how to heat his bottles in the night.

But this time she was doing it because she wanted to, not because I couldn't.

"How do you do it?" she quietly inquired.

"How do I do what?" I replied.

"How do you put him to bed?" she asked. "Exactly what is your routine each night?"

This was so awkward.

"Don't worry. He's really easy. I'll heat the bottle in the warmer for you," I suggested, "then give it to him in the rocking chair. After that, you just put him in the crib, and then you pull his favorite blanket up over him."

I looked around the room. *Oh crap.* Did she know how to put the side rail of his crib down? I'd better put it down so she wouldn't be embarrassed. I could just come in after she leaves to put it back up.

"Sometimes I sing him a short lullaby before I turn out the lights," I continued.

"Can I rock him a little after he has his bottle?" she inquired.

"Yes, of course you can rock him," I said, looking at Brandon. "He loves to cuddle."

I left mother and child alone, my mind whirling. I felt so sad for her. She didn't seem confident about meeting the needs of her own baby, but I knew she could do a fine job. She just didn't know it because she had given all the responsibility—and joy—to others.

Did having a nanny mean living with this kind of uncertainty about your own kids? Michael seemed to have it, too. He stopped by the nursery nearly every morning to kiss Brandon good-bye, but one morning he stood there quietly with me for a few moments. When he reached toward Brandon to hold him, Brandon nuzzled into me.

Michael sighed. "Do you think he knows I'm his father?" he asked reflectively.

"Well . . ." I paused. "Yes . . . I think he does know."

"I'm not sure he does," he replied, leaning over and kissing Brandon.

I watched him walk down the hallway like he usually did, as fast as possible, the lower half of his body moving while the upper half remained motionless and in control. I could only imagine all the thoughts running through his head, the lists of the "important" things that he needed to accomplish that day. I felt gloomy standing there clutching Brandon. It occurred to me that Michael barely knew his own children. He revered them as the most important thing in his life, and I had no doubt that he would do anything for them. Yet he barely laid eyes on them for more than a few minutes during the workweek. And since he wasn't a part of their everyday lives, he hadn't really learned how to play with them. He wasn't the type to take Joshua fishing or to the batting cages, to play tea party with Amanda, or to take Brandon on a walk. He hired people for this kind of activity, so the kids wouldn't miss anything.

But what were the parents missing? Did the hired help not actually help anybody at all?

One evening after Joshua and Amanda fought terribly at the dinner table and were sternly sent to their rooms to cool off, Michael and Judy started discussing their kids' behavior while I helped Delma clear the dishes. Judy offered her thoughts, and then Michael expressed his opinion. He then asked me why I thought Joshua was so often unruly and prone to outbursts. Surprised to be consulted, I added my two cents' worth.

"I think Josh is such a perfectionist that he gets frustrated when things don't go perfectly for him," I ventured. "He has such high expectations for himself."

"I don't think that's it at all—" Judy began.

"Shut up!" Michael said coldly, setting down his wineglass.

I looked down, embarrassed for Judy and for him. It was the first time I'd ever witnessed anything but their chilly, formal interactions.

"Suzy, would you go on?" he asked. "I wanted to hear what you had to say."

*Oh, great. This was really gonna help my relationship with Judy.*

"Um, well, he is a really bright kid. I think his brain is working much faster than his six-year-old writing skills are able to display on paper. I just try to give him plenty of quiet time while he's doing his homework so he can work at his own pace and not have outside distractions. I also think—"

But then Judy rolled her eyes and interrupted me to lean across the table and buzz Carmen for some more pepper.

Whoa, can't believe that Michael was so rude to Judy tonight. On the other hand, it was nice to be treated like somebody with a valuable opinion for once. And about child psychology, my favorite topic! But was it ever awkward. Did we have a lecture in nanny school about what to do when the parents don't seem to like each other all that much? Don't recall one.

Mom called tonight to see how I was doing and said that she talked to Ryan and he told her he really missed me. He didn't think he would ever find someone who he loves as much as me. It's kinda bittersweet. I miss him. I am happy that he still feels that way. But realistically where would he even fit into my life right now?

We have moments where she's sleeping in her crib and we're like, "Oh my God, there's another person in our house, and she's not leaving!"

—Denise Richards

chapter 12
# nothing but trouble

The one thing I *had* made very clear when I took the job was that I needed to go home in June to attend my uncle Skinny's birthday party.

Thank the Lord. I was more than overdue for a break from my day-to-day responsibilities and from the whole LA scene in general, and I longed for a place where I understood the rules and rituals. And I couldn't wait for some time alone to recharge my batteries.

But from the moment I stepped into my parents' car at the airport until the time I left three days later, my so-called vacation was spent answering one question: "What are they like?" That's all anyone wanted to know, along with the occasional inquiry about me: "How does it feel to be a nanny for the stars?"

Technically, I had to explain, I'm not a nanny for the stars. My employers weren't actors, and anyone outside of LA who didn't subscribe to the *Hollywood Reporter* didn't know the Ovitz name. So, I would say patiently that my employer was the guy who was important to the people *we* think are important. I guess I shouldn't have been surprised by their curiosity. My letters and phone calls home had described my experiences talking to the likes of Barbra Streisand and John Travolta, and star power seemed magnified by distance. In Cottage Grove, people's imaginations made the wattage even brighter.

By the third day of my visit, it almost seemed easier to go back to work than to tell one more story. But one of the guidance counselors at my high school had asked me to come in and speak to the students on Career Day, and I felt I owed her. Besides, I've never been one to pass up a chance to talk.

Girls packed Mrs. Pittman's computer room, wanting to hear all about the "Hollywood Nanny"—or, rather, the people she'd met. They had the same question as everybody else: "What are they really like?" I wanted to explain to them the reality of my life, but I realized that I couldn't publicly admit how demeaning my job really was. And I certainly couldn't confess all the negotiation mistakes I had made. I saw in their eyes that rubbing elbows with legends was glamorous beyond belief, so that was what I talked about. Once I got started, I couldn't stop. I did touch on the craziness of my household, carefully dodging any description of my duties. I told them how it was difficult to get them to buy new clothes for the baby, while vacations on private jets were as common as changing socks. I recounted how little things like losing a Barbie doll's shoe were cause for uproar and accusations.

I began to feel a bit like a celebrity myself, laying claim to my proverbial fifteen minutes of fame. A reporter from the local paper interviewed me, and the *Cottage Grove Sentinel* ran the story next to an awful picture of me. It appeared that I was looking off into a faraway galaxy, contemplating the meaning of nannyhood.

Boy, is fame funny. The position that equaled servitude and low status in Hollywood had made me a hometown star.

The shock of moving between Cottage Grove and LA is huge—I almost feel like this flight isn't long enough to prep me for the cultural shift. Going home seems to put things in perspective, and I can't shake one thing in particular. Why don't people with a great deal of money realize that their wealth is providing them with so many choices in life? I see their abundance of resources allowing them to be able to spend more time with their family, not less. I grew up with so many of my friends' parents constantly being limited by a work schedule they had to follow in order to provide income for the necessities of life. They would have given anything to never miss a Little League game or be able to volunteer each week in their child's classroom. It got me thinking about why Michael never drops by Josh's reading class or Amanda's ballet school. Why in the world would any parent miss that stuff voluntarily?

I didn't have time to psychoanalyze much more after I got back; somehow I'd managed to get into trouble without even being there. Apparently the day I left, Gymboree had changed to the spring schedule. Brandon's class was moved up an hour, and Grandma Ovitz showed up late and found herself surrounded by older children. She was livid. Delma and Carmen said she and Judy couldn't stop talking about me. Maybe it had embarrassed her to be in the wrong place at the wrong time; I didn't know. What other explanation could there be? My time at home had shaken my brain up a bit, and I was as frustrated with them as they were with me. How hard could it have been to play with him on the floor at the gym? What in the world would this family do if they ever had a real problem?

At least I was about to take a positive step, one that would get me more independence from my job. I had saved enough money for a down payment on a brand-new Celica. Finally, wheels of my own. When I mentioned my plan to Michael, he surprised me by offering to help. He had his CFO call a dealership in Marina del Rey to negotiate a contract. When I went to pick up the car, the salesman complained that he wasn't making any money because some big shot had bullied him into selling the car at cost. I felt sorry for him, but I was also thrilled to be able to afford my first new car. I was really grateful to Michael—he didn't have to help me out. I just knew life was going to be a whole lot more fun now.

I called to tell Mandie the good news. She didn't have a car, either, unless you counted the battered Ford Escort station wagon that the Goldbergs let her drive once in a while on her days off. We both continued to be boggled that these people let their employees drive their children around in automobiles that weren't exactly highly rated in safety crash tests.

"Just think how cool we'll be, tooling around in a car that isn't ten years old or covered in rust!" I said dreamily.

"Speaking of cars," Mandie said, "I have a car story you're gonna love. Last weekend, Mr. Goldberg ended up with three cars at the beach house, so he asked me to bring the Porsche home. I wanted to ask him if he was feeling all right. I didn't mention that it'd been a couple of years since I'd driven a stick shift. But I figured it out after a couple of false starts, lunges, and squealing tires. And there I was, sailing down Pacific Coast Highway."

"You had the convertible?" I exclaimed.

"Well, yeah, except I couldn't figure out how to work the roof thingy. It was hot as Hades, and I wanted to put the top down and let my hair blow in the wind. But I was worried that he'd be able to tell that I had opened the roof, so I pulled into a gas station and tried to figure it out. I poked around at things for a few minutes, but I was kind of scared that I'd screw something up. I figured I'd just settle for rolling the windows down, but I couldn't find those controls, either, or the air-conditioning buttons. And I didn't want to just start pulling random knobs, not knowing what havoc I might cause. So I gave up. I was dripping wet by the time I got back. I'd been sitting in a mobile sauna for an hour." She paused. "And then I worried I might be screwing up the leather upholstery with my sweat."

I laughed. "Was it fast?"

She snorted. "Like hay flying through a baler!"

You can take the girl out of the country, but you can't take . . .

"I got it up to seventy, but then I got scared and slowed back down to the speed limit. But that's not the whole story. As usual, there was a fiasco at the end."

"Oh my God, you didn't crash it, did you?"

"No, thank God. When I got to the house, I realized that Mr. Goldberg didn't have a house key on the Porsche ring."

"Oh no!"

"The Goldbergs weren't going to be home until Sunday, and I wasn't about to call back to the beach house to say I had no house key. Mrs. Goldberg would have had a fit over my irresponsibility. Then I remembered that Graciella had a complete set of keys. So I decided to go to her house and get them. Unfortunately," she added, "Graciella lives in a pretty seedy part of town."

"Like where I got my nails done?"

"Yeah, only worse. This place was Gang Central as far as I could tell. Everywhere I looked there were bars on the windows and very scary-looking people. I mean, it was spooky. I got to Graciella's, but of course I didn't want to get out of the car. There was no way I was going to leave Mr. Goldberg's precious Porsche parked on Florence and Normandie, especially since I didn't know how to use the keyless lock."

"Good decision. So what did you do?"

"I sat below Graciella's window, laying on the horn. She probably thought it was just one more car alarm going off in the neighborhood. But finally she poked her head out of the window, and I yelled to her that I needed the house key."

"What did she say?"

"Well, she doesn't speak very good English, and my Spanish still consists entirely of food dishes so it took a while to sort it out. We finally settled on going down the street to a place that makes duplicate keys. When she pointed out the place, I knew I was in trouble because I can't parallel park, so I slowed down to a crawl and Graciella kind of rolled out of the car. I circled the block twelve times until she showed up on the curb again with the key. I'm positive that the police officer on the corner thought I was a drug dealer looking for a sale."

Mandie sighed. "God, what an afternoon. But what a car!"

I could almost hear the smile in her voice.

My shiny new Celica wouldn't have impressed the likes of the Goldbergs, but I adored it. The Saturday after I bought it, Michael asked me to do him a favor. (Sure; anything to use my wheels!) He wanted me to go down to Spago and pick up some lox that they had special-ordered. Now, Spago isn't exactly a carryout place; in fact, I didn't think they prepared takeout for anyone. But Michael had convinced Wolfgang Puck to do him a special favor.

I took Amanda, and after parking near the front of the restaurant, we walked up and pushed on the two huge glass doors. They were locked.

That struck me as odd. It was the middle of the afternoon. Why would Spago be closed? The sun reflected off the doors so brightly that it was difficult to see inside, but I cupped my hands around the sides of my head and pushed my nose on the glass, trying to get a peek.

"Are they closed, Suzy?" Amanda asked.

"I don't know. I don't think so," I answered. "There are people running around in there. I can see Wolfgang. Maybe they're doing a private party or something."

I pounded on the door to get their attention. Nothing. Perhaps they hadn't heard me. I pounded harder and pushed my face back up to the glass. Inside, several chefs stood around, resplendent in their white out-fits, glaring at me with fingers to lips as if to shush me. *Don't shush me!* What in the hell was going on?

Irritation overwhelmed me. More drastic measures were needed. I took off my loafer and used the heel to pound on the door repeatedly. Then I peered back in. This time the men were gesturing with sweeping motions of their hands and arms as if to say, "Go away, little girl, we're closed."

*Damn it, why aren't they opening the door for me? Don't they know I'm Michael Ovitz's nanny?*

Bang, bang, bang. I pounded again, and now Amanda joined in. They couldn't ignore us now, I thought pointedly, walloping the door. Then I saw Wolfgang approaching. His lips were pursed tightly together, eye-brows pulled down toward his nose, hands on hips. Oops.

"Just what in the hell do you think you're doing?" he yelled at me through the still-locked doors.

"Mr. Puck, I'm picking up some lox for Michael Ovitz," I said, smiling weakly.

I don't think he heard a word I said. "Get the hell out of here. We are filming a television commercial. You're costing me money! Go away!" he yelled as he shooed me with his hands and stormed back to the kitchen.

Luckily a crew member took pity on me and cracked the door to ask what I needed. Salmon, I repeated. For Michael Ovitz. He told me to try around back where all the staff was taking a break. Behind the

Dumpsters, Amanda and I found the employees outside, sitting at tables. They kindly handed over the lox.

I trudged back to the car with Amanda, humiliated. The worst part was that I so quickly slid into the role of a "don't you know who you're dealing with" Hollywood bore. I had never been that rude in my life. What was happening to me?

I decided that if the traits of a cranky LA coattail-rider were rubbing off on me, I could at least pick up some of the highbrow cultural trappings as well. I vowed to learn at least a little about the art that practically wallpapered the house. The lines and squiggles confounded me, and I constantly twisted my head at different angles, trying to find something familiar in the dozens of abstract paintings: a dog, a vase, a tree, anything recognizable. Michael kept a stack of art books on the table in the living room, and I sometimes thumbed through the pages hoping to soak up something. One day I saw a picture of the very same painting that was hanging in the living room. No! It couldn't be, could it? This silly-looking picture—of nothing I could come close to identifying—might cost millions of dollars. The next morning, the construction foreman, Carl, came in to use the phone. (An endless supply of these workers roamed in and out of the house every day, doing exactly what, I never did figure out. Mostly small projects such as the ones Oregon husbands tended to do on weekends; but Michael was not the kind of husband I was used to back in Oregon.) Carl was only a few years older than me, a chatty and friendly guy. This gig paid his way through college.

"Michael's art collection is really something," he commented, coming into the room after his call and staring at the wall. "Wow. That's a Picasso. Is it a copy?"

"No, that's the real deal," I chimed in confidently, having just boned up on the subject. I motioned for him to come closer. "Look, can you see that streak of paint?" I asked as I touched the canvas.

WAAA! WAAA! WAAA! Oops. A shrill alarm sounded, like the car version I set off when Kristi visited. Only a hundred times louder. I clapped my hands over my ears. It was so loud that Carmen came running out of the kitchen howling, frantically waving her arms in the air. "Miss Soo-zita, it is the Picasso alarm, oh my."

I couldn't think.

"Miss Soo-zita, you must call Mr. Ovitz."

*He'll kill me.* But at least the horrible racket would stop. I ran to the relative quiet of the other side of the house to make the call. I dialed frantically. Was the phone even ringing? Or was that just the alarm echoing in my ears?

*Oh my God*, I thought, they'll never answer. They've probably got a hundred calls backed up, as usual.

"CAA," one of the receptionists finally answered.

"I need Sarah in Michael's office!" I screamed. "Right now!" The still-shrieking horn slowed down our discussion, but finally she transferred me to Sarah.

"Suzy? I can hardly hear you," Sarah said. She never got too riled up about anything. "Is that the Picasso alarm?" she asked calmly.

"Yes!" I shrieked. "It won't stop!"

"Oh, don't worry, Michael's not here," she said smoothly, with the practiced air of someone who'd been through this before. "Just wait for the security company to call. It'll stop in fifteen minutes, anyway."

"Really?" I panted.

"Yes. And I'll have the alarm company reset it," she assured me.

As soon as I put the receiver down, the phone rang. "Hello. Hello?" I boomed.

"What's the code word?" a man asked.

Damn it. "Carmen, come help me!" I yelled. "What's the code word?"

"I have no idea, Miss Soo-zita. I only know the code for the house alarm; I don't know about the Picasso."

By now the awful noise had been going for almost ten minutes, and my ears were hurting.

"We'll notify the police, ma'am," the man said.

"No, no, no!" I pleaded. "Mr. Ovitz's secretary is calling you right now to take care of this. Please, please don't send the police!"

Carmen and I both scooted out into the front yard, Brandon in tow. The sound was so piercing that I was afraid his hearing would be damaged if we stayed inside any longer. Big tears rolled down his cheeks, and it was all my fault. And as we stood by the front gate, nearly forty yards from the door, I realized that the entire street could hear the damn thing. Fortunately, no one came out to investigate. Maybe they were used to alarms going off in this neighborhood.

I tried to avoid Michael that night and the next day at all costs. But oddly enough, he never said a word about the incident. Maybe he was distracted by his work, or maybe it was really no big deal. Who knew? I wasn't getting any closer to figuring these guys out. Then again, maybe Sarah didn't tell him.

I had a great weekend—I didn't set off one alarm! And I saw someone from home. Mark Gates was in town visiting his dad, who lived in a neighborhood called Miracle Mile. While I was looking up directions in my Thomas Guide, Judy said she couldn't believe I had a friend who would ask me to drive into such a seedy neighborhood. Miracle Mile sounded pretty nice to me, but with her comments I was petrified that I'd have to drive through Gang Central. Instead, though, I just had to drive through Beverly Hills. Mark and I had a barbeque and played cards all night, and I had so much fun being with people from home. But I'm still puzzled by Judy's comment. I guess in her world, friends don't let friends drive to middle-class neighborhoods.

"You're not going to believe this, Suzy." I could hardly hear Michael's assistant Jay, who was on his cell phone, barreling down the freeway in the family's brand-new SUV. "It's a friggin' tank. Whoa! Watch out. I think I might have sideswiped a semi with the mirrors. This thing is as wide as a motor home, I swear. They don't expect you to drive this monstrosity, do they?"

"Uh, yeah, they do. I've told Judy I'm kind of worried about it. How about you sticking up for me and saying it's probably too much of a vehicle for the poor little nanny to drive?" I teased.

"This thing is too much for *me* to drive." Jay laughed. "Okay, I'll do what I can for you. I'll be there in about fifteen. Open the gates so I can get this 18-wheeler on through."

I had been dreading the arrival of the new behemoth. Brentwood's streets were narrow and lined with cars parked on either side, not to mention the ever-present fleet of construction vehicles—cement mixers, dump trucks, etc. Just piloting a sedan to the grocery store made me feel like a rat triumphing over a maze. Judy knew I was nervous and took me out immediately for a spin. She wanted to assess my driving ability.

*Driving* wasn't the problem, for heaven's sake. I had been driving since I was six, when my uncle Tubby took me out to the hayfields and let me behind the wheel of the flatbed while he threw in the bales of hay. (Yes, I have an uncle Tubby. He's Uncle Skinny's brother.) I could even handle a stick shift; the issue was not the mechanics of a flippin' automatic SUV. It was the *size* of the thing, especially relative to the skinny streets. I couldn't help imagining that Judy was wishing she had a brake on her side of the car like the old driver's ed cars did.

"If you're so nervous about driving this, you should keep both hands on the wheel," Judy informed me.

Ten and two . . . ten and two . . .

We got through the lesson somehow, but I didn't feel much better about driving it. And I clearly wasn't much better *at* driving it. A few weeks later, I was wheeling down our street when I heard a loud scraping sound.

"Suzy, what was that noise?" Amanda asked, alarmed.

"Oh, probably a dump truck unloading some gravel, honey. Don't worry about it," I said casually, glancing in my rearview mirror just in time to see an old work truck rocking back and forth in my wake. Oh my God, had I just sideswiped that pickup? I must have—why else would it be moving?

I began to sweat profusely. In my mind, a jagged, ugly scrape now marred the shiny new SUV. I just knew this would happen. I frantically pulled into the driveway, parked, and jumped out. Cringing, I peeked at the side. Nothing. Just minimal damage to the driver's side mirror.

Still. I hustled the kids inside, found Carmen and Delma, and begged for help. They found me a rag to buff up the chrome on the mirror. Barely noticeable, thank God. How would I have explained it to Michael?

Yours truly came too close for comfort today, literally. I'm afraid Michael's going to find out. He notices everything. Just yesterday Judy told me that he never makes mistakes, and that's why he has no tolerance for incompetence. I also heard her telling Mrs. Eisner that she's worried that all the pressure and demands and stress he puts on himself will kill him, and she wishes he would just quit the business, although she knows he never will. I could never live like that. It is not looking good for me. I wonder if I'll ever have more than one week running without some kind of calamity.

Note to self: Call Mandie and hear her latest story and hope she did something worse.

We say no to 99 percent of the parties and events we're invited to, because if we can't bring the kids, we don't want to go.

—Kelly Ripa

# chapter 13
# house party

"Where are the caterers?" Judy asked in a panic.

It was 1 P.M. The guests, including many luminaries who had attended the last Academy Awards ceremony, were scheduled to arrive around five.

I shrugged. Carmen didn't know, either.

June and July were apparently big party months in Los Angeles. If the Ovitzes weren't going to one, they were throwing one. This was nothing new. Every year, Judy showed her flair for organizing and managing large events by hosting a party for the premiere of one big studio release. Huge, star-studded affairs, these gatherings required Judy to coordinate legions of caterers, publicists, decorators, and studio executives. I wasn't on the guest list, but I saw the frantic preparations: invitations that played music, colossal ice sculptures, place settings that cost as much as my monthly car payment, champagne fountains, and over-the-top gift bags with the latest electronic gadgets and jewelry from the hottest designers (that part always seemed like such a paradox to me. The richer you were, the better the freebies).

This particular event was only a dinner party, but I could see from Judy's panicked face that any problem would be cataclysmic. By the time two o'clock rolled around, she had shifted into full freak-out mode. At that point, even I began to realize that a fiasco loomed.

"Oh my God, where are the damned caterers?" Judy kept asking, dashing aimlessly around the house. "Do you think they could have written down the wrong day?" She phoned Michael's office and chattered at him. He had no answer, either, but he said he'd be home shortly.

"This is a nightmare!" she kept repeating as she dialed the caterers with shaking fingers. "Where are you?"

Indeed, they had written down the wrong day. Judy let loose with a tirade that would have made a sailor blanch. I was betting the owner of the catering company would remember this particular date for years to come.

"And you can bet Michael will never ever let me use you as a caterer ever again!" she yelled, slamming the phone down. She turned to me.

"Suzy, we've got to do something," she said, pacing the floor. "This is the biggest nightmare of my life. This can't be happening. Everyone is going to be here in less than two hours! Michael is going to kill me."

Judy scurried about frantically as Amanda joined in the fun. "Mommy's having a nightmare! Mommy's having a nightmare!" she chanted over and over, imitating her mom's frantic fidgeting.

I knew my hamburger casserole wouldn't quite cut it, so there wasn't much I could do in the kitchen. I called Sarah, savior of unsalvageable situations.

"Hey, Suzy," Sarah said. "Bad day, huh? Michael called Spago to see if there was any way they could help out. I'll call you right back."

"Oh God, Suzy," Judy moaned. "No one is going to want to—much less be able to—come up here on an hour's notice and feed this many people. This is a nightmare; my worst possible nightmare come true. Do you know I've actually had this dream several times?"

She sighed. "We are going to be taking a lot of people out for dinner with no reservations," she said resignedly.

The phone rang again, and I jumped on it.

"Suzy! Guess what!" The unflappable Sarah was practically bursting with joy. "Wolfgang said he'll send his people right out. Tell Judy that the cavalry should be there shortly."

Within the hour, guests started arriving. Aaron Spelling and his wife were first, the lady leading the way. "Darling," she breathed, loudly placing air kisses at least six inches from her hostess's cheeks. I swear I could hear the smacking sound all the way in the kitchen. Judy looked pained and pinched, even with Carmen plying the early arrivals with wine and champagne.

But within minutes, Puck's people showed up in a large Mercedes followed by a huge enclosed truck. Seven people rolled out, jammed a ramp in the back end of the truck, and began to unload carts and trays and containers filled with food. God knows where they got it all on such short notice. They certainly didn't have time to cook anything. Nevertheless, there it was, a full complement of hors d'oeuvres, salmon, grilled vegetables, you name it, all sizzling hot and ready to serve. Who said Spago didn't deliver? Judy laughingly told several guests about the catering fiasco, turning it into a cute little story. None of the guests would have believed that their perfect hostess had been spitting nails just a few hours ago.

The next event on their social calendar marked the first time I would accompany them to a dinner party. Normally they didn't take the kids to evening functions, and I wouldn't have been invited on my own, of course. (Reminder: *Nannies are not part of the family.*) But this time they wanted Josh and Amanda to come for a short visit and then go back home as soon as dinner was served. Once again I faced the wardrobe dilemma: what the hell was I supposed to wear? I wasn't sure how formal the party was, and I never did get the hang of the LA casual-but-dressy look that came so effortlessly to everyone else. The old cocktail dress and heels? Not too practical while chasing my little charges around the house. I settled for my nanny costume of jeans and a shirt.

Michael and Judy drove in the Jaguar, and I followed behind in the Mercedes. My stress increased with each mile. I had no idea how to find the house on my own. What if I lost them? What if I crashed the Mercedes? What if they looked in the mirror and hated my driving?

At about seven, we arrived at an enormous estate that was surrounded by twenty-foot-tall iron gates, extremely sharp points gracing the tips of each spearlike pole. The home—scratch that, three-story castle—must have been at least twenty-five-thousand square feet. We approached the valet tent, which was set up under an immense porte cochere. The valets were actually wearing ersatz Buckingham Palace uniforms—we're talking red velvet, gold braid, and epaulets—and were accompanied by two gargantuan guard dogs.

Who knows what kind of brand name they were. Rottweilers? Pit bulls? A horrifying hybrid? They were the scariest-looking dogs I'd ever seen, and they were unrestrained. Each one had its own handler, standing by on full alert, but it seemed to me that thick chains and padlocks were in order. Okay, so I'm not a dog person. Jacques LaRivière's yapper knew it, I knew it, and I was willing to bet my unscathed arms that these monsters knew it, too.

I prayed as I got the kids out of the car. All of the guests in front of me passed without eliciting even a doggie blink, and even four-year-old Amanda seemed unperturbed by the vicious guard-beasts. As I got closer and closer, I tried to convince myself that these canines were actually made out of concrete. Maybe they were just elaborate special effects. I had nearly passed them when they began to snap like fasting crocodiles—at me, of course; only at me. I thought my life would end in a flash of bared fangs and flying fur. I sprang three feet into the air and crossed the front door threshold like an Olympic long jumper, propelling the kids in with me.

Clearly, the dogs were trained to sniff out anyone with a net worth of less than a million.

Okay, maybe I was exaggerating about the dogs. But I kept wondering if there was some trick to understanding the upper class. Take my bosses' wedding anniversary. Late that afternoon I had signed for the delivery of a three-foot-wide box, courtesy of Michael and Jane Eisner.

Michael and Judy came home at the same time that evening, and I saw Judy spot the package and light up with a big smile. She was like a bubbly little girl who knew she was about to get a new pony. "What do you suppose it is? It's so large," she asked Michael.

"I have no idea, Judy," Michael said. "Why don't you open it and see."

With that, Judy tore into the box and pulled out a stuffed Mickey Mouse.

Silence. Judy looked at Michael. One eyebrow went up slightly. He shrugged.

"I don't get it," she finally said as she reached in again and pulled out Mickey's bride. "Do you get it?" she asked Michael incredulously. "Do you get it?" she turned and asked me.

Michael didn't have an answer. Neither did I, so I reached into the box and pulled out an envelope.

"Here, Mrs. Ovitz. It's a card," I said, handing it to her.

> *Dear Judy and Michael,*
>
> *Wishing you a lovely anniversary.*
>
> > *With Love and Friendship,*
> > *Jane and Michael*

"That's it? Do you believe it?" Judy exclaimed. "The Eisners have more money than God—certainly far more than we do. And what do they get us for our anniversary? Two stuffed rodents."

Another long silence.

"I'll bet they didn't even pay for them!" Judy said, looking dejected.

The next day she would give the dolls to Amanda and complain to me about it again. I didn't quite follow Judy's thinking: I saw it differently. Maybe the Eisners thought the two mice were a symbol of unity that couldn't be broken, a very appropriate anniversary gift.

Oh well. At least the Ovitzes weren't having an anniversary party. I wouldn't need to worry about my own lack of gift-giving skills.

But I was actually looking forward to the Fourth of July party that they attended each year. I'd heard that it was a huge event in Malibu, complete with a spectacular fireworks display. Just seven doors down from their beach house, so I wouldn't have to load up all the kids, and I knew Mandie was coming with the Goldbergs. What could go wrong?

The party was hosted every year by Frank Wells, a bigwig at Disney.

All the homes on Celebrity Row, as I called it, were tightly packed together to keep the riffraff from accessing the public beach next to their private homes. Everyone gathered on his beautiful, emerald green lawn for drinks, then meandered just a few feet down to the beach. Lounge chairs were scattered about for optimum fireworks viewing, fire pits and volleyball nets were set up, and caterers in crisp white uniforms and chef's hats manned a forty-foot-long buffet table. Music blasted from hidden speakers. Down on the beach where the grass met the sand, several very large, unhappy-looking men in suits stood guard. Joshua and Amanda wanted to play with the other kids on the beach, and I asked if Judy could hold Brandon while I went with them. She said yes and took Brandon, who, judging by his cute coos, was whole-heartedly enjoying the ladies fussing over him.

Strains of reggae filled the air, and I played tag with the kids and a whole group of other children. I was having fun for the first time in quite a while, working up a good sweat. After about twenty minutes, I decided to take the kids up to the buffet. On the way up to the food, I passed Mandie coming down.

"Where have you been?" I asked. "You're missing some actual fun in the sun."

"Oops," she said, grimacing. "Big trouble. Mrs. O is looking for you, and she has mean in one eye and angry in the other."

"Now what did I do?" I said. "Would you stay here with the kids and get them something to eat? I'll go see what she's so upset about."

I sprinted up to the house, where Judy was worked into a lather. "Where have you been?" she snapped. "I've been looking all over for you. We were frantic."

"What's the matter?" I had visions of Brandon lying somewhere hurt, crying, alone. "Is Brandon okay?"

"I couldn't find his pacifier. Where did you put it?" she demanded. "He was getting all fussy."

"It was in his pocket when we got here," I said. "That's where I always put it."

"Well, we couldn't find it. Michael and I searched all over the damned place, and then I had to send him all the way back to our house.

Michael's going to leave Brandon with Carmen. You need to go back up there and help her take care of him right away," she ordered.

"I am so sorry this crisis has been so distressing. But I wasn't sitting in a lounge chair sipping margaritas. I was entertaining your two *other* children. Why don't you just rename me Slacker Nanny?"

Oh, excuse me. That's what I *thought*. What I actually said was, "Oh, I'm so sorry. I'll walk back to the house." *Wimp!*

Irritation washed over me, spoiling what had been, for me, a really fun time. So much for spending the evening with Mandie at a real party. I wanted Judy, for just one minute, to see how things looked from my point of view. I don't think she ever realized that I grew up attending parties at our local Elks club. As you can imagine, that had not been an establishment where it was routine to observe:

—Cheryl Tiegs, wolfing down two hot dogs like she hadn't eaten in a couple of days. By the looks of her, it might really have been that long—or longer—since her last meal.

—Kenny Rogers walking around and not singing. I know, I know, but I had never seen him on TV without a microphone. I kept waiting for him to break into "You gotta know when to hold 'em . . ." But apparently his preferred mode of communication was just plain talking.

—A slightly blitzed Goldie Hawn, who tripped over me, apologized very sweetly, and included me in her conversation with Ali MacGraw about how a baby is such a little miracle.

—Sydney Pollack, whom I recognized from *Tootsie*. I had seen him a little earlier in the day at the beach house, dressed in nothing but a purple Speedo. I was having a hard time getting that disturbing image out of my mind.

—Not to mention Sylvester Stallone, walking around with prominent bags under his eyes, demonstrating unarguable proof of the expertise of lighting and makeup artists.

—Also, the curious spectacle of the aforementioned Mr. Stallone, surrounded by security guards, who appeared to have heat exhaustion because they were in full suits on a sweltering summer day. What possible peril did he fear in this social arena with fellow celebrities? Evidently he did not want to take any chances with some pesky autograph seekers.

Years later I would meet one of Mr. Stallone's nannies, and from what she said, this attitude was par for the course: apparently the staff in his home was not allowed to make eye contact with him unless spoken to first. The nanny also told me that everything concerning the kids went through his wife. The wife, who was considerably younger than her famous husband, tended to become very friendly with her nannies, taking them on shopping expeditions and out to eat, just like girlfriends. But before too long, there was inevitably a spat, and the nanny/friend would be fired.

Speaking of nanny/employer spats, I hoped this one would blow over quickly. After the pacifier scene, I was banished back to the Malibu house for the rest of the evening. Carmen was standing on the deck, and Brandon slept contentedly. She and I stood quietly together and watched as a shower of lights lit up the sky.

Just another day in paradise. The highlight of my day today was talking with the nice mom who was renting the beach house next door. She was playing with her daughter on the sand, and there was no nanny in sight. I still have hope that there are more people in this city who are genuine like her. I called Christine immediately to report that I spent the morning with Ms. "Hell Is for Children" herself, Pat Benatar.

P.S. What the hell is with that song? I have never understood it. Maybe she had childhood issues she was working on when she wrote it, because now she is obviously a loving and devoted mother.

P.P.S. I have got to get a life with friends who actually live in the same state as me.

P.P.P.S. Mom and Dad and Traci went to Ryan's graduation party last week. Can't believe I missed it.

I had better luck the next week at the Malibu house. No parties, so I could enjoy the best part about the beachfront place: my own separate guesthouse. It was detached, near the road, and blissfully private. The bedroom was big and open, with hardwood floors and lots of quiet. I relished such a private space. Either Carmen or Delma always came with us, and wonderful friends that they were, they always offered to get up with Brandon so I could snore through the night uninterrupted. Just the thought of having physical separation from the group lowered my blood pressure, even though I had to creep through the courtyard past the pool very late in the evening and report for duty in the main house at dawn.

I was alone at the beach house with the kids that next afternoon when the phone rang. I jumped up from our hundredth viewing of *Sleeping Beauty* to answer it. "Ovitz residence," I answered automatically.

"Hello, is Michael there?" a man said. His voice sounded familiar. *Dustin Hoffman?*

"I'm sorry, he's not home at the moment. May I take a message?"

"Huh. Who's this?" he said.

"Oh, it's just the nanny."

"*Just* the nanny?"

"Yeah."

"I see. Well, this is Just-the-Roto-Rooter guy. We have the same first name, Just The. I never met another Just The before."

"*Okay.*" I groaned inside.

"Hey, Just The, where are you from?"

"I'm from Oregon."

"Or-e-GONE. I know a guy from there. Maybe you know him, too."

"Um—"

"His name's Ken."

Okay, there are three million people in Oregon. How on earth was I supposed to know the same guy? Oh, the hell with it.

"Uh, what is his last name?"

"Kesey."

Now, what were the chances of that? Ken Kesey is the uncle of my health teacher's wife, and I had been to their house several times in high school.

"Actually," I said, "I do know him."

"You do? Wow!"

"Sure, I know him." I didn't explain my *loose* connection to the man. I also didn't let on that I had figured out it was Bill Murray on the other end of the line. "He lives on that farm in Pleasant Hill."

"That's right. I've been there," he said. "That's amazing. What a small world."

"It sure is," I agreed.

"Hey, do me a favor. Tell them that some guy named Bill is coming over later today."

I hung up the phone and felt slightly guilty. My connection to Ken Kesey, the infamous Merry Prankster and celebrated author of *One Flew Over the Cuckoo's Nest*, was more than a little tenuous. I loved my high school health teacher and his wife, but I had never actually laid eyes on her uncle in my life.

Carmen soon came in from shopping, and I told her what a strange conversation Bill Murray and I had had.

"Oh yeah," she said. "Bill, he's a big jokester, that one. Very nice guy, though."

When Judy came home, I gave her the phone message.

"God, I hope he's not bringing that kid of his. Last time that little monster was over, he hauled off and bit Joshua."

*Yes, that has actually been known to happen with young children.* I clenched my teeth.

"I couldn't believe it," Judy continued. "He bit him right on the face. Can you imagine the nerve of that kid? He hasn't been over since, and I don't plan on inviting him. And why the hell they named him Homer I'll never know."

I didn't pipe up. I liked how Bill had joked with me on the phone. And I was willing to bet that he wasn't like the famous movie-making mogul who had his assistant call Sarah at the office to officially pencil in playdates for the children. Bill's kids probably didn't have their own schedules—he sounded like a real, regular kind of dad.

Bill rumbled in an hour later, without little Homer. "Where's the nanny? I gotta meet the nanny." Then he came bursting into the living room. "Hey! You must be Just The. Come over here, Miss OreGONE!"

He swooped me up in a tight bear hug. "And there's Carmen!" he said, seeing her in the doorway. "Come here, you! I missed you." He picked up Carmen, too, and she started laughing.

Later, after he left, I said to Judy, "Wouldn't it be funny to live with a guy like that? His wife must have a pain in her side all the time from laughing."

Judy just stared at me for a long time. "Yeah, she has a *real* pain in her side all right," she said.

Mom called today to tell me that she ran into Ryan and his dad at the Shriners' annual barbeque. Turns out, Ryan is on crutches. He cut himself with a chain saw last week while he was out chopping wood on his dad's property. Mom said, "Well you know how his dad is. He has a very strong work ethic. So he made Ryan finish throwing the wood in the back of the pick-up *before* he would take him into town to get the gash sutured up."

Mom said Ryan's dad was just *sure* he was trying to get out of a hard day's work with his minor medical emergency. He wasn't about to let him off that easy. Don't think I will share that story with Judy, she may not find the humor in the situation. Judy doesn't ever think anything is funny. She would probably get stuck on the fact that there are people in the world who use a wood stove to heat their homes.

I really should start accepting their way of life. If I don't stop comparing things that I think are odd (like Michael eating chicken wings with a knife and fork) with normal things (like me going through the drive-up and being asked if I would like original recipe or extra crispy along with my coleslaw and biscuit) I will never fit in.

There must be something good to write about. Oh, yes! I got a book today on making homemade baby food. It has all kinds of fun recipes. I think that homemade is so much healthier than buying in jars—Michael and Judy should really be happy about that. Plus I can expand on my culinary skills. How can I screw up pureed zucchini?

My life is very split at the moment. I'm too scared to put on a dress in case the baby vomits on it.

—Cate Blanchett

## chapter 14
# the beverly hillbillies

This name-dropping thing wasn't foolproof.

I was cruising down Pacific Coast Highway, thrilled to be on my way back to Cottage Grove for a long weekend. Judy had approved my leaving the beach house at 2:30, but she and Amanda left at noon for a mother/daughter fashion show in Malibu, and by one I was really antsy. Carmen shooed me out the door, promising to take care of Brandon and Joshua. I thanked her profusely; she knew how excited I was about going home.

But my lead foot got the best of me, and the officer who pulled me over didn't care one whit about Michael Ovitz.

"Well, I guess the most powerful man in Hollywood won't be too happy about your ticket, now, will he?" he retorted sarcastically when I tried to wheedle my way out of a citation. Crap. My fifth speeding ticket in three years.

I wasn't going to let that officer ruin my excitement; I was off to spend a sweet weekend at home. I swung by the Brentwood house to pack my things, and Delma came dashing out to meet me.

"Suzy, Judy's holding on the phone. She's steaming mad," Delma said.

What in the world had I done now? Had the cops called Michael about my ticket? Did he have spies at the LAPD?

"Suzy, she just went off on me," Delma cried, wringing her hands. "I've never heard her so upset."

I tried to catch my breath, gulped, and grabbed the nearest phone, holding it a healthy distance from my ear.

"Yes, Mrs. Ovitz, it's Suzy," I said timidly.

"I know who it is," she snapped. "What do you think you're doing?"

"Huh?"

"Carmen is not your boss, I am! And I'm very unhappy with you. What did you do, just run out the door after my car left the driveway? I was already letting you go early. And by the way, I am not happy about uh . . . uh . . . the fact that sometimes you don't pick up the kids' toys," she ranted.

*Come again?* I couldn't think of what to say, and I'm not sure I could've managed the words if I'd had them. The pit of my stomach dropped out as she kept yelling. Mercifully, she finally hung up.

I immediately dialed Sarah, practically engulfed in tears.

"Suzy, calm down," Sarah said, trying to console me. "Judy must be under some heavy-duty stress or something. Surely it couldn't really be you. They always tell me how happy they are with you."

"But she complained that sometimes I don't pick up the kids' toys," I sobbed.

"That's ridiculous." Sarah snorted.

Ten minutes later, Judy called again, apologizing for losing her temper. Had Sarah called and told her how upset I was? I tried to stop crying. Judy even said that she was looking forward to my return, and she sounded sincere. Was she? I didn't even bother trying to analyze it; I just wanted to hold on to any shred of appreciation I could find. If she was willing to throw me a crumb, I was willing to accept it.

I heard Joshua whining that he wanted to talk to me. Great. Having just heard his mother's earlier tirade, I was sure he was going to join in on the fun.

"Suzy? Will you still bring me back pictures of you water-skiing like you said?"

I began crying all over again.

This is the first time Josh has ever opened his heart to me. And he did it even after he heard his mother berating me. It may seem trivial, but for Joshua to take any interest in me, to extend himself even that much, is a monumental breakthrough. I really have hope now that things can be better. I think this may be a turnaround point with us.

Speaking of my male relationships, I went and visited Ryan and his family. His dad said he didn't think Ryan was ever going to grow up, and he was really proud of me for moving on. I don't think I *have* really moved on. I can't imagine ever getting over him. Ryan and I stayed up and talked until 2 A.M. I gave him the world's longest hug goodbye.

It's not easy to remember why I left. Oregon exists on a different planet than Hollywood, a planet that cherishes fun and relaxation. I can't even describe how much I enjoy myself here, waterskiing and having fun, but there is always a nagging voice in the back of my mind reminding me that I'll be back in Bizarro World very soon. I'm trying to let myself fully relax, anyway, knowing that I'll just have to deal with the reimmersion when it happens.

Apparently my subconscious really didn't want to go back. On the morning of my flight to LA, my alarm didn't go off. I had to connect in Portland, and if I didn't catch the right plane, I'd be hours late. I was petrified of Judy's wrath, especially given how I'd left things. Mom screeched out to the airport with me, yelling "Go faster" the entire way. I checked in at 8:42 for a 9 A.M. flight. Miraculously, the agent said I might still be able to make it if I ran—the Eugene airport is very small, and passengers walk right on the tarmac to the planes. I tore off across the asphalt, my enormous purse swinging behind me. Even from fifty yards away I saw the flight attendants waving for me to hurry up. I could only imagine what was running through the minds of all the passengers staring out at me from the little windows.

And then I tripped.

The entire contents of my bag—four tampons, wallet, a banana, two magazines, four sticks of Doublemint gum, my ticket, a paperback book, a pair of socks, a small can of Mace, nail polish, about four dollars in change, several loose slips of paper with notes for journal entries, pictures of the kids, and a backup toothbrush—spewed out across the tarmac. I lay there sprawled out amid it all, some free preflight entertainment for those infernal staring passengers. One of the flight attendants—laughing uncontrollably, I might add—dashed down and helped me pick up the stuff. Humiliated, I finally boarded the plane. My seat? Perhaps I should have known that it would be at the very back of the plane, past rows and rows of snickering people.

Thankfully, when I got back to Brentwood, it looked like there might be some good news. While I was home, my sister Cindy told me how bored she was with her accounting job at the headquarters of a national restaurant chain. In a flash of brilliant inspiration, I persuaded her to apply for a position in the accounting department at CAA. She had to send in a photo with her résumé—why they cared what the back-office number crunchers looked like, I'll never know, but she must have been cute enough, because she got an interview. Cindy had an outstanding work ethic and was very good at what she did, and I wasn't surprised when she got the job. Sarah had briefed Michael, and he said in passing one night, "I hear your sister is moving down here and coming to work for us." It was the most personal remark he had ever made to me.

Just two years older, Cindy and I had always been great friends, and we were both excited to live close to each other. She aspired to do great things with her career, and I aspired to get an occasional Saturday night off and stay at her apartment. She put me in charge of finding a place for her. My priority was proximity to *me*, of course. The best I could do was a two-bedroom box that cost $1100 a month. Poor Cindy couldn't muster up the rent herself, so she ended up convincing two of her friends to move down and share a two-bedroom five-hundred-square-foot flat not far from my house. One of the girls had to take up residency in the walk-in closet. I am not kidding.

At first, Cindy's job seemed no different from shuffling paperwork in Eugene. She processed clients' compensation in a room with eight other women and no windows. Though CAA's clients weren't employees, money they received from movies, TV, commercials, whatever, came through the office first, and CAA deducted its commissions immediately.

Then the balance was sent on to the clients. On her first day, Cindy took a call from an actor's manager demanding that CAA pay interest on the money that he was supposed to have received the month before. Apparently the check had still not arrived at his mansion. Cindy didn't understand why such a wealthy actor would be worried about some measly interest—until she realized that the check was in fact two months late and was for four million dollars. Of course she wouldn't ever tell me *who* it was; she has this confidentiality thing hardwired into her brain, and it has always been impossible for me to get information out of her.

During Cindy's first week on the job, she was asked to handle the phones for the CFO while his secretary went to lunch. She was told to interrupt him if anyone "important" called. Since it was only her third day, her first thought was "How am I going to know who's important and who isn't? What am I supposed to say? 'Excuse me, but before I can put you through, I'll need to know how much your last film grossed.'" No, that wouldn't work. She had *no idea* what amount made a movie a blockbuster.

The truth is that my sister never knew which actors and actresses were currently hot in the media, let alone the names of behind-the-scenes people. To this day she's probably not quite sure exactly what Steven Spielberg does.

The very first call she received was a memorable one.

"Hello, Bob Goldman's office. How may I help you?"

"Is Bob in?" came the stressed-out reply.

"I'm sorry, he's not available right now. May I take a message?"

"Yes, it's extremely important. Tell him to call . . ." Cindy didn't know what to do. She hadn't heard clearly; the caller was talking so fast that she hadn't caught the last name.

"I'm sorry. I didn't get that. Could you give me your name again?" she asked politely.

"It's Michael . . ." Still she couldn't catch the last name.

"I'm sorry, sir, one more time?"

"O-VEE-EYE-TEE-ZEE." He spelled it loudly and dramatically. "OVITZ!!!!" he screamed into the phone.

She gulped. "Thank you. I'll put you right through."

One night Cindy called, all proud of herself, informing me that I was wrong about thinking she was not up to date on the latest happenings in Hollywood.

"Suzanne, you know how you are always saying that I don't know who anyone is?"

"Of course, yes," I confirmed.

"Well, I will have you know that Nancy in the office just invited me to go with her to a wedding for that girl who played Lucy on Dallas, and I knew exactly who she was talking about."

"Of course you're up to date on it; no one watches that show anymore," I explained. "Maybe we can rent some current movies this weekend. It might be helpful if you are going to be in this industry."

The poor girl had a lot to learn.

Less than a week after she began her new job, Cindy realized that it provided more entertainment than an issue of *People*. The government had just required a new form in accounting, an I-9, which served as proof of U.S. citizenship. CAA tapped Cindy to gather the necessary paperwork on all of CAA's clients. She needed to make copies of several documents: a passport, driver's license, and social security card, and the law required that she "physically" see original documents.

Since CAA's clients included some of the most notable and reclusive actors and directors in Hollywood, what might have been a relatively mundane accounting procedure at any other office quickly became a hot issue among the celebrity clientele. These folks maintained their privacy at any cost, and things like birth-date verification could be quite upsetting to actresses of a certain age. I told Cindy that this was a job better suited for a *National Enquirer* reporter.

The adventure began when she went to the local clients' homes with her portable copier on wheels. (She looked like a flight attendant perpetually headed to the airport.) In the first few weeks, she dropped by the homes of Demi Moore, Cher, and Dolly Parton. She could deal with looking like an overworked insurance saleswoman, but then came the complication of the out-of-town clients. Driver's licenses and passports aren't exactly the kind of documents you want to be mailing here and there. Cindy kept hearing some of the same comments over and over: "Oh, the government didn't care if I was an American citizen during the past ten years when I paid millions of dollars in taxes, but now suddenly it's imperative" or "Who's going to see these documents; why do you need it?" Translation: Who's going to know how old I *really* am, or how I lied about my weight on my driver's license?

She persevered despite their protests. One day she was sent to track down Chevy Chase in a suite at the Beverly Hills Hotel. When she pulled up, she was mortified that she would have to use valet parking. Cindy drove an old clunker, and suddenly she found herself surrounded by Ferraris and Range Rovers. She said she felt a little like the girl in class who was wearing faded jeans from the Goodwill while all the cool kids had on name-brand clothing.

She nervously found Chevy Chase without a problem (although she hated interrupting him during a meeting), but as she headed back down to the lobby, she rummaged through her purse and discovered that she was virtually broke. Outside the hotel's massive glass doors stood two valets. In queue were a Rolls, a Bentley, a Mercedes, and a Lamborghini, each driven to the entrance by a valet who would then dutifully stand by the open doors, awaiting guests. And a big fat tip.

Cindy stood frozen, not knowing how to handle her predicament, when a young valet in a purple uniform approached her and asked for her receipt. She winced and handed it over. A succession of cars came and went for nearly ten minutes. Evidently her jalopy had been trundled to a far lot.

Cindy soon realized Chevy had followed her and was now waiting for his car as well. She felt sick. What would he think about CAA if he saw that the accounting person entrusted with valuable, personal information drove an ancient Toyota with two bald tires and a "nonstock" baby blue paint job? She could only hope that somehow her car would be hidden on the other side of one of the limos.

The valet was quite tall, so his arrival in the tiny rattletrap—in front of more than fifteen waiting businessmen and dignitaries—was even more ridiculous than it might have been. His legs were so long, he had tangled one of them between the steering wheel and gearshift knob. As if the appearance of the lovely blue Toyota had not been embarrassing enough, the sound of the horn blaring under the valet's twisted knees certainly was. There might as well have been a contingent of marine honor guards firing a twenty-gun salute along with a loudspeaker announcement:

"Will the very poor person with a very old foreign car please come to the valet station immediately and take this pile of trash off the premises before more of our important guests are further offended?"

By the time she reached the car, my sister had managed to find a single dollar bill in her purse. She carefully folded it in fourths so that the numeral one wouldn't show, not so much to hide the denomination, but to make it look like there was more than one bill.

The valet opened her door and stood formally by as she climbed in. She then engaged the clutch, put the car in first gear, put her other foot on the accelerator, and tossed the tiny green square of paper at the valet. She careened down the driveway, knowing that by the time she cleared the hedge protecting the hotel from street view, he would just be unfolding his largesse, and she would be safely out of sight. Cindy's first Hollywood lesson in Class Consciousness 101:

- It's not who you are, it's what you drive.

- Appearances really are everything.

- Fake it while you can, then bolt.

After Chase, Cindy continued to work her way through the Cs. She came upon a name that seemed out of order: Mapother—a name she didn't recognize. Certainly not a big star; perhaps a director? When she asked Mr. Mapother's agent why his client was in the Cs, she was quickly ushered upstairs by two male employees.

"Here, make a copy of this passport and be quick about it," he said, tossing the paperwork at her.

"Now listen to me," the agent said while Cindy stood there, bewildered. "This Mapother guy is really Tom Cruise. That's why he's in with the Cs. You're not to tell anyone else about this, ever. Do you understand?"

"Yes. Yes, I understand," she replied, feeling as if she had been kidnapped momentarily by the Secret Service. She had just entered the secretive Society of the Keepers of the Name, and her lips were sealed. She wouldn't betray it to a soul, not even to her own sister. And she knew how much I adored Tom Cruise. (I had to look up his real name to write this book.)

It's so refreshing to have Cindy's perspective here in Glitter Land. None of the status stuff matters to her, and we can laugh at the craziness together. I also am excited to have a retreat, even if it is a sofa in her cramped apartment. Except that I am a wimp. It is currently 9:15 on a Friday night. I want to go stay at Cindy's. But I am afraid to ask. I think I might get an ulcer, it's so stressful pacing back and forth upstairs, contemplating in my head all the reasons I should get to leave, but unable to get up the nerve to go downstairs and announce that I am doing so.

Here is what Ms. Doesn't Have a Backbone has done the last three Fridays.

**7:50:** Get Brandon ready for bed—pajamas, rocking, etc.

**8:00:** Take him down for kisses and hugs from the family and then lay him down for the night.

**8:05:** Get bottles on ice, and put in upstairs bathroom.

**8:08:** Confirm with Delma that she will get up in the night with him.

**8:14:** Pack my bag to stay Friday and Saturday night over at Cindy's.

**8:32:** Pace back and forth, attempting to get up the nerve to ask to leave.

**8:40:** Go in the kitchen to get moral support from Carmen and Delma, hear that *yes*, I should be able to leave.

**8:46:** Tell myself that I should be able to leave; it is Friday night, Saturday is my day off, I have put everything in order, Brandon is in bed, and I should be off duty now.

**8:51:** Get a knot in my stomach thinking about what Judy will say.

**9:02:** March into the dining room and announce, with as much confidence as I can muster (with my bag over my shoulder), "I am going to stay at my sister's now!"

**9:02 AND 30 SECONDS:** Michael says, "Great. See you later." Judy says, "Huh, what? Where are you going? Is Brandon in bed? Did you tell Delma you were leaving? When are you coming back?"

**9:03:** Hug kids, say good-bye. Michael says, "Thanks, Suzy." Judy continues to look confused by the events that have just transpired.

**9:04:** Get in my car and scream, "Yes, I am off work!"
OR
As is the case tonight at 9 p.m., I chicken out, come up to my room, and decide to wait and leave first thing in the morning, as soon as Michael shuts the alarm off. While silently steaming that I SHOULD be able to leave the house on Friday nights.

Note to self: Stop by the bookstore tomorrow. There must be some self-help book out there called You and Your Boss: Working Together for a Mutually Satisfying Relationship.

I decided to stop stewing about Judy not liking me and start stewing over baby food. I was so eager to try my new recipes for healthy veggie purees. One night I was feeding Brandon my carrot and squash medley, but he didn't seem all that interested. Judy walked in right when he was craning his head as far away from me as possible.

"What is that?" she asked in disgust.

"Well, I don't think he likes it," I said.

She looked down at the orange slush. "Well, look at it, of course he doesn't!" she said. "Would *you* like to eat that?"

*Well, no, I have teeth.*

I needed my nightly conversations with Mandie more and more.

As bad as I thought I had it, she had it worse. Mrs. Goldberg once sent Mandie on a routine errand to Rodeo Drive to pick up some clothes she'd ordered. Price: $700. Mandie only had $83 in her checking account, so she returned empty-handed and was promptly berated.

"Mandie, where are my camisoles?" Mrs. Goldberg demanded. "Or did you forget to stop by the boutique?"

"Sorry, Mrs. Goldberg, I didn't have the money in my checking account."

"But you know I always reimburse you for it on your next *paycheck*," she responded.

"I know and I appreciate that; it's just that I didn't have enough money in my account at the time I was writing the check, and my dad has always told me to—"

"You always need to have enough money in your account to be able to run errands for me," Mrs. Goldberg interrupted.

Mandie said nothing. For her first six months of work—until she paid off her half of the agency fee—her bimonthly paycheck had been $428 after taxes. She was now making a whopping $478 every two weeks, but her next paycheck wouldn't be coming until the following Friday. She didn't want to bounce a check, but she didn't want her boss berating her for only having $83 in available funds.

Hearing the story worked me into a rage. "Then tell her to pay you more if she expects you to keep that kind of money in your checking account!" I screamed. "Or, for that matter, have her give you a credit card for her stuff. This is totally ludicrous."

Mandie seemed embarrassed, and I hung up quickly. But I kept stewing about the money thing. I got out my calculator and started figuring out how much money middle America generally has to spend on childcare. When I was finished, I figured out if our employers were paying the same *percentage* of their income that a family earning $80,000 a year spends on childcare, a nanny to the wealthy would be paid a six-figure salary. Ridiculous. Well, not so ridiculous for a suburban family who is *actually* paying 14 percent of their gross income to their children's caregiver.

I know, I had to get a life.

Why was I spending all this energy being angry when I could be working on changing my own situation? I had to stop criticizing Mandie all the time. Maybe my mother's little saying about walking in other people's shoes, washing their socks or whatever, had some validity.

I guessed part of the reason was that I didn't care that much anymore. I no longer wanted to be the perfect employee and I wasn't at all interested in spending all my time and energy trying to please my bosses. My take on the world was a galaxy apart from theirs, so I figured I might as well enjoy myself as much as I could during the day, have fun with the staff, and engage the children in as many activities as they would tolerate. I ordered myself to stop worrying every morning about whether Judy was mad at me. She seemed to be unhappy most of the time, and I decided to stop automatically assuming that it was because of me. I was done being a stress case.

But then I had a horrible suspicion. I rounded up Delma to help me test it out.

"Delma, stand here, outside my door," I directed, heart pounding, then closed the door and sat on my bed. I chatted to myself, in a normal tone, pretending that I was talking to Mandie on the phone. Finally I jumped up and opened the door.

"Well, could you hear me?" I asked.

Delma proceeded to recite, verbatim, my entire fictional conversation.

Oh my God. The countless phone conversations I'd had with Mandie flew through my head. Who knows what I'd said while Judy was listening? No wonder she acted so strange around me. Maybe I should wrap a pillow around my head to muffle my voice from now on. Oh, it was probably too late. The damage was done.

My mother called to tell me that my younger sister, Traci, and her best friend, Nancy, were taking a trip through California with Nancy's family. "Of course they want to come and visit you when they're in LA," my mother said.

"That's great!" I said. "I'm dying to see some Oregonians."

"I'm very happy for you, honey, and Traci's excited, too, but I think you should keep a couple of things in mind. Now, you know we love Nancy and her family, but let's face it, they're not exactly going to blend in down there. And you should keep in mind that the Ovitzes might be surprised that people take their road trips in an old truck and camper."

Great point. Nancy's dad was the greatest guy you'd ever know, and he'd give you the shirt off his back if you needed it. But he was kind of like Jed Clampett without the millions, even though he did live close to an old gold mine near Cottage Grove. I started praying that Nancy's uncle wouldn't be traveling with them. He was a dead ringer for the kind of people Larry the Cable Guy likes to talk about. Even their dog,

Blue, was a character. He could drink more beer than a human when he had a mind to.

I thought about my employers' lives and what they didn't experience on a daily basis, insulated as they were by wealth and power. Little things like the signs I had seen all my life:

NO SHOES, NO SHIRT, NO SERVICE

LOGGERS BREAKFAST SPECIAL $4.99

BONANZA BURGERS: 3 HAMBURGERS FOR $2.99 (ONIONS 15 CENTS EXTRA)

TEN-FAMILY GARAGE SALE OUT LORANE ROAD—LOTS OF GOOD STUFF

RETURN BOTTLE AND POP CANS AT THE BACK OF THE STORE

Several days later, the old Chevy pickup pulled up out front. There was Nancy's dad, Gary, behind the wheel, his latest hunting trophy—a large pair of antlers—strapped to the grill. Suitcases and duffel bags piled up in the uncovered truck bed, and the Chevy was towing an ancient camper trailer that looked a little dented and rusty. I bolted downstairs as I heard the front gate buzzer ring. I found Judy staring openmouthed out the front door of the house.

"What on earth is that out on the street?" she gasped.

"Just a sec, it's my sister," I said, flying past her. I ran to the gate to meet them. Just as I approached, Blue jumped out and proceeded to relieve himself on a palm tree. At least he wasn't lapping up Bud Light.

"Sorry; he had to go real bad," Gary said. "I 'spect this neighborhood has some kind of rules about pets. It's pretty upscale." A wave of homesickness suddenly swept over me, hearing his familiar voice. I wanted to be with "regular" people again.

I hugged everyone, holding Traci especially tight. Overjoyed barely came close to describing how happy I was to see them, but I also knew that my boss was still standing in the door zapping us with her disapproving radar. But I didn't care. Today was Saturday, my day off. I could stand out here all day if I wanted to.

I just hoped she wouldn't come closer and say anything to embarrass them. She'd probably have a nervous breakdown if I opened the gate and let them pull in. Traci kept looking at me like, *Okay, now what? Aren't you going to invite us in?*

But I knew I couldn't. We stood and chatted for about thirty minutes, and I grew more and more angry with myself. I was strong enough to stand there and withstand Judy's stares, but I knew I couldn't bring myself to show my sister and her best friend into the house where I lived.

I was so afraid of what Judy might say to Traci and Nancy's family that I didn't even invite them in. I wanted to scream from the street, "Yes, Judy, there are people who go on vacation in an RV. And yes, that does require pulling over at rest stops to empty the contents of the toilet into a drain." This is how a lot of America actually *lives;* it is this thing called "going camping" where you build a fire and roast marshmallows to make s'mores. It is actually quite enjoyable to be out in nature looking up at the stars with your family.

Why am I beating my head against a brick wall, or in this case, a brick mansion? I knew my sister knew why I hadn't given them a tour and that hurts even more than the realization that I am losing part of who I am because I'm afraid my boss will criticize me.

Traci mentioned that she had seen Ryan and he was miserable without me and really wanted to come visit. I am really missing him now.

And I am *really* homesick.

Our sex life has been ruined since the arrival of our first baby . . . we can't be so spontaneous, because we don't want the nanny to hear us. We manage, but it is a big change—we can't scream and yell like we used to.

—Cindy Crawford

# room service

Fall rolled in, and Halloween passed without any fanfare. I'd been wondering how it would work. Would we buzz each gate and scream "Trick or treat" into every intercom in the neighborhood? I needn't have worried; the kids didn't dress up or go out at all that night. Guess their parents didn't want them to collect bags full of artificial flavors and colors.

Chin up, chin up; on to Thanksgiving in Hawaii. After six long hours on our ill-fated flight, we landed, thank God. Later our entourage met up with Al Checchi's group: Al, his wife and three kids, plus their nanny, Jenna. She was a cute girl about my age with long, shiny black hair and a wide smile, but she was a lot bolder and wilder than me. I didn't know much about Mr. Checchi other than that he was a bigwig with some airline, and Judy said he had more money than they did. (But after the first twenty million, did it really matter who had more?)

While we were checking in at the Hilton on the Big Island, Jenna asked me if I'd join her that evening for a night on the town. I gaped at her.

"You get to go out?" I inquired. "I mean, you really get to *leave?*"

"Of course. I'm off at six while we're in Hawaii."

*No way.* The thought of being "off duty" on vacation had never even entered my mind. Because she watched three kids of similar ages, I had assumed that our situations were the same. I tried to breathe. *Okay, don't get angry. You did this to yourself. Just one more example of you not asserting yourself.*

"Just ask Mrs. Ovitz if you can go out with me," she said, carefree.

"Are you out of your mind?"

"Never mind, I'll do it," she said, as if it was no big thing. My knees shook at the thought.

She did it right then, all confident and direct. But Judy's cold silence made it clear that she wasn't exactly crazy about the idea. Later, when we were alone, I was told that Jenna's request was impossible to accommodate, and I would not be going out that night or any other night. In short, Jenna had not gotten on Judy's good side. The next day, Jenna raised Judy's temperature a few more degrees when she started massaging Michael's shoulders as he sat in a lounge chair. It wasn't like she was coming on to him, but I thought it was quite strange and could see why his wife would be annoyed with her unwarranted familiarity. To top it off, after she assessed his rigid neck muscles, Jenna told Michael that he should lighten up a bit, just as casually as you please. For once Michael was too stunned to take control. Or maybe he was silently enjoying the rubdown. Judy didn't say anything, either, but I can still picture the look on her face. I think the casual violation of personal body space had so shocked her sensibilities that she couldn't even begin to formulate words. I didn't think she, herself, would be comfortable enough to touch him like that without an invitation.

The next day, in the living area of my suite, Judy made a point of telling me that "that girl," which became Jenna's name for the rest of the trip, "did not know her place."

While she was rambling on, a knock came at the door. Jenna. When I invited her in, Judy immediately bolted. Jenna and I flopped on the bed while I related the story, which started us on a whole litany of comparative tales. Instant nanny camaraderie! It's funny how the subject of money always comes up when nannies get together.

"Did you guys come to the airport in a limousine?" Jenna asked.

"Yes," I said. "We always do when we go places as a family."

"Mr. Checchi would never allow that. He made the cook drive us all in the old Suburban; he said a limo was frivolous." This was the same man who paid for his nanny to fly first class?

I laughed knowingly. Oh so knowingly.

"You think that's weird? Get a load of this. When we got here, they made a big to-do about no one using the honor bar. Under no circumstances were the children and I to eat or drink anything from it. Judy said she'd buy juice at the grocery store for the kids. And yet she has no problem sending the kids' underwear out with the bellman to be cleaned and pressed."

Jenna laughed. "My friend, who's a nanny for a big director who gets six million dollars a picture, actually had the mother speak to her about using too much toilet paper. The mother requested the nanny be more conscientious about the children's wastefulness."

"And get this," I said, just warming up. "The best part was last night after we checked in and I helped Judy unpack, a bellman rolled in this enormous basket of fresh fruit, soda on ice, and an assortment of cookies. When Michael came in and saw it, he had an absolute conniption.

"'Suzy, did you order this? Judy, did you?'

"'No,' we said.

"'Well, I'm not paying for that! Call them to take it back.'

"'Michael, I *didn't* order it,' Judy attempted to explain.

"'Well then who sent this?' Michael demanded.

"'I suppose they're going to charge us for this now,' Judy grumbled.

"'Call them and tell them to pick it up,' Michael ordered.

"Judy picks up the phone and punches the button for the front desk. 'Hello. This is Mrs. Ovitz in room 77. Would you please send someone to pick up the rolling cart that was just delivered to our room? We didn't order any fruit, and we can't be expected to pay for it.'

"Silence as she listened for a minute.

"'What's that? Oh, I see . . . the . . . the manager did. Oh . . . with the suite. Well then. Okay. Just leave it, and tell the manager thank you. And uh . . . you have a nice evening as well.'"

"Turns out our suites are so flippin' expensive, it's standard to get this assortment of goodies as a gift every other day."

"Yeah, we do, too. Do you believe the service in this place? It's gonna be a blast!"

Right.

Maybe *she* would have a blast.

I did have a gorgeous two-bedroom suite adjacent to the main hotel building. Amanda and Joshua shared one bedroom and Brandon and I the other. We were on the ground floor. Everyone else was in the hotel proper, I guess. I never did get a chance to see anyone else's room.

"Bet you never dreamed you'd have your own hotel suite in Hawaii," Michael's brother commented one day as he breezed by.

*Yes, it sure is unbelievable!* I wanted to say. It's great to have a convenient spot for everyone to drop off a wallet, grab a towel, or make a phone call. Sunscreen? Have at it. Flip-flops? Sure, just root around in the pile of them there. Don't worry about my privacy—it's much easier to let yourself in through the patio rather than go around and knock on the front door. Yes, it's really quite something having my own suite in Hawaii!

Aloha! I can't go anywhere. I've actually seen Hawaii twice so far, both times from inside a van when we were riding to a restaurant for dinner. Then on the way back to my room. Brandon has been acting like he doesn't feel well, so I take him out in the sun very little. He just wants me to hold him most of the day, and he isn't interested in playing with his blocks like he usually does. I think Josh and Amanda are having a good time, though, splashing with their parents in the fancy pool and paddling around in the ocean. I'm working my normal hours here, without the weekend off. When I get home I'm going to ask if I can combine the two extra days I worked with my normal weekend so I can have four days off in a row. I AM going to get up the nerve to ask. Come hell or high water!

See, I'm looking at the bright side: long time with no days off equals four glorious days in a row of freedom when we get home.

One morning the phone rang while I was shooing out several non-Ovitz kids. Brandon felt feverish, so I wanted to settle him into a nap.

Amanda sat grumpily in front of the TV, complaining that I'd turned down her *Sleeping Beauty* video too low. I was tempted to just let the phone ring, but I picked it up.

"Suzy, is Michael in your room?" Sarah sounded tense.

"Good guess. I had a crowd of ten here a few minutes ago, but no, he isn't here now."

"There's a message for him. I called his suite but didn't get an answer."

"Okay, I can take a message," I said, transferring Brandon to my other arm while I grabbed for a pen.

"No, Suzy, the client wanted to leave it in his own words so Michael would get it straight. He made me write it down verbatim," Sarah explained. "Listen to this."

"Wait, do I have to write this down exactly?"

"I'm sorry, yes."

"Shoot," I said. Brandon was whimpering now, and I just wanted to hurry up so I could go take his temperature.

"Okay, here goes: 'Michael, I can't believe you're on vacation again!'" Sarah began. "'Isn't this the third one this year? That must be nice.'"

"Sarah, am I supposed to be infusing the anger and sarcasm into the phone message?"

"No, just keep writing. 'Damn it, did you get the FedEx package? I want to know what's in that contract, *now*. What the hell is going on there? This is the last time I put up with this horseshit. You tell me you've got this handled—handle it! Call me back *immediately*.'"

"Okay, I got it; now what do you want me to do?"

"Wait, Suzy, Jay wants to talk to you. We were both here when we got the message."

"Hi, Suzy, you have got to make sure he gets this right away," Jay said breathlessly. "I promised Redford I'd deliver the message."

"When did he call?" I asked.

"A few minutes ago. Can you find Michael right away?"

"Yes, sir, I will. You gotta love this work, don't you, Jay?" I laughed.

The adults were down at the beach. Great. Amanda hated the hot sand on her feet, and I couldn't leave her in the room alone. I slung Brandon on one hip, wiggled Amanda into my other arm, and we waddled slowly down to the shore. As soon as I gave him the message, Michael went bounding back to the room ahead of us. I told Judy what had happened, and she said, "Oh, Bob. He is the worst, just the worst," shaking her head in disgust.

I told Judy I thought Brandon was coming down with something. I then casually tried to encourage Amanda to stay on the beach with her mother, so Amanda wouldn't catch whatever Brandon was coming down with. But she insisted that she wanted to finish watching *Sleeping Beauty*.

When we finally made it back to the room, Michael was spread out on my bed with the phone to his ear. Sarah was patching him through to Redford. I tried to usher Amanda back out the door to the patio, but she began to wail. Michael had been leaning back against the headboard, but now he was leaning forward to brush sand off his legs onto the floor.

Was he motioning to me to keep her quiet? That's what it looked like, but that couldn't be it. He had to know there was no way I could control the noise level in the room. I tried to coax Amanda outside again, but she just started to fuss more, and then Brandon chimed in. *No, that's not good; reverse course.* Poor Brandon started to lunge out of my arms for his crib. Wow. He really must not be feeling well if he wants to get in his crib. I had to let him lie down.

By now Michael had evidently reached "Bob." He threw himself back onto the pillows and launched into high-voltage appeasing mode. Oh no. He was going to need his full concentration for this. Amanda kept crying. She wanted to finish her *Sleeping Beauty* video, *right now*. I told her I would read a book to her quietly, but she insisted we sit on the bed to start the story. Nothing was working! *Please don't have a tantrum. Please don't have a tantrum*, I prayed. Then I remembered my gumdrops. I desperately searched through my bag for them to use as a mouth-stopper. She took the bait. I jiggled Brandon a little in his crib and discreetly tried to see if Michael was distracted by the ruckus. Although of course I was desperately curious and listening as hard as I could.

I leaned down to Amanda, whispering and crooning. We perched as far away from her father as we could and still be on the bed, and then I started the story.

"I promise as soon as Daddy's done talking, we will start the movie again," I said, smoothing her hair. "Thank you for being so quiet, sweetheart." *Positive reinforcement, positive reinforcement; don't have a tantrum, don't have a tantrum.*

Finally Michael wound up his business with a smile, laughing and promising Redford that he'd be in touch again soon. Then he jumped up off the mattress and smoothed down the comforter. "Thank you, Suzy," he said. "I appreciate all your efforts; thanks for keeping the kids quiet."

I let out a breath I didn't know I'd been holding in.

"Why did you bring that jacket?" Judy asked Joshua one night as we got in the van to go to dinner. "You're not going to need it."

He reluctantly toted a light windbreaker.

"'Cause Suzy *made* me," Josh said sarcastically, sticking his tongue out at me.

Judy didn't turn around. She just shook her head, like she was trying to repel a mosquito. "I doubt you're going to need it. It's eighty-five degrees out."

"I know, but she *maaade* me." He flipped around in his seat and made another face at me. How nice. A bonding moment for mother and child as they shared a snort of scorn at the expense of the "weather-forecasting-impaired nanny."

It wasn't like I asked him to bring a *snow parka*. How was I supposed to know it never cooled down in Hawaii? I'd never been here before. And now that I was here, I'd hardly left the hotel room.

It only got worse. Brandon threw up in my egg drop soup at dinner, and that was curtains for the two of us. I stayed up most of the night trying to soothe him. Eventually I ordered in room service, the highlight of my trip so far. A completely delicious and interruption-free meal. Poor miserable Brandon never did improve much. He was beset with diarrhea and attacks of vomiting the rest of the trip, and I was beset with record numbers of diapers and dirty laundry.

The following night, after finally settling down to sleep, I woke up, startled, at two or three in the morning. I froze under the covers, sensing someone in the room other than the kids and myself. I was disoriented, but the scent of Fendi perfume tickled the air, and my gut said it wasn't a burglar. Turning very slowly under the covers, I peeked out, and there, lying next to me, was a blond woman, sound asleep. *Judy! What the hell was she doing in here?* A hundred thoughts raced through my mind. Had she gotten drunk and gone to the wrong room? Did she feel terrible for the way she'd been treating me and wanted to apologize to me after all these months? Oooh, maybe. Oh. Or maybe she and Michael got into a fight. That had to be it. It made perfect sense. I mean, she'd had to use her key to our room to get in, so I doubted it was a mistake. I feigned sleep when she beat a hasty retreat at dawn, and neither of us ever brought it up.

On the return trip, we had to go through customs, or at least it seemed like customs. Since we weren't in a foreign country, it couldn't have been. Maybe it had something to do with gypsy moths trying to hitchhike in on fruit? The fact that I don't remember what they were looking for shows how tired I was. Everyone was already cranky, though I don't know how you can spend eight days in paradise and end up cranky. Unless your trip consisted of one outing to the beach and one dip in the pool and the rest of your stay in a hotel room.

Out of our army of first-class passengers, I was the first one in line, with Brandon in the stroller. Judy and Michael stood behind me, about ten people back. The inspector rummaged through my things, looking for contraband. The wait was interminable. Would it never be over?

"What the hell is the holdup?" Mr. Checchi asked, loud enough for everyone in the airport to hear.

Oops. Me. I had put two apples in my backpack for the kids to snack on. Once those strident inspectors found the illegal fruit, they had to fill out a report and confiscate it. Then they grilled me for another fifteen minutes about any marijuana, food, or plants I might have. Of course, Michael marched up to the head of the line to see what all the ruckus was. I was mortified.

As we were boarding the plane, I overheard Judy asking Michael what had been the problem. "Oh, one of the kids had put an apple in one of the bags," he explained. I remained silent, fussing over the baby. Thank God he thought it was the kids' fault and not mine.

On the plane ride back, I broke open my backpack, looking for something to read. I had forgotten that I'd brought the latest nanny newsletter. The headline on a front-page article read TRAVELING WITH MARY POPPINS: NEGOTIATING THE ROAD WITH CAREGIVER IN TOW.

Caregiver in tow? That's just about how I felt: I was a flatbed trailer, and they were cranking the winch to load me up with a minivan full of kids. I read on. "To many, bringing a nanny on family journeys would be antithetical to the notion of quality family time. Increasingly, however, many parents are finding a pair of extra hands the best excess baggage they can bring."

Excess baggage was right. I felt like an old dented Samsonite.

The brief positive attitude I'd had when thinking of my four days off had vanished. Shortly after the trip, my mother called. "Did you have a good time on your vacation, honey?" she asked innocently. "Did you stay in a fancy hotel?"

"I have just spent a long week with a group of people who never appreciate all that they are fortunate enough to have," I snapped, feeling my blood pressure rise. "They make everything an ordeal and hardly ever smile, even when they're sitting in the lap of luxury, surrounded by paradise. There was absolutely nothing about it that was enjoyable."

Undaunted, my mom mentioned that her friend Earleine had said, "Wow, Suzy sure has it good with all the trips she goes on. Sure must be rough being paid to travel all over."

"Mom, why don't you give her a rundown?" I yelled. "I pack up all the kids and get criticized for what I choose to pack. I travel with a family that never experiences any joy. Everything in their life is a hassle to them. Everyone they encounter is out to screw them over. The kids are crabbier when we're in paradise than when we're at home, since they don't have all the stuff they require to be entertained. When they're around their parents, they treat me like crap. And they can get away with it. I never know exactly what to do. I just know they expect me to know what to do."

Venting felt good. Nice mom that she is, she continued to listen to my tirade.

"I've got Judy asking me why Brandon still takes two naps while I am trying to inform her of her youngest son's sleep schedule. I have the nanny from the other family snapping back, 'You don't *even know* how many naps your own son takes?' It's all just splendid," I said, shrieking by this point. "Add to that, I'm with two miserable adults who don't enjoy each other's company. Oh, I'm living inside a fairy tale all right. Just like good ole Cinderella after she married the prince and lived happily ever after."

I realized that maybe it would be best to hang up and call her back after I'd finished venting in my journal.

Boy, did Mom's questions bug me. Maybe it was just my exhaustion talking. I get so frustrated because nobody can begin to understand what it's like to live with these people. Most people go on vacation for fun. Not this family.

Talking to Mom about how Brandon's sleep schedule was unfamiliar to his parents only reminded me of a depressing pediatrician's visit not long ago. The doctor asked if Brandon was sleeping through the night and Judy said of course. Then I had to pipe up and admit that he was actually still getting up one or two times a night for bottles. Judy raised her eyebrows, and the doctor scolded us, saying that Brandon was just in the habit of getting up and that we needed to put a stop to that. Then Judy turned to me and said, Yeah, you do.

Thanks, Judy!

Mom said everyone missed me at Thanksgiving. I told her I missed having stuffing without eggplant and tofu in it.

You can be very, very, very spoiled and be an extraordinary person. It's how you raise them.

—Celine Dion


chapter 16
# the nightmare before christmas

"Do the Goldbergs have a tree yet?" I asked Mandie in December.

"Oh my gosh, yes. It must be twenty feet tall. And get this: they aren't going to decorate it themselves."

"They're not? So you just have a big naked evergreen in the living room?" Another strange Hollywood custom?

"Only for another day. They hired someone to come in and do all the decorating—not just the tree, but also the entire house. Can you believe it, a professional tree decorator?"

"Yeah, that makes sense. Judy's got the holidays all figured out, too," I said. "There's a woman who goes out and buys some of her Christmas gifts and comes back with them all neatly wrapped. Plus, she has a florist come by the house to pick up twenty crystal vases. He returns them the next day filled with gorgeous fresh-cut flowers. When those die in a week, she repeats the whole thing. On top of that, she hires someone to write all her thank-you notes. She told me that after Brandon's baby shower, the girl who came from the office to write the notes left with carpal tunnel."

"And you know those dog walkers and tree decorators make way more than we do!" Mandie exclaimed. "Can you imagine anyone in Montana or Oregon hiring a tree decorator?"

I snickered. I pictured the hardworking men of my little logging community coming home to an interior designer named Pierre who was gleefully decorating their home in a trendy holiday motif, say lime green snowflakes. I could hear the lumberjack saying, "Honey, whadja do with Clyde?" pointing to the spot where his prized elk head had been mounted. "And who is that guy in the living room? I never seen a guy in a pink shirt before."

I tried hard to imagine Judy standing in a sea of lights on one side of the tree and Michael on the other, yelling, "Here, I'm going to jiggle this strip and you tell me if any bulbs are burned out." The scene just wouldn't form in my brain.

Actually, there was no tree at our house. The family celebrated Hanukkah instead of Christmas. I hadn't known much about the Jewish religion, but NNI gave me sort of a Judaism for Dummies—tutoring on traditions, customs, and beliefs. (This had already come in handy at Rosh Hashanah and Passover.) One Friday night in December, Judy decided to light the menorah. Hanukkah struck me as a chance to reflect and think, and I was up for a little divine peace myself. We could have used some that day—rowdy and revved up probably best described the kids. But just as she lit the first candle, Joshua yanked Amanda's ponytail, triggering much squawking.

"Goddamn it!" Judy yelled. "You kids have no respect for anything."

Needless to say, eight nights of light stopped short right there. I got the distinct feeling that Judy viewed the whole holiday ordeal as one big inconvenience. I started wondering what her holidays had been like as a child. Probably not the kind of loving, haphazard gaggle of fun I remembered.

The whole Hollywood holiday felt quite surreal to me. Christmas Day was probably going to be a perfect Southern California eighty-degree day, and I was used to snow. I was eager to get back to it. I couldn't wait to leave for my four-day Christmas vacation in Oregon. Delma had agreed to work the Christmas shift in Aspen with the family. But Judy was having second thoughts about my time off.

"Suzy, I don't know what I'm going to do," she said worriedly. "Carmen will still be on vacation when we get back from Aspen, and I'll have to let Delma have two days off, and I won't have any help here on the day we get back. I know you want to go home and be with your family, but can you make it back before the twenty-seventh?"

I said of course, whatever she needed, and booked my flight accordingly.

It was the season for giving—and for Michael's annual bonus checks. I learned from my sister and Sarah that bonuses were the mainstay of CAA agents. Apparently most of them actually made 75 percent of their entire year's earnings in bonuses. Of course, these were people with six-figure incomes. My sister heard that the accounting department had all received CAA-inscribed watches for a holiday gift last year. But Delma and Carmen promised that I would get a bonus, too. I could hardly contain my excitement. Carmen told me Michael had given her $10,000 the year before. Of course, Carmen had been there for seven years, and a big bonus kept her in the kitchen. Delma's check had been $1,000. What kind of money would I get? The high-flying LA lifestyle prompted outrageous sums to dance in my head. Like an eight-year-old staring at all the gifts under the Christmas tree, I just had to know.

I was obsessed. I could not get it out of my mind—and I sunk to a new low. The next morning I began my search. I looked in drawers, peeked in stacks of mail, and opened cabinets. No luck. I was just about to give up when I noticed a note from the CFO saying, "Please verify these are the amounts we decided on." Attached was a list with the names of each of the household staff and an amount beside each name. *Suzy: $2,500.* More than two months' pay! I danced around the room, waving my arms in the air in an awkward attempt to give myself a silent high-five.

I did a horrible thing today. I snooped to see if I'd get a Christmas check. And I can't believe what I found. They are so generous to me! Maybe they do notice my hard work. Maybe this is Michael's way of showing that he appreciates me. On the other hand, it seems like Judy might have had a say in the amount. I wonder whether she thinks it's too much for me or if she suggested the amount. Okay, here I go again, trying to overanalyze every situation.

Note to self: Try not to be so nosy.

P.S. I wonder what Ryan and his family are doing for the holidays. I hope I get to see him when I go home.

My conscience churned in overdrive. I felt absolutely awful and couldn't get my misdemeanor out of my mind. Why did I search for the check even though I knew it was wrong? Maybe I had a problem. I never *had* been very good at minding my own business.

I decided I would try to make up for it by not snooping around my parents' house to find the Christmas presents. I needed a little childlike magic for myself, and I thought a Hansen-style holiday would be the perfect tonic.

And it was. My family seemed like an old-fashioned Norman Rockwell painting compared to the abstract and modern people in LA. We played board games, opened presents, and laughed uproariously. We frosted sugar cookies and hand-delivered them to friends, and plenty of company stopped by to drop off mouthwatering holiday desserts.

I trekked to a kegger at the lake with my high school friends. Some of them were home on semester break from their second year in college. I was beginning to wonder why I hadn't gone to a real school. I fielded everyone's questions about my glamorous job in Southern California. It didn't seem nearly as glamorous as it had only six months before.

Of course Amy and I saw Ryan at the party. He was still handsome and muscular, and I felt a rush of emotion when I saw his familiar face. I immediately forgot everything I'd highlighted in my *Women Who Love Too Much* bible, and in a rush of holiday sentiment, we decided to get back together. How we thought this would ever work since we didn't even live in the same state I'll never know.

Looking back, it's clear to me how needy I was at the time and how desperately I wanted to have *somebody* in my life who cared about me and valued me.

Before everyone had left for Aspen, I had been given one last official duty, a minor one. Judy asked me to pack the children's clothing for the trip, including snowsuits. I packed the snowsuits for Joshua and Amanda, but I somehow forgot to include Brandon's. When I returned to Brentwood, Delma filled me in on Judy's rage. Joshua made sure I understood: he pointedly told me how mad his mom was at me and informed me, triumphantly, that they had to go buy a new suit for Brandon because I foooooooooorgot to pack it. He then stuck out his tongue at me, just so I wouldn't miss the point that I was a real loser.

I clamped my lips shut to avoid screaming my thoughts at him: *You know what? I don't even care that I messed up! If your family with their screwed-up values ever ran into a real problem, none of you would have the slightest idea what to do. You want to hear a real problem, kid? It's when the mill lays everybody off and your parents go on unemployment and you have to join the school lunch program because your parents literally don't have enough money to buy food! Now that's a problem!*

I succeeded in squelching my anger and calmly told Josh that I was sorry to hear they'd had to buy an additional snowsuit. Then I calmly went up to my room, where I proceeded to lie on my bed and stare at the ceiling.

Was there ever a time that I was sick and couldn't work? No. I had been sick several times, but I still worked. Was there a time when I was late to work? I was tardy after my hair fiasco, but that was it. Had I ever missed a day of work? No. Did I ever complain (well, not out loud) or not do exactly what was asked of me? No. I offered to help even when I wasn't asked. Did I say yes to every request they ever made of me? Absolutely.

Even though I had taken some prearranged breaks to go home briefly, I had more than made up for them on vacations when I worked nonstop. Barring those quick breaks, for an entire year I had been "on duty" twenty-four hours a day with less than forty-eight hours off on the weekends. I was absolutely forbidden to leave on weeknights, and I had not challenged that. And yet, Judy still showed disdain for me, and over a $40 snowsuit.

I realized I couldn't stay in a place that drove me to the brink of yelling at a child who was simply imitating the behavior of his parents.

This is ridiculous. I'm finally losing it. It is none of my business how they spend their money; I did forget to pack the snowsuit, and I am sure it was a big inconvenience to them. Problem is, I should feel apologetic about it. I *don't!!!* And I want to scream,

"GET A LIFE!!! You wouldn't know a real problem if it ran over you with an 18-wheeler." What was I thinking when I told them I'd stay two years?? Simmer down, Suzy. Remember, you only have 364 days of service left.

I knew many nannies stayed in jobs with conditions far, far worse than mine, because they felt the children would be so devastated if they left. A British nanny I'd met at Gymboree, who had cared for her charge since birth, brought him home with her so much that he actually called her husband "Papa." She had a boss just like mine; she knew that if she left, she would never be allowed to see the boy again, and she loved him, just as I loved the kids. "They never spend any time with him," she had told me in a rare moment of frustration, losing her British cool. "These kinds of people would be better off getting a couple of well-bred dogs instead of giving birth!"

I called Mandie. Maybe her vacation had gone better.

"Remember Mrs. Goldberg told me I could go home for a few days in December since they were taking the housekeeper with them on their vacation to Aspen?"

"Uh-huh."

"They told me I had to be back on the twenty-third, the day they were coming back. They wanted me to help them get ready for their annual 'day after Christmas' trip. When I was making my plans to go home, I told Mrs. Goldberg I could get a less expensive ticket if I stayed over on a Saturday night. She said that this wouldn't work because I had to be back when they returned from their trip. She offered to pay the difference, since I was getting very few days off. I was thrilled, but when I told her it was two hundred dollars more, she said that Mr. Goldberg would never pay that much. So I ended up buying the more expensive ticket and planning a shorter time with my family. Of course, I was bummed, but I was still excited to go home. Then they called me in Montana and said they were going to stay in Aspen until after Christmas, so I didn't have to come back on the twenty-third after all. I guess it was pretty thoughtful of her to at least give me the option of staying home longer."

"So did you?" I said sarcastically.

"I wanted to. But I checked on changing the ticket and found out it would cost three hundred and fifty dollars. My family suggested I ask the Goldbergs to help me pay for it, but I didn't have the nerve after she said they wouldn't pay the two hundred dollars to change it in the first place. I was in tears on my way back. Christmas Eve and Christmas Day I spent with some surfer guy who was house-sitting, a guy who watches their beach house, too. We had to order pizza from the only place that was open for miles and miles. It was pretty uncomfortable trying to make small talk. Not exactly a great Christmas dinner."

My God, did Mandie's employers have a heart? How could they happily ski and down hot chocolate knowing that Mandie was sitting in their home with some stranger, instead of with her family on Christmas. $200! Surely they had spent more than that on *lunch* at some point.

I had held on to my faith in people until now, but the rising degree of my anger and bitterness surprised me. I began to think about the practicalities involved in leaving. Obviously such a move had crossed my mind many times, but because of the two-year commitment, I'd never considered it seriously. Now that I saw how resentful I was becoming, I knew I needed to reconsider.

The next morning, I secretly called a placement agency just to test the waters. Apparently someone of "my caliber" could literally pick and choose, news that substantially lifted my spirits. The woman at the agency started rattling them off: "I've got an opening with Cybill Shepherd; a nightmare job, I might add. She just fired all of her staff. I also have Zuckerman, he's a producer. . . . And we just got a call from Shelley Long. You would qualify for any of these positions."

When the woman asked me when I could interview, I told her weekends only. When I tried to explain how impossible it would be to get time off during the week, she chuckled and brushed it off.

"Oh for God's sake, just tell your boss you've got female issues and that you have to go to the doctor," she offered.

"No. You don't understand," I said, almost smiling at her naïveté. "That would be out of the question. If she ever found out, I would be drawn and quartered in downtown Brentwood, and if I lived through it,

I certainly wouldn't get a decent reference. I'm afraid they'll be so angry when I quit that they won't give me a good reference, regardless."

"Oh, I'm sure you're exaggerating," the woman said breezily. "I've never even heard of this guy, and if he's as big as you say he is, then he's far too busy to spend time giving *you* a bad reference. What's he going to do to you?" She laughed.

I hadn't yet figured out how to end my misery when I got a call from my friend Tammy.

"Suzy, you're not going to believe it," she squealed. "I'm here. Here in LA!"

"What do you mean?"

"Sally called on Sunday and said the baby nurse she hired instead of me didn't work out. She said she wanted me to start this Tuesday, as in today! I drove down in my old GTO with my mom, and I started work today."

"No way!" I tried to imagine kind, sweet Sally Field as my boss.

"Yeah, I'm here now. I was in such a hurry to get here to take the job, I was driving ninety-five miles an hour in the desert."

"Just like in *Smokey and the Bandit*?" I laughed.

"Well not *exactly*, 'cause there was no beer transportation involved, and I had my *mother* in the car."

"Okay, sorry I interrupted, go on."

"Anyway, who knew my car could go that fast? And then we got pulled over."

"Well you're preaching to the choir here. The story of my life. So what happened next?"

"So Mom comes up with the brilliant idea to tell the cop that I'm on my way to be Sally Field's nanny and see if he'll let me off. So I take a chance and tell him, and it works! He even tipped his hat and said, 'Well, say hi to Sally for me,' and we were on our way."

"I've found out in Southern California that the name-dropping thing with the police works quite well," I said dryly. "Well, sometimes."

"That's not the best part. You will not believe this," Tammy chattered. "I got here and Sally's just out of the shower, holding the baby. She says she's having a big dinner party tonight, and that's why she needed me to start immediately. People are coming to this party to see the baby for the first time. Sally says, 'Go upstairs and get him dressed in something cute, and I'll come and get you when it's time to come down.' Can you believe it?

"She came up to get me about eight, and as we're walking down the stairs, she says to me casually, 'I don't think you'll know anyone here tonight except Kurt and Goldie.' I stop walking, grab her arm, and shriek, 'No way, they're here? Kurt Russell and Goldie Hawn are here?'"

"My God, Tammy," I interrupted. "You said that? You can't talk like that."

"Why not? Anyway, Sally says to me, 'Is that a problem?' I blurted out, 'Sally, I don't think you understand. Two days ago I was living in my hometown with a population of less than eight thousand people, and now I move into *your* house, and *Goldie's* coming over. I always go see your movies. You guys are so great!'"

"I can't believe you said that stuff!" I exclaimed. "I've never been able to be that honest about my celebrity encounters. I've been too scared. I was given strict instructions not to act like meeting these people is anything out of the ordinary."

"Well, there's more. I went down and there at the table, along with other people, was Kate Capshaw."

"Oh my God," I gasped. "So Spielberg was there, too?"

"I don't even know. After I laid eyes on Kurt, I almost dropped dead."

"Well, then what happened? Wait. I've gotta go. Brandon's crying. Give me your phone number. Oh, never mind, I have it here somewhere."

"Okay . . . wait. There's more, Suzy!" Her breathless excitement reminded me of myself one short year ago.

"Yes, yes, I know. Welcome to Nanny World."

A movie director came to see me and brought his nanny. In the dressing room she pulled her pants down and showed me a picture of my face, which was tattooed on her rear end.

—Jon Bon Jovi

# the great escape

By the second week in January, I realized that I would *never* work up the nerve to actually say, "I quit."

I finally decided I needed to talk about this with somebody. I called Mary, the insightful instructor I had become close to at NNI. She listened intently, as usual, this time for over an hour. "Suzy," she said, "you didn't commit to stay at this job under *any* circumstances." That hit a chord. She was right.

The very next evening around 10 P.M., I was sitting on my bed engrossed in my nightly phone call with Mandie. Suddenly someone knocked at my door. I froze. I knew it could only be Judy—Delma and Carmen never ventured out of their rooms at night. But Judy hardly ever came to my room. She thought it was important to give her nannies privacy, something I had always appreciated. Had she heard part of the conversation? I told myself maybe she hadn't, completely forgetting about the results of my controlled experiment with Delma a few months earlier.

"Come in," I said softly, pulling the covers up over my pajamas. She opened the door.

"I have to go," I told Mandie. "Judy's here."

"OH MY GOD, WHY?"

"I'll talk to you tomorrow," I said calmly.

"WHAT IS SHE SAYING? ARE YOU IN TROUB—"

"Okay. Bye-bye." I hung up on her midsentence.

Judy sat on the twin bed next to mine. My heart was racing, my mind a blur. *Why in the hell is she in here? What in the world is she going to say to me?*

"Would it be okay if I talked with you?" she began.

"Yes, of course," I responded awkwardly.

"I've noticed lately that you seem to have a chip on your shoulder. What's wrong with you?"

Well, that was direct. I couldn't believe she had noticed *anything* about me. *Had* I been acting differently? I didn't quite know what to say, but it didn't matter because she didn't pause.

"You know, I was pretty disappointed in you about the snowsuit, because I asked you if you packed all the kids' clothes and you said yes. Then when I told you it wasn't in the suitcase later, you didn't seem to even care about your mistake. You know snowsuits aren't cheap."

In that split second, before I had a chance to organize my thoughts, I just started talking. "I'm not happy here," I blurted. "I've been thinking about quitting, that's what's wrong with me. I work nearly twenty-four hours a day. I can't even leave the house in the evenings, and I don't want to keep on doing this. I have no life other than work."

*Oh God. What was I doing?*

She looked stunned. Awkward silence hung over the room. Then she scowled at me, and her chest heaved with labored breaths. I felt myself cringing. What would she say? I wanted to put my hands over my ears. The lump in my throat must have been the size of a baseball.

"What do you mean?" she asked in disgust, not waiting for me to answer. "What exactly do you think a nanny *does*, Suzy?"

*Well, I think some of them work nine to ten hours a day.* But I didn't have the nerve to say that for fear of what else might come out.

"I've been thinking of quitting," I muttered sheepishly, in case she hadn't heard me the first time.

"We do a lot for you. I don't think you understand that," she said, shaking her head.

"Judy, I am very appreciative of everything you've done for me."

She rolled her eyes, as if to say, *Yeah right, I don't believe you.*

"I feel very bad, and I'm sorry," I said pathetically. "But I'm just not happy."

"So what are you saying? You're just going to leave tomorrow?" she said, the sarcasm thick and heavy.

*My God, I could never do that to the kids.*

"No, of course not. I'll stay until you can find someone else."

"This is just like you. I tell you something I don't like about you, and you just up and quit."

*Wait, what?*

This conversation was moving too fast.

Just like me to do what? As if every time I was reprimanded I had threatened to quit? I'd never mentioned *anything*, ever, about leaving.

"I wish I would have known you were going to do this before we gave you that Christmas bonus."

With that, she let out a deep stage sigh, stood up, swirled around, and left the room.

I curled up under the covers, my stomach in knots. I broke out in a sweat when I heard Michael get home that night. I heard Judy's angry voice. Apparently she had stayed awake to talk to him, something she didn't usually do. Not a good sign. I couldn't hear what they were saying, only a murmur of voices.

But there were no more knocks on my door that night. My anguish lingered, and I hardly slept the next two nights. Certainly Michael was going to have a talk with me, but I didn't know when the axe would fall. I began rehearsing the scene in my mind, playing both characters. I heaped guilt on myself by the shovelful. I wondered if I should give the Christmas bonus back. But my biggest concern was the kids. I felt love and affection for Amanda, and I sympathized with Joshua's angry behavior and cared for him more than he could ever let in. But the kind of love I felt for Brandon was the reason I became a nanny in the first place.

I worried about the impact my departure would have on him. After all, I was his primary caregiver. Would he have the same feeling as a child raised by a stay-at-home mom would have if she just suddenly disappeared one day? I hoped not. I couldn't bear that thought. I wanted him to keep laughing—he was the only one in the entire family who laughed, a big hearty belly chuckle. But the saddest thought that crossed my mind was that maybe I wouldn't be missed at all; Leticia, Suzy, and then the next nanny in line. Would Brandon even know I ever existed a month from now? I was going to be a blip on the radar screen of his life.

> When Magic Johnson called today, the whole time I was thinking that this should be an exciting moment in my life. But no. I can't express those kinds of feelings around here, that I'm actually thrilled to talk to such a sports star. I'm supposed to be businesslike and blasé. The stress is not worth it. Giving up joy is not worth it. The money I make is certainly not worth it. And yet I'm so scared I'm going to wimp out when Michael finally confronts me.

For the next couple of days, I walked on eggshells waiting for the king to signal the hooded man to release the heavy blade. But nothing. Then Wednesday morning, two days after my conversation with Judy, Michael approached me calmly and asked me to sit down. I was sure he could see my heart pounding through my T-shirt.

"I understand that you want to quit." There was a long, awkward pause. "Suzy, would you please reconsider?" he asked in a soft, nearly pleading voice I'd never heard from him before. "Can't you just finish out the year?"

*Finish out the year? It's mid-January!*

"You know we have the Aspen vacation scheduled for spring break, so how about just hanging on until after that?" I was too afraid to answer. I put my head down and sat there in silence with my shoulders slumped around my chest. I couldn't believe I was about to wimp out again, but I couldn't muster up the courage to quit.

"You could at least stay until after Judy's week in February at the Golden Door Spa. You know she deserves this vacation."

I had told Judy that I would stay for four weeks, which would carry me beyond the Golden Door vacation. And I'd said if they found someone to replace me before that, I'd leave earlier. But it didn't sound like she had been listening that night. She'd been so angry. I wondered what she had told him about my sudden notice.

I steeled myself for the next question. I knew him well enough to realize that his campaign to have me stay would quickly escalate from two controlled, peaceful questions to a flat demand. And then things would get ugly.

Instead, he said, "You think about it and then let me know in a few days what you decide."

"Okay, I'll think about it," I told him, knowing full well that there was nothing to think about. I wanted to leave. I just didn't have the nerve to say so.

It wasn't as if the actual leaving would be easy, either. I knew I would dearly miss the three children for whom I had been pseudomother, nurse, playmate, diaper changer, referee, emotional punching bag, and chauffeur. And then there was Carmen, Delma, Gloria, Rosa, Sarah, and Jay. We had been a family within a family, or rather, a little family attached to a family. As for Michael and Judy, well, I wouldn't miss devoting my life to them, but I didn't dislike them. They were the parents of the kids I loved, and I wanted the best for all of them.

In the days following our conversation, I did mull over my decision like Michael suggested, turning it over and over in my mind. But the answer always came out the same. My misery was affecting my caregiving, and I was no longer doing a good job in helping to raise healthy, happy, well-adjusted kids.

I braced myself for the inevitable confrontation. I had to stand up to him. I knew there were two choices. If I stayed, I would be depressed, the kids would suffer, but Michael would be happy. If I left, I would have a feeling of freedom, and the kids would find an eager new caregiver and eventually adjust, but Michael would not be happy, to say the least. I suddenly remembered how easily he had intimidated poor Carmen all these years, wearing her down every time she asked to move out of the house. I rehearsed the conversation in my mind, this time coming up with an answer to every objection he would make, creating a script for myself.

A few mornings after our first talk, he came into Brandon's room when I was pulling a shirt over Brandon's head.

"Have you reconsidered, Suzy?" he asked politely. "You know that I've always loved your work. I really don't want to see you go."

The more he talked, the more afraid I became that I'd back down. He never took no for an answer. What made me think he'd take it from me?

He repeated his request for me to stay until after the Aspen trip, or at least until after Judy returned from her vacation at the Golden Door Spa.

*No. I had to leave. I had to leave. I didn't want to stay another two months. I couldn't wimp out.*

"No. I really do want to give my notice," I said, hanging my head. "Mr. Ovitz, I'll stay for four weeks. I'm not happy here, and I don't think it's fair to the children to be around them when I feel like this."

"Oh, Suzy," he said, rolling his eyes and speaking in the most condescending voice I'd ever heard. "Don't you think that's pretty egocentric of you? Brandon is just a baby. He doesn't know the difference. And Amanda and Josh are too busy to know the difference."

I didn't answer. *You can't hit much lower than that, can you?*

But for some reason the words touched something within me, breaking a spell. I looked at Michael and saw a sad shell who in reality had nothing but things. I looked into his eyes as his words flew by me and drifted away. My mind raced. *You say your children are the most important things in the world to you, and I know you believe that with every fiber of your being, but those are empty words. You're no more connected to them than you are to your wife. All of this is just another picture, like the ones hanging on your walls. A seemingly ideal life, a position of great importance, lots of money and power, a beautiful home, three adorable children, and a wife who would do anything for you. But none of it goes beyond the depth of a single brush stroke. There's nothing there, only a very thin veneer. Nevertheless, like a talented artist, you've made it appear that the scene stretches into infinity.*

When he realized that I wasn't going to change my mind, his face grew ugly. "Do you ever plan to work as a nanny in this town again?" he said, smirking.

"Um, yes, I think so," I said, surprised.

"Hmm, we'll see," he chortled. With that, he turned in his $4,000 suit and walked down the hall.

"This has really fucked up my week!" he barked to the staircase.

At that moment, as sad and as frightened as I was, as painful as the experience had been, I realized I did have an inner strength. I tried to reassure my shaking body that I had made the right decision. I finished dressing Brandon and took him into my room to play. I didn't want to go downstairs. I knew Judy was there.

An hour after Michael left, Judy appeared. I handed Brandon a toy train and looked up at her. "Michael just called and he wants you out of the house, immediately."

I stood up silently and walked toward her numbly.

"He doesn't want to have to see you when he comes home," she snapped.

"Um . . ." My mouth was so dry I couldn't form any words.

"Was it really that bad living here?" she spat.

I started to answer her, and she cut me off.

"Oh, never mind. You're going to leave, anyway, so it doesn't really matter now. I just wish I would have known that you were going to quit before I gave you that Christmas bonus."

Again with the bonus.

I considered offering to give it back. Instead I pleaded, "Judy, I would still like to continue seeing the kids—"

"No, I don't think so," she said, cutting me off. "I don't think that is a good idea. I think it would be too confusing for the children; it just wouldn't work."

With that declaration, she stalked out of my bedroom. My heart sank. I guess I had always known, on some level, that this would be my punishment if I chose to leave. It was what my British colleague lived in fear of, wasn't it? Maybe that was part of why I had stayed so long.

But that was little consolation, and I was devastated. I walked over to my little Brandon. Would I never see him again? I didn't know what to do first. Did this mean I should stop taking care of the children and start packing my stuff?

Maybe Cindy could help me settle down and give me advice. I dialed her at CAA to inform her of my sudden eviction.

"Cindy, Judy says I have to move out right now. What do I do? Do I keep taking care of Brandon while I'm packing?"

"No, you don't. Just start packing."

"I have several carloads of stuff to take to your house; how am I going to do that all by myself?"

My sister was probably thinking, *To my house? That is all we need, one more permanent resident and all your crap.*

But what she calmly said was, "Can I come help you after work?"

"No, he said I have to be out before he gets home. Can't you come help me right now?"

"No, I can't. I'm working." Great. Now my sister's strong work ethic, the one I was so proud of when I got her the job, was backfiring on me.

"Can't you tell them that you have to leave and do those I-9 thingys?"

"No, Suzy, I can't do that," she said firmly. "What if Michael was to show up while I was there?"

"All right, fine," I answered. "I have to get started. I don't have a key to your apartment, so I guess I'll just have to pile it all up in the hallway until you get home."

"Sorry, Suzy, but I have to go. Bob Goldman is walking up."

I walked downstairs with Brandon in my arms, hoping to God I wouldn't see Judy. I found Carmen and her boyfriend in the kitchen.

"Can you watch Brandon?" I asked. "I have to get out right now, and he hasn't had his breakfast this morning."

"Yes, I know. I heard," she said. "Here, give me the baby. Don't worry, I'll feed him."

I couldn't say much without my throat constricting.

"Thank you," was all I whispered. I hurried back upstairs. How was I going to do this? I had no boxes and a lot of stuff. What if my sister hadn't lived nearby? Where would I have gone?

It ended up taking me about four hours to fill garbage bags (the cheap kind, not the ones used for the trash compactor, of course) with all my worldly possessions. I packed my Celica to the brim twice for the round-trip to Cindy's apartment.

Before the last round, I hugged Carmen good-bye. I told her to give Delma my best; sadly, it was her day off. We both cried. "I'm so sorry," Carmen said. "You know how they are."

Amanda and Joshua sat at the kitchen table, wolfing down snacks and watching TV. I knelt down next to Amanda. "Honey, I have to go, but

you can call me anytime," I said in what I hoped was a calm and soothing tone. "I am leaving my sister's phone number with Delma and Carmen, and whenever you want to talk to me, you can call."

"Where are you going?" she asked, wide-eyed.

"I'm going to live with my sister," I answered.

"Why? Why are you leaving?" I was at a loss. What could I tell a four-
year-old to help her understand?

"Yeah, I know you're leaving," Josh interjected. "My mom told me
that my dad's really mad at you."

I ignored him. I hugged Amanda for as long as she would let me, and
then doubled back to the kitchen to hug Brandon one more time. I then
faced Joshua and hugged him, telling him I was sorry I had to leave him.
He didn't hug me back.

Michael and Judy just don't get it. They have no idea how this
will affect Brandon. I've been his primary caregiver for over a
year; then one day he wakes up, and I'm not there. Until this
moment, I had no idea how terrible it would be to leave the kids.
They didn't talk about this at nanny school. I feel a terrible sense
of loss, like I'm leaving my own family.

I figure if a little voice calls for Mommy in the middle of the night, that's who he should get.

—Deborah Norville

# searching for debra winger

In the days following my eviction, after the numbness wore off, I started to worry. I knew that Michael and Judy were angry, and I kept replaying in my mind his threat that I'd never work in this town again. Oh, I was being silly. Would Michael really spend his precious time answering calls from some random Santa Monica stay-at-home mom calling to inquire about his former nanny?

Nevertheless, what if the busiest man in Los Angeles *did* feel motivated to concern himself with my job prospects? I'd heard far too much about how Michael did business. That he always eventually got his way, that he never took no for an answer or forgave a grudge. This could get ugly. My gut said that he wasn't going to let a little girl from Podunkville say no to him without making sure she experienced the consequences.

But I forged ahead, calling the nanny agency and speaking with the woman who had previously suggested that I was making "too big a deal" of my fear that my employer would be angry with me after I quit. She was thrilled to hear that I was available ("lots of jobs for someone of your caliber!") and booked me for an interview the very next day.

I discovered that the nanny-hunting parents had made their reputation by writing for *The Golden Girls*. The mom, who was pregnant,
recognized my name right away.

"Oh, I've already heard about you, Suzy."

Uh-oh.

"Oh, really?"

"Yes, you're that great nanny," she said warmly. "You're the one who
diagnosed Michael Ovitz's youngest son with meningitis."

*Excuse me?*

There isn't much that's missed in Hollywood. Except for the truth,
which would make the story much less interesting.

"Oh that. I didn't actually diagnose him. In fact—"

"Yes. Michael's our agent," she interrupted, beaming at her husband. I
could read her thoughts: *This is great. Michael only settles for the best, so
this girl must be outstanding.*

Good grief, this wasn't looking good. Not only were they clients of
Michael's but there was also the ever-so-small matter of the location.
These people lived ten doors down from my former residence. I ask
you, in the huge metropolis of LA, what were the statistical chances
of that?

"Tell us about you," she continued.

I mumbled something halfheartedly. *Why bother? You're not going to
hire me after Mr. Überagent gets a hold of you.*

I knew Michael would tell them not to hire me, but I couldn't figure
out what possible explanation he could find. Maybe that I quit after I
accepted the Christmas bonus check. Of course he could always talk
about the time he almost suffered a public humiliation when I tried to
wear that hideous NASA jumpsuit. But really, what else was there?

I tried to think positively, and the rest of the interview went well. I
could tell they liked me. They gave me a tour of their elegant home,
which had been featured in *Architectural Digest*, and then showed me
the room I would live in. When they walked me out to my car, both
smiling from ear to ear, they said they thought I would fit in perfectly
with their family.

As I started my car, I told myself that I had just been paranoid. It
apparently hadn't bothered them at all that I'd worked for Michael. The

more I thought about my previous concern, the more I convinced myself that the king might not even bother to take a call at his office from a couple seeking a reference.

But then the agency called and told me very nonchalantly that the couple had decided to pass on me. As if they were playing Monopoly and decided not to buy Baltic Avenue.

"They're *passing* on me. I told you!" I reminded her. "They must have talked to Michael."

"I checked it out, and you're right about that," she said calmly. "But I talked with Michael at length today, and I think I managed to work a deal with him."

*Oh, really? What kind of deal? I can tell by your voice he has you running scared, lady.*

"I can send you on any interview I want," she said, "as long as it isn't with someone who works in the entertainment industry." She said this as if it was just a minor detail, as if it didn't matter at all that the clause to which she'd agreed cut out 90 percent of the population who might have a nanny job available.

The paranoia came crashing back. How far did his influence reach? If I went back to Oregon to start college, was he going to put a bad word in with the dean? Okay, that was probably ridiculous, but I could not believe that intelligent, talented, professional people were so afraid of him that they had to bow down to his every edict.

But they did. Oh, so many of them. I interviewed with a couple who had never worked for or with Michael, but they knew him socially, just like everybody else in town. Despite a great interview that ended with smiles all around, two days later they called and declined.

I knew that a person with my experience was in great demand in Southern California. The majority of Hollywood types wanted a nanny who was intelligent, hardworking, and devoted to children. But the unspoken, politically incorrect reality was that they also wanted someone who was thin and spoke English as a first language. I fit all categories, but it was starting to look like the word from the Ovitzes trumped everything. And it was clear that Michael didn't mind using his valuable time to sink me. If I wasn't going to work for him, he didn't want me working for *anybody*.

Michael's blackballing made me angrier as the days passed. How could he possibly justify his behavior? He had begged me to stay, and now here he was telling everyone in LA what a terrible nanny I was. If I was so unfit, why had he tried so hard to get me to finish out the year? How far was he really going to take this silly vendetta against a nineteen-year-old? I was broke and completely powerless in Hollywood. What kind of joy did he get from making sure I stayed that way?

Since the placement coordinator—Ms. It's Fine, I Worked Out a Deal with the President of CAA—suddenly wasn't returning my phone calls, I decided to take my résumé to a place called Malibu Mommies. I didn't have much hope, but maybe this agency would be a little more understanding. Malibu Mommies sounded so wholesome and friendly. I began by telling them about my stint at the Ovitzes. Surprisingly, Malibu Mommies didn't run scared. They said that they'd be willing to work with my situation because they had seen it happen to many other nannies, quite a few times, actually. In fact, so many employers gave their nannies bad references when they wanted to leave that the agency now recommended that *all* nannies get a written review of their work every six months, some proof on paper that their bosses really had been happy with them—at least until they had the nerve to inconvenience them by quitting.

To my great relief, two days after I applied at the new agency, they called to say they had a nanny-hunting parent—with one infant boy—who was okay with the fact that Michael wouldn't give me a glowing report. *Such a person really existed?* I was beginning to think that no one could have that kind of independence in this town.

I found the address off Pacific Coast Highway in Malibu, just a few miles from the Ovitzes' beach house, on a quiet little street with a front gate and a hedge all the way around the property.

Large and unpretentious, the house seemed welcoming. Seconds after I rang the bell, a barefoot Debra Winger greeted me with a hearty handshake. "Welcome, Suzy," she said in a familiar husky voice paired with a big smile.

Although I had never seen her big hit *Urban Cowboy*, I loved *Terms of Endearment*, and I had watched the Academy Awards the night she was nominated for best supporting actress. Her on-screen presence gave me the feeling that she might be a person who hadn't let her fame affect her. When we finally sat down, I discovered my intuition had been right. She seemed genuine and unassuming, and her home reflected this attitude. There were no Chinese artifacts glued to tables or famous paintings on the walls. An alarm system existed, but she rarely used it.

Debra offered me tea, and I dove in by explaining my unhappy departure from the Ovitz house, making a point of how hard it was to leave the children. She listened and seemed genuinely compassionate. Her only response was "Well, that Michael, he is a shrink's dream. . . . Or maybe would that be nightmare?" She laughed. I stayed silent. I didn't want to open up that can of night crawlers. She said she'd tell the nanny agency she didn't need a reference from him. Besides, she had already called all my Cottage Grove and practicum family references, who had raved about me. I was pleased but puzzled by her lack of deference to the king.

I soon learned that Debra was one of the few clients in CAA's history who had jumped ship. Since I knew all too well how much Michael hated the word *no*, I could only imagine how he reacted when she told him she was leaving.

"I like Michael, but I couldn't continue to work with him," she explained. "It was as if I knew my boss was dumping toxic waste into a playground; I couldn't sit by silently and do nothing." Michael's response, she later told me, was to threaten to tell the media she was pregnant. Before her son Nolan was born, she'd suffered a miscarriage. Devastating in itself, being in the public eye and having to tell her fans only made the tragedy worse. Once pregnant with Nolan, she decided to wait a little longer to reveal her news. Michael had gone right for her jugular with that threat—though he had never actually carried through with it.

Just nine months old, Nolan still woke up and cried several times during the night, and Debra was exhausted. Debra's husband, Timothy Hutton, insisted that she hire a nanny; he couldn't help out much since he was in Baton Rouge working on a new film. Debra herself didn't really think that she needed a nanny. After all, she was home all day. Didn't most stay-at-home moms handle things themselves?

By now, this seemed like an alien concept to me, the idea that a woman wanted to take care of her own child by herself. But Debra breathed some normalcy into Hollywood. She told me she had hired a baby nurse for a short time after Nolan was born, but it hadn't worked out. By the time the nurse figured out that the baby was awake and crying in the middle of the night, Debra had already been in his room comforting him for five minutes. So she had let her go after two weeks.

This story reminded me of what I'd heard about English nannies. Shows like *Supernanny* and *Nanny 911* wouldn't be hits for some time, but Hollywood always seems to be ahead of the trends, anyway, and then it was all the rage to have a proper British baby nurse for the first months of a Hollywood baby's life. These descendants of Mary Poppins were made of much sterner stuff than their American counterparts— they believed in letting babies "cry it out" until they would eventually sleep through the night. I could see that this would not work for a hands-on mom like Debra.

I felt at ease with Debra immediately, and I sensed that I had entered a different dimension. This was the kind of relaxed environment that might be ripe for leisurely lunches and girly shopping trips. During the interview, Debra even asked me if I would be interested in reading scripts for her. Her agent sent her so many, and she asked if I could give her an idea of what the story was about. Could I? Of course! The prospect of some secretarial/assistant work thrilled me, and I told her so.

Debra wanted me to start right away, so we quickly made arrangements. I liked my new quarters on the first floor, a plain, comfortable bedroom and connecting bathroom, with an enormous bed that sat so high off the floor I nearly had to get a stepladder to climb in. A dried flower arrangement was the only decor, but the room felt warm and homey.

But before I left the interview, I had to complete one more hurdle. Money. This time I was determined to assert myself regarding salary. The consequences of not speaking up at my last job haunted me, but that wasn't all. Living in LA for a year had soured my opinion of the rich and their millions. Jaded didn't even begin to describe how I felt about how poorly the wealthy paid the staff who made their lives easier. I'd come to see salary as an expression of value, and celebrities constantly sent the message that nannies were worth merely pennies. For example, I knew a nanny who worked for a socialite who spent all day every day trawling boutiques to feed her ravenous shopping appetite. The nanny got so fed up with her boss never being home that one night she looked through the day's receipts. Just one couture dress that her employer wore to an event for a few hours cost more than the nanny made in two years.

"Do you think you should be paid less than at the Ovitzes because I've just got Nolan, not three kids?" Debra asked.

She had a point, and I'd never thought of it that way. Hmm. This had never been discussed at nanny school. Then she said, "Or do you see the pay as compensation for your time, regardless of the number of children you are caring for?"

Her clarity and fairness amazed me.

But I was through playing the part of the naive young nanny who let employers take advantage of her. This time I would be paid *well* to work twenty-four hours a day.

"I don't really want to make less than my last position," I told her. Then I blurted out, "I want to *net* four hundred dollars a week." Why I threw in the net thing, I have no idea.

She agreed, and suddenly I'd negotiated myself a huge raise. Okay, so I had once again neglected to bring up the issue of a contract. I know, I know. But this time I was too embarrassed. Debra seemed so casual about everything, and I didn't want to offend her with the formality.

I love Debra! She's so cool, so completely *real*. And yet she lives and works in this town. Amazing. But when my interview was over, I realized that I would be working about half the time I did before, and yet I'd be making more money. Maybe I drove too hard a bargain. It isn't her fault that I've been a doormat. She shouldn't have to "make up for it." She said we could work out what the gross amount would be later. How the hell did I come up with the *net* thing? She seems so easy to talk to; I have high hopes that this will be a great working relationship.

Mom called me tonight to tell me she ran out and rented all of Debra's films, and then she proceeded to give me a blow-by-blow of each movie. Finally I had to cut her off and tell her it really wasn't necessary for me to know the plot. I informed my mother that I wasn't going to be given a movie trivia quiz to get the job.

*Note to self: Try not to be so hard on Mom. She deserves to have a little fun with all the Hollywood hoopla. That's more than you can say for yourself so far.*

Cindy happily helped me move all my stuff from her cramped apartment into Debra's house. Poor Cindy. Not only did she still share the place with her two original friends, but one of the girls had taken in Pedro, a sweet fellow employee who was down on his luck. Cindy would relish the breathing room, and I knew she was glad that I had found such a nice new boss. She, of course, was still working for a not-so-nice boss. Her immediate supervisor had told her that in the wake of my sudden departure from the Ovitz home, Michael had wanted to terminate her from CAA as well. But since her work was excellent, they had no legal grounds to fire her, so she remained at the agency. I was sure her presence was a thorn in Michael's side—a reminder that he didn't always get his way.

I soon discovered that working for Debra was the polar opposite of working for the Ovitzes. For one thing, she loved being a mom so much that she spent far more time with Nolan than I did. The original plan had been for me to start waking up with him so that she could get some much-needed rest. But Nolan and Debra had bonded, and he wasn't too sure about this other person living in his house and coming into his room in the middle of the night. So we had to back up and work on getting him used to me. Debra would coo and cuddle him while I'd just stand there, willing my presence to be familiar.

I found myself with a strange nanny dilemma. When I comforted Brandon at all hours of the night, no one else was even awake, so it didn't matter what I was wearing. But it now seemed inappropriate to report to work with no bra on. How do you maintain a professional appearance when you're standing next to your employer at 3 A.M. in your pajamas?

"You must be Suzy," said a male voice when I answered Debra's phone on one of my first mornings.

"Uh, yes I am."

"Oh, hi! This is Tim calling from down in Louisiana."

"Oh yes," I said. "How are you?"

"Doing great. I'm so glad you're there," he said cheerfully. "Debra didn't think she needed anyone. But I know she's tired with Nolan getting up so much in the night. And I wanted her to have some help while I was gone. I really miss those two. I look forward to meeting you when you all come down here to visit the set."

"Yes, it was nice talking to you, and I hope I can help Debra get rested up. Let me find her for you."

A most cordial conversation. One marital partner concerned about the other. There was even an indication that they valued the childcare provider. It was freaky. Abnormal. It had taken me just one short year to reach this level of cynicism.

In addition to my help, Debra employed a cook and a housekeeper, both live-out. The cook dropped by a few nights a week to make dinner, preparing the rest of the meals for the week in advance and tossing them in the freezer with heating instructions. She also whipped up an amazing thousand-calorie-per-slice cheesecake. Debra loved it. She told me that when she was preparing for a movie she forbade it in the house. At those times she had to ban everything high-calorie from the premises. But since she had just finished a film, the "no sweets" rule didn't apply, and she liked to indulge herself.

Thrilled, I indulged right along with her. No need for sneaking homemade cookies, looking over my shoulder the way I did at the old place. Not that Judy kept a cookie count—it was Carmen who watched me like a hawk. After she had found out who was gobbling down her creations, she restricted me to two a day. If I exceeded my limit, my cookie-eating punishment was to help her make another batch. Remembering this made me miss Carmen, Delma, and the kids so badly that I ordered myself to put the entire situation out of my mind. The whole thing just hurt too much.

I did place one last call to Sarah, though. "You'll never believe who I'm working for," I blurted out as soon as I heard her familiar greeting. "Apparently someone Michael hates."

"Suzy, it's so good to hear from you!" Sarah said. " Hmm . . . you're not working for *Spielberg*, are you?"

"No! Debra Winger," I said, and we both laughed. It was good to talk to her again, but I knew she didn't have much time to chat.

"They really hate me, huh?" I said finally.

"No, they don't hate you, Suzy," Sarah said. "You made their life convenient, and leaving was an inconvenience. And you know how they hate being inconvenienced. But you personally, no, of course they don't hate you."

The conversation made me feel a little better, and I decided to close the book on that chapter of my life and enjoy my new job.

It didn't take long for me to realize that Debra deeply valued her principles—she was well-known in Hollywood for being "difficult" and unwilling to "play the game." I found out that she had moved from California to Israel when she was just sixteen to live in a kibbutz, even serving time in the Israeli army. After she came back, she got a job at Magic Mountain, where a serious accident left her in a coma. Partly paralyzed and blind in one eye for several months, she told me that the accident had given her plenty of time to think long and hard about where her life was going; it had been at that point that she decided to pursue acting.

Debra took things such as the environment very seriously. If I'd been paying more attention, I could have guessed that from our first conversation. She based many of her personal decisions—what she bought, where she shopped, what she ate—on how it impacted the planet. No pesticides—not even when ants invaded my bedroom. Organic baby shampoo for Nolan. No disposable diapers. Once she tried them, in place of her standard cloth ones, when she and Nolan flew somewhere. When he got a horrendous rash, she researched what the absorbent material was made of and vowed to never use them again. And then one day she told me a story about her parents, who had just phoned to tell her about their harrowing flight from hell. Their plane had to make an emergency landing, and her parents feared their lives would end in a fiery crash landing. Standard operating procedure in such a situation is to dump all the excess fuel out of the fuselage before landing, which the pilots did. "Imagine all that toxic fuel polluting the air and landing all over everything, Suzy, can you believe it?" she asked. I couldn't, but I was a little more worried about her mom and dad.

Debra mentioned that her cook had previously worked for Steven

Spielberg, and she said how funny she thought that was. I didn't get it. She went on to explain how she thought it was her karma to have these people come to her—people who had been previously employed by someone she'd had problems with. I hadn't known she'd had a falling out with the famous director. What was not to like about her? I wondered. I found her amazing. I never asked about the problems, but the cook's stories about one of Spielberg's children made Josh sound like an angel. It was kind of funny that two of the biggest moguls in Hollywood had essentially sent her their castoffs.

I hadn't been working long at Debra's when I caught a cold. She said that this would prevent me from getting up in the night with Nolan and that I would need to rest and take a lot of vitamin C. I couldn't believe my ears—for more than one reason. First, it blew me away that she would even notice that I had a cold. Second, I was flabbergasted that she would suggest I lighten my workload so I could get over my minor illness quicker. I immediately called Mandie to report that my new employer had noticed I was blowing my nose a lot and was concerned about my getting enough sleep.

She laughed heartily into the phone, and then complimented me on the little comedy routine that I was trying out.

One morning, Debra abruptly announced that Timothy's mother was coming to town to see Nolan, and she asked me to pick her up at LAX. We found a very sad daisy in the yard and pinned it on my jacket. Look for the girl wearing a flower, Debra told her mother-in-law. We giggled, realizing that the poor woman would have to be leaning right up against me to see the wilted thing.

The flight was due in at noon, so I got there a half hour early. I didn't have any idea what this woman looked like, but I certainly knew how cute Timothy was. I'd just keep my eyes peeled for an adorable grand-motherly type. Between that and my little flower, I figured I wouldn't have a problem.

At 12:15 the plane arrived, and I stood smiling, looking to catch the eyes of anyone who might fit the part. Hordes of people filed past me, but there wasn't one woman who acted like she was looking for anyone.

Apparently, either I'd missed her or she'd missed the plane. I immediately called Debra, but the answering service picked up. This wasn't like the Ovitzes, where someone always grabbed the phone. Debra preferred her privacy. She let the service take care of calls and dialed in whenever she felt like getting her messages. I told the answering service I was Debra's nanny and that I was at the airport. I asked her to try to ring through to the house and she did.

The answering service of a very well-known actress believes anyone who calls? What if I was a reporter from the *Star*? The trick to contacting celebrities, I decided, was getting the private phone number in the first place.

But Debra didn't answer the phone. I realized then that I had never actually *heard* the phone ring in the house, unless it was Timothy. He must have some special number.

*Oh great, I am going to spend the entire day waiting.* I called the answering service back ten minutes later. This time the operator told me to leave a message, and she would see if she could get it to Debra sometime today. *Swell. Sometime today would be great for me!*

"Tell Debra her mother-in-law did not get off the plane. Find out if she called," I snapped into the receiver. The operator, hearing the frustration in my voice, tried patching me through again. This time Debra picked up.

"Hello, Suzy. Where are you?" she asked.

"I'm at the American terminal. She wasn't on the plane."

"That's odd," she said.

"Wait. Wait a second. Maybe this is her. She might have gotten past me and . . ." I put my hand over the phone and squinted at a woman with large brown eyes and light brownish gray hair, talking on the phone next to me.

"Say her name and see if she turns around," Debra suggested.

"Um," I stammered, "what is her name?" I couldn't believe I forgot to get that crucial information. Debra told me.

"Maryline. Maryline," I said as loudly as possible without shouting. The large woman ignored me.

I spotted another possibility. "This might be her. This woman's a classy dresser, with beautiful skin and silver gray hair," I reported.

No answer, just an immediate throaty laugh.

"Oh no, Suzy, I don't think she's the one, keep looking. Look, call me back in ten minutes. I'll call her house and find out what happened." Ten minutes later, I called and got the answering service to patch me through.

"You're right," Debra said. "Her husband said she didn't get on that plane, but she'll be on flight 456. It's due in at four. Do you mind waiting?"

"Oh, uh, no, um, no problem," I responded, in a tone that was definitely lacking in enthusiasm. "When did she plan to notify you of her change of plans?" I was miffed on my own behalf as well as for Debra. Didn't Maryline realize someone was waiting for her? What if it had been Debra and Nolan? Maybe she just thought there was a limo on call, but she had to know that wasn't likely.

Contrary to popular belief, movie stars don't usually send limos to pick up people at the airport. Most of them send employees, in their personal cars, as chauffeurs. Well, except for Sally Field, who sent a limo to pick up Tammy at LAX when she returned home from visits to Oregon. Why did I always have to remember Tammy's good fortune at the worst times? I repeated my mantra I'd begun chanting whenever I talked to Tammy: *Bitterness is not becoming. Bitterness is not becoming.*

There was no mistaking Timothy's mom at four o'clock. She carried a strapping black purse, and, well, let's just say she looked like she had worked outside most of her life and didn't wear any sunscreen.

"Hello, Mrs.—" *Oh, crap. I don't know her last name.* Debra said she had been married several times, so I knew it wasn't Hutton. I kind of mumbled my way past her last name. "You're Tim's mother, aren't you? I'm Debra's nanny, Suzy. So nice to meet you."

"Yes, dear," she said, pointing toward the floor and leaving my outstretched hand floating in empty space. "Can you carry that bag for me?"

I looked down to see an enormous red leather bag. How did she cram it in the overhead compartment? Then I lifted it. My God, what was in there?

"We'll have to go to baggage claim for the rest," she said as I struggled toward the escalator with her.

The rest? How long did she plan to stay?

"Grab that black one; that's mine," she directed as the luggage whirled by. "Oh, oh, that big one with straps, that's mine, too."

"There. I think that's it," she said as I pulled a fourth suitcase off the conveyor belt. "Where are you parked?"

"Uh, maybe I should go get the car and bring it up to the terminal," I gasped, trying to keep the baggage upright.

"Good enough. Why don't you hail that skycap?"

He brought the luggage out to the curb, where she elegantly settled on top of the pile of suitcases, lit up a cigarette, and took a deep drag.

By the time I wheeled my Celica up to the doors, she was on her second cigarette. Oh no. What was I going to do? Was she planning on smoking in my car? It still smelled brand-new. I despised the smell of smoke just about as much as I hated those ankle-biting dogs.

I had made a lot of progress during my year in LA. For heaven's sake, I was now *netting* $400 a week. But I still couldn't bring myself to be assertive about anything that involved confrontation, especially with the chain-smoking, yellow-fingered mother-in-law of my new boss.

Mentally kicking myself, I even took the change out of my ashtray when she lit up her third cigarette. I immediately rolled down my window. She left hers up. My nausea grew. I tilted my head toward the fresh air for the excruciatingly long ride back to Malibu.

As soon as we got back and unloaded her piles of luggage, I dashed back to my car. Maybe the damage could be reversed. I rolled down the other window, put one fan in the front seat and one in the back. I wiped down the ashtray with a rag soaked in Pine-Sol, left the doors wide open, and kept the fans running until it was time to go to bed that night. Our guest, meanwhile, was banished outside to indulge in her forty-year habit, which she did quite frequently. She showed up in the driveway soon enough and watched my frantic efforts with a small grin.

Several days later, Debra announced she was going out with a friend to a movie for the first time since Nolan's birth. This was one movie-star mom who most certainly hadn't parked her son with help as soon as he was born, jetting off to a movie set or rafting trip. She treated this first separation almost ceremoniously.

This was a big deal for me, too. Okay, a huge deal. I was a nervous wreck. I'd fed Nolan finger food before, but never a bottle. What would

I do if I spilled the six ounces of precious breast milk she had pumped and frozen? There was no formula in the house. No way was I going to interrupt Debra's first evening out, no matter what. I was beginning to see why the other name for mother's milk is liquid gold.

When I finally managed to defrost the bottle and bring it to the living room intact, Mrs. I Still Had No Idea What Her Last Name Was sat in a large chair near the fireplace, cradling Nolan and staring at me. Did she sense my trepidation? Was she judging me? Carefully, I put the bottle down on a table beside the couch. Then I crossed the room and reached out for Nolan, silently. She held him out to me as if to say, *Are you sure you can handle this?*

But Nolan relaxed in my arms and smiled at me. This anxiety was ridiculous. I'd fed babies a thousand times. When I finally eased the bottle into his mouth, he sucked furiously, and I began to relax.

"Don't you think you should switch sides?" Maryline said a few minutes later, breaking the glorious silence.

"Excuse me?"

"That would make it more like you were Debra, and she was switching boobs," Maryline offered. She did have a point. I knew Debra took breast-feeding seriously because she had joked with me that she was planning on weaning Nolan when he was eighteen . . . years, that is.

But should I risk it? What if I dropped the bottle? I went for it anyway. Thank God he drained the bottle. Maryline beamed, Nolan gurgled gently, and I was so happy.

Debra came home much earlier than expected, upset and out of sorts. Some teenagers had thrown bubblegum into her hair from the movie theater balcony where she'd gone to see the latest blockbuster. She thought it was a karma thing, a sign that she shouldn't have left Nolan. A lot of things were karmic to her. Maryline, unexpectedly an expert at removing gum from hair, found the peanut butter and got rid of the Bubble Yum. I felt bad that Debra's big night out was cut short, but she didn't seem to mind.

She was thinking only of Nolan. She was thrilled that her son had done so well.

If you bungle raising your children, I don't think whatever else you do well matters very much.

—Jacqueline Kennedy Onassis

# chapter 19

# down and out in beverly hills

One of the best things about Debra was that I could so easily identify with her. She didn't care at all about gowns or looking glamorous. She didn't artificially enhance her appearance or her attitude; what you saw was what you got. Nolan mattered to her more than anything, and I had a feeling that one day I would be just as devoted to my kids. And then, well, we had the same approach to the open road. One day we passed a California highway patrolman on a motorcycle, and Debra slammed on the brakes, saying that she had to slow down because if she got one more speeding ticket, her license would be suspended. Now that's my kind of gal: one misdemeanor away from public transportation.

Actually, the scant attention she gave her wardrobe shocked even me, queen of the jeans and T-shirt ensemble. Sometimes she would wear her pajama bottoms and a T-shirt, kicking it up a notch to a sweat suit when she went out—a ratty, high school gym-type thing, not designer activewear. Her attire never got much fancier. She didn't want to go to red-carpet events or wear couture.

One afternoon, she asked me to go with her to Beverly Hills, and when I saw her outfit, I actually thought about declining. Then I realized I must have been gaping the way the Ovitz family did when I wore that ridiculous white jumpsuit. Putting it plainly, Debra resembled a gypsy. Her skirt sported three tiers: one purple, one red, and one green with small jingle bells lining the hem. Her top might have best been described as fluorescent tangerine. She didn't care, but *I* did. I wanted to send a recon ahead to shoo away any photographers just waiting for a picture to paste prominently on one of those when bad clothes happen to good people pages. I couldn't figure it out. It wasn't as if she couldn't afford great clothes. Her style was loose and free, almost hippielike, and she just seemed to prefer stuff that looked vaguely like remnants. Maybe it was an environmental thing?

We wandered down Rodeo Drive, weaving in and out of places like Chanel, Armani, and Giorgio. Debra peered in the window of one of the haughtiest boutiques, the kind you have to ask permission to enter. The saleslady looked away. "She has no idea who I am," Debra giggled. "She isn't going to give me the time of day." I shook my head. I had never gone shopping with Judy, but I was sure that *giggling* would not have occurred. The relief of a relaxed attitude felt like heaven.

Only once during our shopping day did I watch Nolan alone, staying on the sidewalk with baby and stroller while she dashed inside a shop. "My, ma'am, you sure have an adorable child," she drawled when she came back outside.

"Oh, thank you, ma'am!" I said, playing along. "Many people say he looks just like that actor Timothy Hutton." She hooted and we strolled on.

I sometimes forget how different it is at Debra's than it is in the rest of this town. When I look around me, it seems like most people's lives are more like the Ovitzes': hurried and worried. Debra told me today about this actor friend of hers (she didn't give a name) who was so caught up in the business of being a star that at one point he realized he hadn't even *seen* his own child in five months, let alone spent any quality time with him. How could anyone forget to see their own child? What kind of parental Alzheimer's is this—a special Hollywood strain?

* * *

"Suzy, would you like to join Mark from MGM and me?" Debra asked one day. "We're going to have a Debra Winger slide show."

"Sure. What are we going to watch, your vacation pictures?"

"No. These are the studio stills they've sent over. You can help me weed out the worst ones."

This was a task all actors with a big role faced each time they did a film; generally it was in their contract that they got to approve which pictures the studio could use for posters and promotion. Like many actors, Debra didn't much like to watch her own movies or even look at the slides. She never felt she had done as good a job as she could have. I could relate to that.

"Go ahead, Mark, crank it up." Mark had set up a projector in the family room, very informal, and he closed the blinds and started clicking through the slides. "Hate it. I'm not in character," she said to the very first one.

I smiled.

"Ohhhh, look, too fat. Out."

God, she was a rail.

"Too tired. Look at the luggage under those eyes."

I squinted. I couldn't see anything.

"Ah. That's a keeper," she said. "What do you think, Suzy?"

"Uh, I like it." I thought she was a doll. "You look happy and full of energy."

"Right. Good one, Mark. Keep it."

And so it went until we'd gone through a hundred slides and vetoed what seemed like half. I hadn't seen much difference in most of them, but then, they weren't mine. If they had been, I probably would have burned them all. I was every bit as self-critical as she.

"You know, Suzy, those pictures remind me of Richard Gere."

"Why is that?"

"When I went through the stills for *An Officer and a Gentleman*, I noticed that a lot of them were missing," she said. "I found out that when they showed Richard the slides, he chose the ones he liked and threw out all the good ones of me before I had a chance to see them. When I drove down Sunset Boulevard and saw the billboards, I had to laugh because the shot they used was a great one of him. I, of course, looked dreadful. I never did get along with Gere," she mused. "He seemed arrogant to me. The love scenes were just an expression of the tension between us." Her voice trailed off as she walked to the other side of the room.

When it came time for the Academy Awards, Debra showed me the fat, official-looking nomination packet she got in the mail. She cast her vote for Timothy's latest movie, saying she was probably one of very few. She told me that Jack Nicholson had given her a piece of advice when she'd been nominated for *Terms of Endearment:* if you don't vote for yourself (or your hubby, presumably), how can you expect anyone else to vote for you? That's good, I thought. I should be voting for myself more often.

Nolan was inquisitive and loved exploring, and he reveled in digging through the Tupperware drawer, banging wooden blocks, and ripping up magazines. Debra said it was great that his name started with the word *no*, because she didn't like the thought of saying no to him. She wanted him to have a "yes" attitude toward life. So she said his name worked well because if we accidentally started to correct him, we could say, "No-No-No-lan."

I had been hired primarily to give Debra time off at night so she could rest and spend nearly the entire day with Nolan. But we soon found that when I tried to take care of him at night, he only wanted his mom. We gave in, not wanting to upset him. So Debra took the night shift. And the day shift. On the rare occasions that I did take Nolan for walks, Debra wanted to come as well. I spent my days mostly talking to the cook in the kitchen, folding Nolan's tiny clothes in his dresser, and generally trying to help Debra around the house.

But I was beginning to feel like a third wheel on a bicycle.

One afternoon, the three of us went to a park in Malibu. I put Nolan in one of the swings and pushed him gently, and he began to giggle. Debra giggled, too, and climbed into one of the "adult" swings. She kicked off her shoes and began thrusting her legs into the air to gain momentum. Just then an older man walked up to us and said, "Hello, Debra."

I glanced over. Jack Lemmon! Wearing shorts, a golf shirt, and tennis shoes. Though he was getting up there in years, I recognized him right away because I had seen *The Odd Couple*, one of my dad's favorite movies, about twenty times. When Debra introduced us, I gulped before shaking his hand and smiling. I thought I was over my celebrity shock, but apparently not.

"Can I buy you two a falafel?" he asked.

I was too embarrassed to say I didn't know what a falafel was, so in unison, Debra and I said, "Yes. Thank you." I just hoped and prayed that whatever the thing was, it didn't have mushrooms on it.

As I munched my odd concoction, which appeared to be the Arabian equivalent of a taco, I glanced around at the hordes of mommies and nannies. Parks were a popular place for moms to go "steal" other people's nannies. You could find someone by the merry-go-round and avoid paying a hefty commission to a placement agency, and there were plenty of women living in five-million-dollar homes who thought nothing of heading out to the swings for a day of stalking. I mean, who wouldn't want to save a thousand dollars on something as unimportant as the person who would be spending more time with your child than you would?

It would be years before the real stalkers came along, before the paparazzi peered out from behind the jungle gym with any sort of regularity. The day would come, though, when media-savvy celebrities would station themselves and their adorable offspring by the sandbox, angling toward the lenses as if to reassure the public that they were regular parents. They, too, got their knees dirty! Photos of the stars and their adorable offspring playing in the park or shopping for organic produce would run almost weekly in *People*. Undeniable proof that they were just average working moms—except that they had two assistants, an accountant to pay their bills, a housekeeper at each home, a chef to cook Zone-perfect meals, and a personal yoga instructor.

Yep, just a typical family.

Suddenly I spotted someone I recognized. "Oh my God," I leaned over to Debra and whispered. "That's Michael's brother's wife. What do I do?"

"Just act like you're having the time of your life." She laughed. Of course Debra would find this amusing.

The woman walked toward the swings with her son. Closer to us. I gulped.

"Hello, Linda," I said as casually as I could.

"Oh, uh, hi, Suzy," she said awkwardly. "What are *you* doing here?"

"Oh, I work for Debra now." I pointed and smiled. "You know her, don't you?"

What else could I say—*How 'bout those Lakers?* I knew she'd heard plenty about my resignation. What would she tell her sister-in-law?

"Umm, of course," Linda mumbled, nodding at Debra, and then she left as fast as she could. She was probably going to break her ankle running to her car to relay the news that I was now working for the original mutineer from the CAA ship.

I voiced my fears to Debra, and I could anticipate her response even as I was telling her. For the second time that day, we spoke in unison: "So what?"

*So what! So what! So what!* A new mantra. As long as I could remember it, Michael and Judy had no control over me. I was voting for myself, *starting now*.

Just weeks ago it had been far too painful to hear Delma describe how Brandon wandered hopefully in and out of my old bedroom, but I finally thought I was ready for another update.

"Oh, Suzy, it's you!" Delma exclaimed when I called. "You should hear how they're talking about you around here."

"What are they saying?" Why was my stomach suddenly churning?

"Judy and Grandma Ovitz are saying bad things because you are working for Miss Winger," she whispered. "I can't tell you the horrible things they said."

I didn't really want to know, anyway. I could just imagine. *She left us high and dry to work for a traitor!*

"Amanda has had me try and call you many times at your sister's, but there's no answer."

That figured; Amanda could only call during the day, when Michael and Judy were out, and everyone was at work then. My heart sank. On the one hand, I was happy that Amanda wanted to talk to me, but on the other, that meant she did in fact miss me. It hurt to know that I was another loss in her short lifetime. I gave Delma the number of the new phone I had installed in my bedroom at Debra's.

"Delma, how's Joshua?" I asked, switching topics.

"You know, Josh is Josh. He will always be the same." Neither Delma nor Carmen understood the reason he was so difficult, and I hadn't helped matters. In a way, I had confirmed his belief that if you start to love someone, they leave. And now that I was banned from ever seeing the children, there was no way to show him that I did still care about him and that I saw more in him than a defiant little boy. As far as he knew, I never loved him enough to ever call or visit.

Then the conversation took a turn for the better.

"Would you like to see Brandon?" Delma blurted out of nowhere.

"Oh God, I'd love to!"

"They just left for Aspen last night. I could sneak him out and meet you at the park. Carmen will stay with Joshua and Amanda, so they won't know," she said in a conspiratorial tone. I couldn't imagine what Michael would do if he ever found out that Delma sneaked his son out to see me.

"He hasn't been himself since you left," Delma continued. "He's walking now, but he still seems so sad. It would do him good to see you."

"Don't tell me any more, Delma. Please," I managed to get out. I missed him so much that my throat constricted as I tried to hold back tears. As much as I wanted to see him, I didn't know if I could do it. No matter how long the visit, I'd just have to leave him again. I paused and caught my breath.

"Let's do it," I said emphatically.

I met them the next afternoon in the park where I had often taken Brandon. I gently glided in a swing, waiting, anticipating. Then I spotted Delma's car, parking in a far lot.

I could see that she was telling Brandon I was here by the way she whispered to him and pointed to me. Sweet little guy. So cute. So innocent. He craned his head up, looked around, and finally saw me. I stood up. He toddled off across the grassy field straight for me. He threw his little arms around me and squeezed me with all his strength, not uttering a sound.

My heart felt like it would collapse in on itself, aching, yet joyful. How could it be possible to feel all these things so strongly at once? I had guessed it would be hard, but I had never had an inkling of the reality. I squatted there, holding him for a long time. When I pulled away slightly to look at his beaming face, I had to quickly wipe my eyes so I could see clearly.

Delma and I embraced silently.

"Suzy, I didn't tell you, but I'm the nanny now," she confessed. "When you left, Judy asked me if I wanted to quit doing the housework and start taking care of the kids. I jumped at the chance. I knew it would make you happy.

"Plus I get to wear regular clothes now!" she beamed. "I don't think she likes it, but I told her that the *other* nannies didn't have to wear a uniform."

"Oh, Delma." I hugged her. "That makes me feel so much better—for both of you."

I was grateful Delma had brought me some of my mail. She said she had begged Judy to stop sending all my mail back, saying that she could take it to me. But apparently Judy didn't like that idea. She had been marking everything, bills and bank statements, with "return to sender."

I hoisted Brandon into a swing as Delma and I kept chatting. Knowing someone he trusted and loved was his nanny made me feel so much better. He wouldn't have yet another person coming into and then leaving his life. And even though Joshua had always been hostile to Delma, even more than he was with me, I was glad he, too, didn't have another new person he felt he had to put his guard up against. This was the best situation possible for all three of the children. Maybe I didn't need to feel so guilty anymore.

But was I in the best situation?

The scene at the park really tore me up. I loved that little guy so much. And even though I wasn't paid to worry about him anymore, I still had a big emptiness in my heart. I almost felt like I was holding myself back from giving Nolan the love he deserved because I didn't want to go through another gut-wrenching departure. Maybe I should give some serious consideration to moving home.

Delma and I arranged a few more clandestine meetings, but I could feel that Brandon's memories of me were slipping away. I was happy he was bonding with Delma. It would be best for me to duck out. I thought of what a woman at one of the placement agencies had told me, that some Hollywood mothers were so paranoid that their children would become more bonded to the nanny than to them that they changed nannies every year, regardless of how good a job they were doing or how much their children liked them.

How could anyone be so cruel?

The third-wheel feeling grew, and eventually I couldn't ignore the fact that Debra didn't need me at all. Once I accepted that, I started feeling really guilty about the great salary I'd negotiated. Just when I'd decided to say something, Debra came to me and said that she realized that she didn't really need help with Nolan, especially full-time. She said she just wasn't the kind of mom who would give time with her child away to someone else just because she was paying for it. Relieved, I confessed how awful I felt for taking so much money for so little work. Debra said not to worry about it, but she thought it would be best if she went to visit Tim in Baton Rouge with the housekeeper, who could serve as a backup babysitter if needed. No entourage of trainer, makeup artist, psychic, chef, masseuse, and hairstylist for this movie-star mom.

"I liked you as soon as I met you, Suzy," Debra said. "The karma of living with yet another castoff was great. Don't worry; I'll be happy to give you a good reference. Actually, why don't you stay here while I'm visiting Tim in Louisiana? You can take the time to find a new job."

So I did, luxuriating in the quiet of the house for two full weeks. I checked in with Tammy, perhaps the happiest woman to ever hold the title of nanny. Every single time we chatted, she told me how great it was to be working for Sally and Alan. During our last conversation, she'd been all excited because her name was going to appear in *Cosmopolitan* magazine, in an article on Sally. When I wasn't overwhelmed with envy, I loved her upbeat attitude.

"Hi, Tammy, what's the latest with you? Go on, share with me your latest tale of nanny bliss," I joked. "I can take it." I braced myself, anyway.

"I got to fly on the Concorde," she said joyfully. "I brought some pictures back for you."

"Of what?"

"I took a whole roll of film of the interior of the plane. Every time Sally and Goldie turned their backs, I took a picture. I wanted to send some to my mom to show her what it looked like. I even took a photo of the hors d'oeuvres. I've never seen butter in the shape of a swan!"

"Silly girl, don't feel bad. In Hawaii I took a picture of my room-service cart. I felt like a knight at the round table; there were so many silver serving trays. Even my pizza had one of those huge covers you see in the movies, and it came with cloth napkins." We both laughed.

"Yeah, our idea of fancy dining was hanging out at Pinocchio's pizza parlor after football games," Tammy said. "I miss the times we had there."

"And I really miss the pizza," I said wistfully.

"Oops, gotta go," Tammy said abruptly. "Sally and I are off to go shopping."

"Great! Have a wonderful time!" I replied with forced cheer. It was time to hang up, anyway. As much as I hated to admit it, her experience grated on my nerves. If I had to hear one more thing about Tammy's wonderful life, I was going to have to borrow one of Nolan's pacifiers to soothe myself.

By the time Debra and Nolan flew back to LA, I still hadn't decided what the next episode of my Hollywood career would be. I wasn't sure I even wanted another role as a nanny. But I had to go somewhere, so I moved back to my sister's Brentwood box. Five, sometimes six of us, crammed ourselves and our stuff into that tiny five-hundred-square-foot space. She didn't have a closet big enough for me to fit in, so I just used a sleeping bag.

I was confused and lonely and instinctively reached out for Ryan. We'd been talking frequently since we'd gotten "back together," and I finally asked him if he wanted to come for a visit. He was more than happy to come to LA to lend moral support. He got the couch.

Why do I feel compelled to stay and take another nanny position in LA? I know I don't ever want to get attached to any children like I did with Amanda, Josh, and Brandon. But I have to get some sort of job; I need money for my car payment. I should have taken the SATs when I had a chance.

The percentage of working mothers is very high, and they end up with two weeks off a year to be with their children. They don't have help. I don't know how they do it. So I certainly cannot complain.

—Demi Moore

chapter 20
# get shorty

Living like a sardine motivated me to get serious about finding a new job, pronto. I quickly revised my résumé to reflect my stint at Debra's. I couldn't stop the nagging voice in my head, though. What if Michael still wouldn't give me a good reference? For most people in this town, Debra's word wouldn't trump his.

I called the placement coordinator at Malibu Mommies, but the openings they had were farther away from Cindy. I wanted to be close to her in case I did get some evenings off, so I decided to keep searching. Driving to a new placement agency I'd found in the phone book, I tried to stay positive. Ryan, who had thus far spent his days soaking up the California sunshine, rode along.

This agency was named after the founder, Beatrice Dart. It occurred to me that the same woman who greeted me had probably opened the original doors sometime back in the sixties. The room smelled as musty as she looked. I introduced myself and sat down, sliding my résumé over to Beatrice, who peered at it over a pair of granny glasses perched on the end of her nose.

"Hmm," she muttered after giving it only a cursory glance. "I think I might have someone for you right away. Sit down over there," she said, motioning to a waiting area without ever looking at me. She buried her nose in a Rolodex and dialed an ancient black rotary phone, which had probably been installed the same day she opened.

"Hello. This is Beatrice down at Beatrice Dart's," she said.

Silence.

"I think I have someone for that position you called me about. . . . Yes, uh . . . let me check." She stood up, scrutinized me, and went back to the phone. "Yes, she's attractive. What? Oh, can you hold a moment?" she said, cupping her hand over the mouthpiece.

What was she going to say now? *On second thought, she's not drop-dead gorgeous, so your husband probably won't make a pass at her like he did with the last girl I sent you.*

"Can you go over to Paramount Studios right now, dear?"

"Uh, yes . . . yes," I stammered. "I suppose so. How far away is it?" She didn't answer me.

"Okay then, right away." With that she banged the phone down.

She handed me a slip of paper with directions and a name. *R something, something, Pe something, something, something. Set of chairs.* Poor old Beatrice's handwriting reminded me of a doctor scrawling out prescriptions. Completely illegible. Was I going to be a nanny or a furniture mover? Maybe Beatrice hadn't spent enough time reading my résumé. She did look nearly eighty. Perhaps she was placing me as a domestic house manager?

"Ms. Dart," I ventured. "Uh, I can't quite read what you've written. Does this say set of chairs?"

"No, dear." She laughed and coughed. "It says, set of *Cheers*—you know, *Cheers* the TV show."

Cheers? Oh, *Cheers!*

"You're going to talk to Rhea Perlman, my dear. Don't worry. The studio isn't far. I'll show you how to get there."

Oooh. I'd never been on a studio lot or on a sitcom set. (Well, except for the time Cindy and I got tickets to a Dolly Parton special and we got to wait in the green room with Patti LaBelle's family.) Sure, I knew that it was probably a waste of time. Beatrice hadn't even checked my references, and obviously the person whom she was talking to hadn't asked. Once I mentioned my little problem, I knew I wouldn't get a second interview. But maybe I'd try to enjoy the Hollywood glamour for what it was.

Suddenly I remembered the hayseed sitting in my car. Who would have known that Beatrice would send me on an interview *that day*? There was no way I was going to drive onto the Paramount lot with Ryan in the car. To be honest, he was the kind of guy who looks a lot better in his own habitat. Did I mention that he was a fourth-generation lumberjack? His rugged good looks and casual style belonged in a small logging town, not Southern California. Ryan truly believed that *ain't* was an actual word, because they used it on his favorite show, *The Dukes of Hazzard*. (He prided himself that people often remarked that he looked just like Bo Duke.) This—and many other things—drove me crazy. I always wanted to change him. This is what happened every time we got back together. I realized I loved him in a "can't live with 'em but how am I ever going to get over him" kind of way. Why I didn't just leave the poor guy alone, let him live his life and forget about things like trying to convince him that the WWF wasn't real, I will never know.

Ryan's entire wardrobe consisted of T-shirts, faded 501s, tennis shoes, and several baseball caps in various colors. Occasionally he topped the ensemble with a pullover zip-up "hickory shirt" (if you don't know what that is, don't ask). But his signature accessory was a faded circle on his back left jean pocket: Copenhagen chewing tobacco. He had been dipping snuff for so long that even when the can found its way to his left front shirt pocket, the ring remained.

I hurried to my car but made the mistake of telling him that I was going for an interview. I should have just taken him back to the apartment in silence.

"Hell no, I don't want to go back to the apartment," he argued. "I wouldn't miss this for the world. I'm here in Hollywood; I want to see some movie stars."

Right. I wasn't really one for confrontation. He stayed in the car. When we pulled into the parking lot, past the big wrought-iron gates with "Paramount Studios" emblazoned across the top, he started fidgeting like a kid on his first trip to Wally World.

"Do not move!" I ordered emphatically, pointing my finger at him like I was his mother. "I'll be back as soon as I'm through."

"Who're you gonna see?" he said, not moving an inch.

"Some people on *Cheers*," I answered. "Now promise me, Ryan, that you will not get out of this car."

"Oh my God," he said, holding his hand over his mouth. "You're gonna see Sam Malone? I gotta come!"

"*No,*" I commanded. "If you move from this car, I will never speak to you again. Just sit here and look out the window. Sooner or later some movie star is bound to walk by." I checked my hair, pulled and smoothed my skirt, and began looking for the *Cheers* set. I wandered around the lot and watched employees whiz by in golf carts. All the stages had numbers painted ten feet high on their sides, so it was easy to find the right set.

I could feel the energy the minute I walked onto the huge sound-stage. People scurried about impatiently, pointing, huddling. Just before I stepped through the door marked QUIET. CHEERS TAPING, I glanced over my shoulder to see Michael J. Fox. The one and only Alex P. Keaton! I'd had such a crush on him when I was younger. And there in front of me on a cavernous stage was the familiar bar scene.

I'd never been a big *Cheers* fan, though I was familiar with the play-ers. I did know that Rhea played a waitress. I asked someone who looked vaguely official where I could find Ms. Perlman. He pointed to a set of bleachers, which I learned held the audience during the show's taping. That day, Ted Danson, Kelsey Grammer, and the others sat scat-tered throughout the stands, rehearsing. I looked into the uppermost row of seats and there, sitting by herself, apparently going over lines in a script, was Rhea. I clambered up and introduced myself, and she smiled pleasantly, giving me a quick head-to-toe scan. She told me that she and her husband had two daughters, who were three and six, and the girls already had a nanny. They were hiring someone for their infant son. Then she asked me if I wanted to meet her husband.

I liked Rhea immediately. She had the same qualities I admired in Debra; down-to-earth, easy to talk to. I could just tell that she would be a wonderful boss. Could lightning really strike twice? But then, as we walked up the stairs behind the set, I remembered I would have to tell her—and her husband—about my employment with Michael. Debra would give me a good word, but I knew that Michael would be my downfall.

Rhea led me into a modest room with some banged-up couches and chairs. Good God, Danny DeVito was her husband! It would have been nice if Miss Senile Beatrice had been less worried about me winning a beauty pageant and more concerned about informing me who Rhea was married to! I'm sure I was gawking, but I tried to use some of the composure I had learned at the Ovitzes'.

I could tell right away that Mr. DeVito was as pleasant and kind as he seemed on-screen. I had always liked him, even when he played the villain. Somehow you could see that underneath it all he was a good guy, mellow, laid-back. I extended my hand, told him my name, and then started in. "Mr. DeVito, I have to tell you about Michael Ovitz," I said before he'd even had a chance to take his hand back.

"Michael? What about Michael?" he said, smiling. "He's our agent."

*Oh great. The worst-case scenario. I might as well get up and leave right now. Let's stop wasting our time.*

"Uh, he's pretty upset with me," I blurted again, wanting to grab the words back.

"Why, were you fired?" he asked.

I paused. "Well, technically I quit. I gave him a month's notice, but he wouldn't take it. When he asked me to stay longer, I said no, and he wasn't really very happy about it."

Mr. DeVito smiled, and then he laughed. "Oh, I can see that. I know that Michael does not like anyone telling him no," he said as he wagged his finger back and forth in warning. "I'm not worried about Michael, so don't you be. We will decide for ourselves."

*What? Isn't everyone worried about Michael?*

"We're about done here, so why don't you just follow us over to our house?" he suggested. Still in shock over his lack of concern about Michael, I couldn't keep up. Didn't he need to see my references?

"Sure, I'd love to see your place," I said. Then I remembered that I had Paul Bunyan in my car. "Oh. I forgot. I've got my boyfriend in the car. Could I come by tomorrow?"

"We wouldn't think of it," he said, smiling and putting his arm around Rhea. "We'd like to meet him."

*Sure you would.* But I didn't want them to witness my great judgment in men. Oh my God. What was I going to do? One look at Ryan and Danny would think I just fell off the turnip truck.

My brain whirled with possibilities as I scooted back to my Celica. Miraculously, Ryan had remained in the car. Oh, it was worse than I thought. I'd forgotten he was wearing a tank top—one size too small, of course, with a Chicago Bears logo on the front.

"Okay," I yelled, getting in the driver's seat. "Get that Copenhagen outta your pocket right now so we don't look like a couple of *complete* rednecks."

"Suzy, you're never gonna guess who I saw while you were inside. Robert Blake! Do you believe it?" he cried.

I sighed. "Any chance you have a collared shirt in the trunk you might be able to put on?" I asked, already knowing the answer.

We followed Danny and Rhea's old BMW to their home high up in the Hollywood Hills. Somehow I convinced Ryan to stay in the car, and I dashed into the house.

I met six-year-old Audrey and three-year-old Lexie, and then Rhea showed me to Max's room. I would share the room, sleeping on a twin bed next to the baby. She apologized for the accommodation, explaining that Danny's mother and sister were coming soon from New Jersey for an extended visit, and they would need the guest bedroom. We had a pleasant conversation, and I left my résumé and thanked them for their time. They told me they would call me that night with their decision.

They were as good as their word. Danny called my sister's apartment to say that they would indeed like to hire me, asking if I could start the *very* next morning.

When I arrived at 7 A.M., most of the family was asleep. Danny let me in, and I stood in the slate-rock entryway while he finished a phone conversation. I soon realized that he was talking to Debra. So they must have looked at my résumé after all. He spoke as if they were old friends. Encouraging. Danny seemed to be chatting about his latest film, and she was apparently updating him on what Timothy was doing. Danny looked up from his phone conversation and smiled at me winningly. It seemed possible that, just like at Debra's, I might be a real person to this family; not just a milk-server, burper, and stain-remover.

I stood there awkwardly, not knowing whether to sit down, stand until he was finished, or pitch in and start cleaning the kitchen. It was an uncomfortably familiar feeling. I realized that this was the problem with my career. It was always so hard to know my place and what was expected of me. It occurred to me that the awkwardness of living with your employer wasn't something that would be solved by new circumstances.

But why was I thinking about problems? Here I was, getting an opportunity to work for a picture-perfect family, one that needed me, seemed normal, and would possibly appreciate my efforts. But as I stood there, I couldn't muster up any joy.

I spent the day getting unpacked and finding my way around, but my heart (and head) was someplace else. My first night there I jotted down the thoughts that had been bugging me.

> I'm angry with myself for questioning my good luck. This is just the kind of position I've been looking for, but somehow it doesn't feel right already. Maybe I'm selfish. I know I should vote for myself and all that. I've been thinking about becoming a nurse-midwife. I can't be a nanny forever. I've got to start making plans for college, but in the meantime, here I am with two kind people, and they want me to help them care for their baby. How bad can that be?
>
> Rhea and I have agreed that we'll have a trial period for a few weeks. I think she's giving herself an out in case she doesn't like me. When that's up, we'll draw up a contract. This time I'll discuss everything I should, about money and hours.

Danny and Rhea seemed to have it all figured out. They were public people who had busy lives working and raising their kids, but somehow they balanced everything well. They doted on their children and each other, and they didn't fret over appearances. Their house in the Hills was unassuming. No long driveway with iron gates at the entrance; you just parked on the street and walked from the sidewalk through a gate into their courtyard. Just being around them made me feel better. It was easy to see that they really cared about the employees who helped them run their busy household. They used to jump in the car to drive their housekeeper home themselves, and former employees were always dropping by to visit.

Lisa, the nanny who watched six-year-old Audrey and three-year-old Lexie, had been with them for three years. She lived in her own exterior apartment attached to the side of the house. Lisa loved the grunge scene, which seemed odd, given Danny and Rhea's all-American demeanor. Lisa was nearly six feet tall and was as thin as a breadstick with jet-black dyed hair, a navel ring, occasional black lipstick and matching toenail polish. She also had something stuck through one eyebrow. It looked like a safety pin. I was kind of worried about her getting tetanus. I couldn't picture chatting with her like I did with Carmen and Delma. But then again, I didn't need the support here the way I did there.

Although I shared a room with the baby, I had the privacy of my own bathroom. Max took to me immediately. He really resembled a miniature Danny, except he had lighter hair that stood straight up on his very round head. He giggled a lot and fussed rarely. He was sweet, but I would not fall in love with him. No matter how much I enjoyed him, I had to guard myself. I couldn't force myself through a heart-wrenching separation again.

Maybe I finally understood why Joshua didn't let new people get close.

Every day Rhea and I would head off to Paramount Studios with baby in tow, where I took care of Max while watching the rehearsal. (We might have had more room to play at home, but he was very young yet, and Rhea wanted every opportunity to be with him during her breaks at work.) On the first day, everyone sat at a long table right in the middle of the bar area that was the center of every episode. The casual dress of the cast members surprised me. Most of them looked like they had just rolled out of bed. When Rhea walked up and introduced me, they all said, "Hi, Suzy the new nanny," in unison.

"Did you come from that Baby Buddies agency?" asked Ted Danson. "That's the one we always use." Apparently, they had to use nanny agencies frequently. I learned from Peggy, the DeVitos' house manager, that Ted's wife, Casey, hired one of Rhea's former nannies to work for them.

Casey, whom Peggy described as a little odd, had thrown the girl out on her ear one day with very little explanation. Since she had no money or family nearby, she had turned to Rhea for help. Rhea kindly took her in. Casey then called the house a few times to give Rhea an earful about how awful she thought the girl was, but Rhea cut her short: "I don't want to hear it. I want to help her out, at least until she gets another job. She has nowhere else to go." I was learning how much Rhea really cared about others, regardless of their social status.

Rhea then showed me to her dressing room. Nothing fancy. In fact, the stairs leading up to it were sort of like what you'd find in a warehouse (complete with not-so-nice graffiti, the kind that you might find in a bathroom stall at a truck stop. I squinted and tried to make out what it said when no one was looking: *For a good time, call Shelley Long at . . .*). Rhea's dressing room was just one small box in a line of small, square rooms. Max and I set up camp there.

I found everything fascinating. Four days a week, the writers and the entire cast would meet around 10 A.M. Rhea said it was a real problem getting everyone there on time, including herself. The director had tried everything to get the cast to be prompt. They had even gone through a period where they had donated money to charity for every minute they were late. But according to her, that hadn't seemed to make a difference. She said the problem was that a few of them would be there ready to rehearse and then someone would be missing. Everyone would get tired of waiting, and then a couple of people would go make phone calls. When the person who was holding everyone up arrived, they'd be missing the other cast members. This frustrating cycle usually occurred *every day*.

When they finally corralled everyone, the show kicked off with the cast sitting at a table reading the script and ad-libbing. Sometimes the jokes would fall flat, and they'd change lines to make them funnier. All the writers would laugh uproariously at their own jokes. It seemed to me that if you had written the line, you knew what was coming. Couldn't be all that much of a funny surprise. But they all seemed to really enjoy themselves. On Fridays the cast conducted a full rehearsal. The taping would take place that night in front of a live audience. Max and I sat alone in the bleachers for the run-through, and it felt as if I was spying on a family that lived in an odd dollhouse. Cameras dotted the set, none of the rooms actually had four walls, and of course there was no ceiling. Guys straight out of the Mr. Universe contest rolled the cameras and cameramen around on some kind of platform on wheels.

I quickly learned that everyone highly valued the actors' time, and the cast only stepped into the shots at the last possible second. The producers used stand-ins to determine the lighting and camera angles. These people didn't need to look like the characters, but it was important to be the same height so the production team could adjust everything correctly. Each of the stand-ins wore cardboard signs that hung around their necks with string, labeled WOODY, KIRSTIE, etc. The stand-ins answered to the actors' names, and sometimes these poor people would literally have to stand in one place for an hour while the cameramen got their angles and marked the spot on the floor with an X. Once the directors got everything perfected, they would call the actors to come and recite their lines. Whenever I felt that others viewed my job as unimportant, I thought about the stand-ins.

About a hundred people—all outrageously enthusiastic—would attend the final taping on Friday night. The cast always seemed to buzz with opening-night jitters, even though the same scenes had been rehearsed countless times before. As the cameras rolled, the director stood to the right and looked into a monitor, watching the action that was going on just a few feet away to see how it looked on the television. After each scene, the director and some of the writers discussed their thoughts with the cast. Sometimes they would reshoot and reposition the props. (No, the beer was not real.) Everything was painstakingly scrutinized and rearranged by the director. Production assistants also had to shuffle walls around because the set next to the bar acted as almost every other room you saw, from the pool room to Rebecca's office to Carla's house. When the scene switches dragged on, a stand-up comic appeared, the same guy who warmed up the audience before the taping with one-liners, magic tricks, songs, and free chocolates.

One morning, Kirstie joined us on the ride to work in Rhea's station wagon. She and Rhea had an easy, friendly working relationship, and she had slept over the night before. Sitting beside her, I noticed that she hadn't had her roots done in a while. I was surprised at how gratifying it was to see such a put-together star look like a regular person, flaws and all. She was hilarious, too. She told us her dad had called the day before to inform her that her prom picture had just run in one of the tabloids. He was not happy about the magazine getting ahold of his daughter's photo; why hadn't anyone informed him that you could get money for that kind of thing? Had he known, he could have sold it himself. In fact, he was planning to haul out some old family albums and see if he could make some quick cash. Kirstie thought her dad's idea was a riot. She had a wacky side, too. She urged Rhea to bring the kids to her house in the Valley, where she kept all kinds of exotic animals. The girls would usually listen wide-eyed to her stories about monkeys and ferrets.

Danny and Rhea had a lot of friends like that—normal and unpretentious. I was beginning to see that the nice ones stuck together in Hollywood. The DeVitos were always taking in actor friends who were down on their luck, getting them parts in movies and even lending them money. They had a lot of faith in people.

Life with the DeVitos had a whole different vibe than life with my first employers. For one thing, the new place was a happy home. I could tell that Danny and Rhea were really in love because they were always so playful with each other. One day while we were driving to the set, Rhea's car phone rang, and she pushed the speaker button.

"Hello."

"Hi, sweetie." I could hear Danny's voice.

"Hi, Dan. What's up?"

"Are you on the way to the set?"

"Yes, dear. Why?"

"I'm just driving the ole Pontiac. Man, this thing is great! And I was just sitting here thinking about how much I'd like to jump your bones in the big backseat of this ole thing. You know what I'd like to do?" He giggled.

"Danny, you're on the speaker phone, and Suzy's sitting right here, darling."

Silence.

"Oh, sorry about that, Suzy." He giggled again. The line went dead.

Rhea laughed and explained that he was driving her car, the first one she'd ever owned as a teenager. This was typical; they saw the fun and nostalgic value in something like a first car. I started thinking that I should have kept my first car, a '66 Mustang, the one my understanding parents let me paint hot pink.

Lisa and I were the only live-in help; the rest of the DeVitos' staff went home at night. The house manager worked Monday through Friday. The lone housekeeper also came in five days a week and frantically tried to keep up with the busy household. She didn't always succeed, but I don't think Rhea even cared that dust lingered on the end tables or that the kitchen floor needed a good scrubbing. The cook appeared for a few hours a day, making dinner each night and serving it. She was from Oregon, and I loved talking to her about Cottage Grove. We both laughed because we actually missed the endless rain in our home state. The staff also included a guy who served as Danny's assistant. He was in his mid-twenties, and he was so funny that conversations with him kept me doubled up with laughter. One day he told me about trying to be a sperm donor when he was hard up for cash in college. He was bummed because the clinic had informed him that none of his "tadpoles ever took," so he couldn't keep donating. There was an awkward silence for a minute. "Oh my," was all I could come up with. Then I started laughing uncontrollably. He didn't seem to mind.

Peggy, the house manager, mainly assisted Rhea. She handled everything that civilian people would take care of in their homes, such as packing school lunches, servicing the cars, picking up the dry cleaning, and grocery shopping. Everyone helped out with the kids, making lunch when necessary or picking them up from ballet lessons. They had lots of vehicles, and everyone seemed to take turns driving whatever was available. The newest automobile was at least five years old. While I was there, though, they did buy a new Land Cruiser to haul the kids around in. I'm pretty sure it was the first new car they'd bought in a long time.

Peggy told me that she had sometimes given one of Danny and Rhea's employees a ride home from work. One day she had noticed that inside the employee's modest apartment some things seemed out of place—like her expensive organic toilet paper and fancy food. It appeared that the employee was helping herself to the contents of Rhea's home. As a test, Peggy left $80 lying out to see if the employee would turn it in or pocket it. She kept the cash, and Peggy triumphantly told Rhea. Rhea was really unhappy, mainly with Peggy. "That wasn't fair to set her up like that. If she needs the money or toilet paper that badly, let her have it!" she said.

I knew Mandie would not believe me if I told her about a day in the life of this rich and famous and *generous*.

Danny's mother and sister Angie did come from New Jersey for a visit. During the day, there were thirteen of us running around making a cozy and crazy house. I grew to love Angie. She and I spent many evenings together, playing cards and sharing stories. Angie told me about when Danny had first come to Hollywood and only had two bus tokens to rub together; he would ride the bus all night just to get some sleep. When things got really bad, he would call Angie and ask for a few bucks to tide him over. She would always send money to him when she could. It seemed odd to hear about Danny's former life, given his fame now.

I loved hearing about how Danny used to cut hair in her salon for extra money. In fact, he still cut Audrey and Lexie's hair. I guess like many so-called overnight success stories, his had actually been years in the making.

It was obvious that both Danny and his sister dearly loved their elderly mother. Angie told me that with her love and care, and Danny's financial support, they were grateful that they would always be able to take good care of her. She looked like she needed taking care of; she was so tiny. Probably about four foot nine. And Angie was shorter than her brother, too. At five foot three, the same height as Rhea, I was actually taller than most of the family.

I fit in well, though. They were a true family in every way I think of families. I was so grateful when they would ask me to join them for dinner each night; it really made me feel like part of the family, not just an employee.

Mandie was thrilled for me that I had found such a great situation. We continued to chat, though I didn't have many stories to share. But she still had plenty, including some I identified with all too well. She called me one night cracking up. "Wait till you see my new look, Suzy!"

Mrs. Goldberg had stopped Mandie in the hall one day: "You're thinking of getting your hair cut, aren't you?"

"Um, no, not really. I just grew it out."

"You might want to consider going to my stylist. He can work miracles . . . on anyone's hair."

Mandie ignored her boss's suggestion. But later that day, Mrs. Goldberg stopped her again. "I had to pull a lot of strings, but I got you into my salon for tomorrow at one." After two suggestive conversations, Mandie felt self-conscious about her hair and kept the appointment. Walking into the salon and seeing all the glamorous people there, she felt like a real Montana hick.

Mrs. Goldberg's hairdresser seemed very nice. Mandie asked him if he cut a lot of movie stars' hair. He said yes, he had a lot of famous clients, but he couldn't say who they were. For a hairdresser, he was pretty closed-lipped. She didn't ask anything after that but listened to all the conversations swirling around her as the stylists next to them gossiped with their clients.

One hour and much eavesdropping later, Mandie was out of there. She had to admit that her hair looked great, but she nearly started crying when she realized she had to shell out $100 for her new look. It killed her to think that in Montana she could get her hair cut for $12 at Sir Cuts-a-Lot.

But there's no doubt she paid for a high-profile stylist. Years later, when Air Force One held up runway traffic at LAX for two hours because President Clinton was getting his hair cut, Mandie had to laugh. Mrs. Goldberg's hairdresser, Christophe, was the one clipping the presidential mane.

I think it's a great lesson in parenting, to allow your child to do what's right for them, as opposed to what you want them to do.

—Maria Shriver

# irreconcilable differences

I still hadn't given up on my spa fantasies. Despite my horrible previous experiences, I did live in the glamour and beauty capital of the country. I knew the magical, relaxing treatment that would make me feel like a star was out there, and I was still determined to find it. This time I booked a facial and waxing appointment at a Rodeo Drive salon that Peggy recommended. Deliciously overpriced and indulgent. And I gave myself plenty of time. What could go wrong?

A large Russian woman with a mustache greeted me at the door, speaking in an accent so heavy I could barely understand her.

"We start with the arms," sounded like *"Vee start vis zee arms."* She looked like one of those Soviet weight lifters in the Olympics, and I'm not talking about the female ones.

I nodded weakly. Working for Debra had boosted my assertiveness, but I knew I was still too timid. And until right now I hadn't realized just how easily intimidated I still was.

I'd been having my eyebrows waxed since I was about twelve, because it was the only way I could prevent a unibrow. I had never waxed my legs, though, and I thought it would be a treat not to have to shave for weeks, maybe even months. And why not do my underarms as

well? Then I wouldn't have to worry about shaving, since the kids and I
were out in the pool practically every day. I envisioned a fairly simple
procedure, the kind of waxing where they douse your legs with warm
wax and then peel it off. I knew it wouldn't be painless, but the eyebrow thing never hurt too much. And after some minor discomfort, I
would have silky-smooth legs, and then I would be treated to a soothing
facial. "You sit there," the Russian matron grunted, pointing to a long
padded recliner, not unlike a dentist's chair. "Here, put on this. I will be
right back." She handed me a tank top.

In about three minutes, the woman returned with her sidekick,
another large Russian woman. Together they looked like a WWF tag
team. Why exactly did we need two people for my waxing and facial?

"Raise de arms, please."

I hesitated. I didn't really want to expose my European-style pits,
even to Andrea the Giant here. I hadn't shaved for about a month; I figured that I needed to grow the hair out somewhat or the wax wouldn't
have anything to attach to.

"Come, come. We don't have all day. Raise arms, please." Okay, okay. I
raised my arms, exposing my extremely hairy underarms. "Owweeee,
you shaved! Tisk tisk!" What did *not shaving* look like to her?

She then slathered a heaping spatula full of hot wax on to one under-
arm, then the other. "Ah-ghuu-u-u-!!!!" I wailed.

The wax congealed immediately and gripped my skin. My arms froze
into a permanent two-fisted declaration, as if I'd just crossed the
marathon finish line in world-record time. The pain was excruciating.
My eyebrow waxings had never been remotely close to this. I imagined
hot bacon grease might feel similar if anyone was stupid enough to pour
it into an open wound. I started hyperventilating in fear of removal.

When she finally did yank off the wax, I cried out like a wounded animal and nearly passed out. I swear she ripped off three layers of my
skin.

Another woman came charging into the room looking quite confused
and dismayed. I could hardly understand her, either.

"What is going on here?"

The large Russian woman shrugged. "She shaved," she said nonchalantly, as if to say, *She made her bed, now she has to die in it.* The new-

comer looked down at my bleeding armpits and shook her head with thinly veiled disgust.

"Oh, well yes, she shaved."

"Come on, let's go. There is nothing we can do for her." And with that, she grabbed the assistant's arm, and they left the room.

"Now we do the legs," the lone torturer said in a suspiciously gleeful tone as she applied thin rows of something that looked awfully close to those fly-catching strips that you hang in a horse barn. I squirmed on the lounge, splayed out like a fish that was about to get filleted. I started groaning even before she began slowly pulling off each strip, my fists still clenched high in the air, armpits still decorated with Kleenex to stop the bleeding. As she pulled a particularly clingy strip off my shin-bone, I vowed right then and there never to give birth if there was any chance it could be this painful. When she told me to turn over so she could do the backs of my legs, I refused.

"No, thank you," I gasped. "I just need the front done. No one really sees the back."

Thank God I hadn't come in for a bikini wax. I never did get the facial; I was in too much pain, and besides, I suddenly couldn't afford it. The Russian charged me $125—a hefty cut above the standard waxing price—because she said I had taken twice as long as a "ragular clieent," and she had great difficulty working with coarse hair that had been previously shaved.

I limped out. Another example of how I never seemed to fit in Hollywood. I just wanted a little piece of glamour, to have the same flawless complexion as the actresses I admired. Obviously, I was going about it all wrong. I wondered what Debra would say about my karma. Did I deserve this torture because I laughed at the need for a class on grooming in nanny school? That was the only plausible explanation I could come up with.

I wasn't even trying to deny it—I was very willing to admit that my appearance could use a boost. Unlike many stars. I couldn't get over the lengths some celebrities would go to in pretending their beauty was genetic. A friend of mine, who was looking for a *clerical* job, was offered a position looking after an award–winning star—well known for taming her legendary heartbreaker of a husband into a blissful spouse—who was recovering from a face-lift. The job required helping her change her bandages for several days while she recovered. Apparently, she thought it would be safer to hire a no-name "temp" to provide her with medical care instead of risking the paparazzi finding her on the way to the usual chichi aftercare center. This, of course, might have exposed her surgically enhanced "natural beauty." Although she and her husband were worth millions, they wanted to pay my friend only $100 a day. We were not clear if they were too tight to pay a qualified RN to come assist or they didn't want the nursing service to know her secret, either. Maybe a little of both. Although my friend was tempted to take the job just to meet the husband, she—who is scared at the sight of her own blood, mind you—passed on it.

After a couple of months, the excitement of watching the *Cheers* set had worn off. In fact, I was a little bored. There were no other kids or babies around, and it got monotonous watching the same scenes played out over and over again. I thought of my friend Katy, who often went on location with the wife and three young kids of a wholesome young blond television star. Katy spent her days cooped up in a trailer far away from the set, with three hyper kids and very few of the toys and games they loved. She was supposed to keep the kids happy and in a good mood for when the star had some downtime to "play" with them (downtime being quite unpredictable, as shooting schedules changed by the hour). My job came nowhere close to that impossible situation, but life on the set became quite dull in a very short time.

I found myself frequenting the buffet table that was set up every Friday for the crew that came in for that night's taping. I think they chose the cuisine with the requirement that it have the highest fat and calorie content possible. Ruffles potato chips with ranch dip, every kind of donut imaginable, cheese rolls, Cheetos, and my personal favorite, an assortment of mini candy bars. I grazed all day.

At one point, I had returned to the buffet so many times that one of the production assistants asked how many maple bars I'd scarfed down. (All of them, actually.) I was humiliated. The next time, I made sure that the idiot who had nothing better to do than monitor my excessive food intake wasn't looking. And I took a plain cake donut. Jerk.

He had a point, though. All my life I had been able to eat exactly what I wanted, and in no way would I deprive myself of something that tasted good. Of course, a 110-pound teenager hatched this theory. Now I was twenty, and I'd somehow avoided noticing that I'd gone from a respectable 114 to an inflated 139.

On my small frame, that was a lot of weight. And here I'd been thinking that the evil dryer had been shrinking all my clothes. No such luck. I hadn't even gone to college yet, so I couldn't blame it on the "freshman fifteen." Especially since it was actually twenty-five. Ouch.

One afternoon, shortly after this unwelcome discovery, I went into the kitchen when no one was around. There on the counter sat a very beguiling bag of freshly baked Mrs. Fields cookies. This was extremely unusual because Danny and Rhea always ate well, avoided red meat, and didn't keep much sugar in the house. I took a peek around the corner.

"Danny?" I called, loudly enough for anyone to hear. No answer. The coast was clear. I opened the bag quickly, my eyes still darting about the room. Inside lay six large, thick, sugary cookies—two chocolate chip, two peanut butter, and two snickerdoodle. Ooooh. I grabbed one blindly, closed the bag snugly, and ran upstairs to my room. It was the snickerdoodle, the largest of the six, and it tasted like heaven. I decided I'd indulge in just one more. I ran back downstairs, listening for footsteps on the way, and opened the bag. I took another one and retreated once again to my room. I repeated this scene three times until there was only one cookie in the bag. You'd think I would have just eaten that one, too, and then had enough sense to throw away all the evidence.

But no. As I hid in my room and licked excess chocolate off my thumbs, I heard the house manager in the kitchen. "Who ate the cookies? I bought these special for Rhea," she yelled. I ventured into the hall, where I stood next to Lisa, who was thin and tall and didn't look at all guilty. We both pleaded ignorance. I discreetly tried to check for crumbs on my shirt.

What was happening to me? I was pathetic, a caricature of the frumpy nanny. Now that the fat had caught up to me, I seemed powerless to stop it. And to top it off, I heard from Tammy again. She spent her twenty-first birthday on a movie set, where Sally was kind enough to have the whole cast and crew, including Julia Roberts, surprise her with a birthday song serenade.

*Bitterness is not becoming, Suzy.*

> My top priority this weekend is to buy the book *Feeding the Hungry Heart*. On second thought, I need the companion book, *Breaking Free from Compulsive Eating*.
> PS. Stop by Mrs. Fields and buy some cookies for Rhea.

After the television taping season ended for the year, Rhea and I stayed at home during the day with Max. Since the DeVitos had so many cars, I let Ryan use mine. But I had given away more than just my automobile, I realized. This was just one more way I had ceased caring about myself. I was chunky, I didn't leave the house, and I'd even stopped wearing makeup.

One day, Peggy spotted a picture of me in my room, a glamour shot Tammy and I had taken for fun a few months before. I was wearing a blue sequin top and a feather boa (it seemed like a good idea at the time).

"Who's this? Is that yoooouuu?" she said incredulously, looking me up and down as if to say, *How is that possible?* Peggy had never been all that kind to me, but this tipped the scale, so to speak.

"Maybe you should wear this much makeup more often," she said, laughing quietly to herself.

*I was considered a hot number back in my day!* I wanted to retort. Oh my God. My day was only a couple of years ago. I had to put myself back together. I already looked like a haggard housewife, and I wasn't even married!

It didn't add up. I loved the way that this family really enjoyed every moment of their lives. They were hardly ever in a hurry. That was what I'd craved at the Ovitzes', right? But just being around them wasn't enough. I couldn't stop thinking about all my friends whose lives were moving forward, to a future. I knew I wasn't getting any closer to where I wanted to go in my life—wherever that was—by staying here and working as a nanny. And as I read self-help books about weight, I knew that this was a big part of the problem. My heart was hungry.

Rhea, on the other hand, looked great. She left the house bright and early each day for the gym near their house, or sometimes she would go to the studio on the lot to work out with a personal trainer and do Pilates. When the girls complained that she was leaving, she would remind them, "A mom can't be a good mom and feel good about herself if she doesn't exercise."

It was hard to believe she was turning forty. To mark the occasion, Danny was concocting a huge surprise party for her in their backyard. Lisa, who was much more hip than I (as if that would have been difficult), knew all the latest music, and she suggested that Danny hire a local band to play for the party, one she'd heard at a club and thought was very good. Danny said he'd never heard of the Red Hot Chili Peppers and didn't think he could risk having a no-name group for such a special occasion. He looked at me and asked my opinion; I nodded in agreement and said that I'd never heard of them, either. I see now that I couldn't have made it as a trend spotter: Kevin Costner, now the Red Hot Chili Peppers—0 for 2.

Several nights before the party, I was in my room when I heard Danny's voice coming from their bedroom next door. I heard him call Michael by name, so naturally I stood at the door of my bedroom to listen in on the conversation. From what I could gather, Danny had never called him for a reference when they initially hired me. I guessed that he had meant it when he said they'd just try me out for themselves.

The two of them must have been discussing a business deal, and then Danny got quiet. I froze. For all I knew, Michael had purposefully tracked me down and called Danny to try and get him to fire me. I heard Danny say, "I know. Wasn't that a coincidence? Rhea found this nanny and she used to work for you . . . uh-huh." There was a moment of silence as Michael said something, then Danny replied, "Oh, so you'd pass on this one, eh?" as if he was still in the interviewing stage. "Yes, okay. Okay. Got it. I'll talk to you later. Thanks for the tip, Michael. I'll let Rhea know."

I was starting to wonder if I might have been able to leave on better terms with the Ovitz family. Michael had made it clear that he valued me. What would have happened if I had tried harder to make things work out? Had I made a mistake by leaving? Sure, I hated confrontation, but maybe I could have talked to him like he was a real person, not a mogul. Maybe if I had gone to him and told him what was really bothering me—that I thought Judy didn't like me, the lack of time off, Josh's lack of respect—this nasty war could have been avoided. I was starting to think that I shouldn't have seen the situation in such black and white terms: stay and be unhappy, or leave and be happy. Lately I'd been doing a lot more thinking about the choices I had made. I now saw that I had been a little depressed ever since I had left the Ovitz family. I needed to start journaling more. It was the only kind of therapy I could afford.

> It kinda seems like the deal with the Ovitzes was as much my fault as it was theirs. I never set any boundaries with Judy. By never requesting what I needed, I made it easier for her to ignore the possibility that I had any needs at all. I settled for what they gave me, rather than asking for what I needed in order to be a good caregiver.
> Why wasn't I clearer about what I wanted when Michael talked to me at the end? I was probably just thinking about Carmen, who never seemed to get any changes she asked for. I never even attempted to tell him what I was so unhappy about. I guess I was waiting for him to ask. I just didn't see that I had other options besides giving my notice.

This was so hard to admit. Here I was at a great nanny job, and I had carried my past mistakes with me. No wonder I was depressed.

I poured out my feelings to Mandie, who was still dealing with economic issues. This time, however, she was the one spending the big bucks. The Goldbergs had taken Mandie and the kids to France, where Mr. Goldberg conducted some business and Mrs. Goldberg shopped. Well, "shop" made it sound so benign. These were spending expeditions of monumental proportions. On the first outing, Mandie fell in love with a $400 purse. She lusted after the purse like she was Dolly Parton in a wig shop. The problem, of course, was that she didn't have Dolly Parton's budget. It was out of the question. Or was it? She approached Mrs. Goldberg, desperately trying to find some rationale for buying the overpriced bag. Mrs. Goldberg agreed that it was beautiful, but even *she* felt it was far too much to pay for a purse. Not the least discouraged, Mandie found a phone and called Montana (never mind that the charges for the overseas call would have paid for a large part of the purse).

"Of course, dear, you must buy it. When will you *ever* be in France again?" her understanding mother responded. Buoyed by this very sensible argument, Mandie went back to the store and maxed out her Visa card. That night she slept with the purse on the pillow next to hers.

Not to be outdone, the next day Mrs. Goldberg spied a Jackie-O-style small clutch purse about the size of two cigarette packages. While forking over her platinum, she remarked, "I'm on vacation. I should be able to do this." The cost of the purse? Six thousand U.S. dollars! Later that afternoon, she paid $343 for a key chain.

Even in my unhappy state I couldn't help but laugh.

Ryan was his usual happy-go-lucky self and he was enjoying LA. He briefly worked as an ironworker, but he decided that the hard physical labor didn't really appeal to him. So he spent a lot of time hanging out in the evenings with me at the DeVitos'. I had weekends off on this job, and on Friday nights I left to camp out in the Brentwood box with him for a couple of days.

Danny invited both of us to Rhea's birthday party. I had it pegged as a dressy event, and Ryan was not happy about the dress code. I finally managed to find a jacket, white dress shirt, and tie for him to wear. (The last time I had made him wear a tie was our homecoming dance, and he had stuffed it in his pocket ten minutes after we had arrived at the gymnasium.) After arguing at Nordstrom's for a half hour about some dress shoes (it was a draw; he bought them but refused to wear them when the time came), we went back to my sister's to get ready for the big party. I pulled out my good ol' standby black dress once again, but I couldn't get the zipper zipped. I decided there was no way I was going to get the dress on without busting a seam, so I gave up.

I heard Ryan in the living room talking to Cindy. "Suzy just doesn't think my Nikes go with these khaki pants." I rolled my eyes in irritation. Why didn't I just admit it? I was dating Jethro from *The Beverly Hillbillies.* I threw on something of my sister's, an odd garment that was a cross between a skirt so short a hooker might wear it and a white jacket that made me look like I belonged in a medical office. My sister, bless her heart, normally doesn't own any clothes that are in fashion for the current decade. This was no exception. So, I had to go with the nurse/call girl/dancer look.

Several valets were waiting to park our car when we rolled up. I stepped out and pulled the knit skirt down for the eighteenth time while my sidekick fidgeted with his tie as if he had a noose cinched around his neck. It was just getting dark as we entered the outside gate, but I could clearly see that we were the only ones dressed up. The rest of the guests wore shorts, golf shirts, and sleeveless blouses. I felt my mood sink even further. Once again I'd forgotten about the chic-casual LA style. After he'd gotten a gander at the crowd, Ryan turned to me with a knowing smirk and hastily bid adieu to his tie and coat. He rolled up his long sleeves as if he were Popeye the Sailorman.

Looking around the patio, I could see that all the *Cheers* people were present, as well as Michael Douglas and Danny's old buddies from *Taxi*, Marilu Henner and Tony Danza, and, oh my God, the last person on earth that I wanted to see—Michael Ovitz. He was still in his office uniform of crisp white shirt and conservative tie. I scanned the crowd for Judy, but I didn't see her anywhere. I kept looking over at him, and I was sure he kept looking back in my direction. Maybe he didn't recognize me? Maybe he didn't remember me! I was really thinking rationally now. But he gazed directly at me, so I made sure I kept enough bodies between us so that I wouldn't have to talk to him. Finally, with a sigh of relief, I spotted him making his way toward the valets. Thank God he had only stopped by to put in a brief appearance.

Ryan saw a major movie star come out of the bathroom with two other people, wiping his nose. "They were snorting coke, Suzy," he told me. I refused to believe it, even after hearing Sheila's stories about piles of cocaine. I couldn't quite wrap my mind around people doing drugs in the bathroom of the house I lived in.

> Seeing Michael at the party tonight was pretty weird. I'm actually getting paranoid enough to think that he might have been following me. I was glad that he left early.
> The struggle with Ryan getting ready for the party just hammered home that we're too different, even though I wasn't

right about the dress code. I can't shake knowing that we're not headed in the same direction. Seems like the most loving thing I can do for him is to let him go, so that he can find someone who appreciates him just as he is. There's just no way I'm ever going to be excited about the monster truck rally coming to town. I keep trying to mask his bad-boy scent in cheap cologne. I'm pretty sure he's sick and tired of my constant nagging and complaining about him doing pretty much everything wrong in my eyes.

Note to self: Get out my book about women who love too much and find the chapter about how to get out of this. And then do it, once and for all.

Second note to self: Go get that book I saw on the talk show yesterday, *Smart Women/Foolish Choices: Finding the Right Men, Avoiding the Wrong Ones.*

Tammy called to let me know she was back from her trip to Aspen. She wanted me to know that Sally's family had gone out to dinner with the Ovitzes, and she had seen Delma and the kids.

"How were they? How did the kids look?" I grilled her for *every* possible detail.

"Well, Mrs. Ovitz didn't recognize me at first. When she made the connection, in the middle of dinner, she gasped, '*Oh*, you're *her* friend!'" Tammy giggled. "She pointed her finger at me as if I were a plague-bearing rodent. The kids looked up at her, then me, in alarm. It's as if she had figured out that I was a part of that 'nanny mafia' that's responsible for so much trouble in Hollywood. 'That Suzy,' she spat, 'she left us high and dry!'"

According to Tammy, the disparaging remarks and finger-pointing continued while Sally and Alan attempted to steer the conversation elsewhere. As soon as they got into the car, Sally made it clear to Tammy that they had attended the dinner for business reasons. She apologized for the uncomfortable incident.

"I'm sure that your friend is a very nice girl, because she helped us find you," she said.

There's a good reason why people really, really like Sally Field.

I couldn't have worked and raised four kids without all the help I've had.

—Meryl Streep

# the goodbye girl

My mom was coming to Hollywood. Ever since she found out how well Danny and Rhea were treating her daughter, she became their biggest fan. She combed her *People* magazine for any mention of them, clipping out the articles. I teased her that her real motivation for the visit was to see them, not me. But in my heart I knew that if I was a nanny in North Platte, Nebraska, she'd be out to see me just the same. That's just how my mom is. But she was probably a lot more excited by the prospect of meeting my famous employers than she would have been to visit farmers in the heartland.

When we walked up to the DeVito door together, I felt an unfamiliar urge to protect the poor star-struck dear. I wanted to give her a hug. Instead, as daughters will, I hissed instructions for her not to embarrass me.

Rhea welcomed my mother as if she was an old friend. No fuss, just an easy warmth and instant familiarity. Within a minute or so, my mother was loosened up, completely in her element, just talking about kids with another mom. Rhea told us that Danny and the girls were watching TV in the office and suggested that we check in on them. We peeked in the room to find Danny lying on his belly on the rug, one elbow propping up his chin while he swatted his free arm at the kids climbing up on his back. I said, "Danny, this is my mother."

The kids looked up and greeted her, and Danny called out, "Yeah, hi!"

Rhea frowned in the doorway. "Danny, it's Suzy's mother."

He jumped up and flashed that big, sheepish, "Whaddayagonnado?" smile. "Sorry, sorry," he apologized as he extended his hand to Mom. "I thought you said 'This is Mariah.'"

My mom was charmed down to her toes.

The morning after my mom arrived, Max woke up at 5 A.M. on the dot, and as he made disgruntled noises, I ran downstairs to get a bottle ready. He was sweet but a fitful sleeper, and when he wrestled his pajamas into a knot during the night, I'd always drag myself out of bed to untie him. I slept five feet away, and every time he shifted, I'd jolt awake, wondering if he was about to wake up and if I should get a bottle warmed up before he really started crying. When I returned this time, he was already letting out little cries of distress, and I lifted him out and held him in the rocking chair until he finished drinking. He fell into a fragile doze as I laid him back down in the crib.

I relished the thought of crawling back into my warm bed for another hour, but just as I had snuggled down, he started fussing again. I knew that sometimes he'd just fuss a bit and then fall asleep, so I didn't move immediately. Instead I did something I'd never done before. I put my pillow over my head and ignored Max for several minutes, hoping he would settle down. The light flipping on startled me, and I looked up to see Rhea standing in the bedroom doorway.

"Why is Max crying?" she asked. It sounded like an accusation.

"I just gave him a bottle," I said sheepishly. "I think he's going to go back to sleep."

"I don't think he's tired," Rhea said, taking Max into her arms and making some cooing noises at him.

She didn't say anything more to me as she left with Max, but I felt horrible. Not only did Rhea think that I didn't care about her son, but for a minute there she had been right. I had cared about my sleep more than him. I was wracked with guilt. What kind of nanny ignores a crying child just five feet away from her? Well, British ones, I consoled myself.

But I was no Mary Poppins. I tried to analyze the situation. I had been awake most of the night, making sure that Max was okay and that he didn't cry too much and wake the rest of the house. But no matter how many times I had gotten up and comforted him, he still seemed restless. Of course this was part of my job description. I couldn't ignore the crying and go back to sleep like an exhausted mother could. I was his nanny, and I didn't get to make those kinds of calls. I could see that I was simply becoming resentful of taking care of others. It was very clear to me at that moment that I just didn't want to be a nanny anymore.

I felt so crappy about what I had done that I wanted to make it up to Rhea. Instead of taking advantage of the extra hour of sleep, I got up, straightened out Max's crib, and went down to the kitchen to unload the dishwasher. My mind was jumbled, but I couldn't shake the feeling that I just didn't want to be a caregiver anymore. I didn't want to be in LA.

All day I wondered how I could possibly tell Danny and Rhea that I wanted to leave. They had been completely accommodating and sweet. I could still hear my mother going on about what down-to-earth people they were and how lucky I was to be working for them. I *was* lucky, I knew that, but I was also lucky to have figured out that I had to move on. I think I finally realized that, up to now, I had been operating from a kid's mentality, waiting for someone else to ask me what I needed. But I was ready to make a major switch: I wanted to be an adult, to take care of myself and make my own life choices.

I wanted to go for a drive, but Mom and Ryan had taken my car so that they could go sightseeing while I worked. I wouldn't have been able to leave the kids, anyway. But I was still frustrated about being stuck there, miserable, with no way of getting out to clear my head. It was another sun-drenched day in California, and I took the girls out to the backyard to play in the pool while Lisa ran an errand and Max took a nap. After spending twenty minutes searching for their swimsuits— which they had worn the day before but had wrapped in towels and left under their beds—and then locating alternate suits, beach balls, floating frogs, towels, and all the other pool necessities, I was ready to collapse in the sun and relax.

I was just settling down in the lounge chair when the girls decided that I needed to be the referee for their water fight. They soaked me to the bone as an invitation. Then I heard the front gate buzz. Mom and Ryan sauntered into the courtyard. They were joking about how Ryan had panned for gold at Knott's Berry Farm but hadn't found so much as a flake.

"I don't think they have any gold in that tub at all." Mom laughed as I stood there dripping. Then she started to tell me about visiting Tammy at Sally's, commenting about how she had such a wonderful job— "Almost better than yours." She smiled. "And she's so appreciative that you got her that job interview."

Mom got to hold Sally's baby and take pictures of all of them together. To top it off, Sally had made lunch for them. Mom was on cloud nine. She said that Tammy had wanted to go to Knott's Berry Farm with them, but she was packing to go on another trip, this time to New York.

"Sally and Tammy get along so well. Tammy seems to just love her job," Mom gushed. "And why not, with such a gorgeous little baby and such a beautiful home?"

That did it! I was already mad that I had never been to Knott's Berry Farm, or to most tourist spots in LA for that matter. But here was Mom, telling me about how much fun she'd had at Sally's without me; how she had wished Tammy could have come with them to the amusement park. *What about me?*

I couldn't help myself. I started yelling at Mom and Ryan, accusing them of trying to make me feel bad and leaving me stuck behind these black gates with no way of getting anywhere.

"To top it off," I said quietly so that the girls wouldn't hear, "I don't even like being a nanny anymore, but neither of you know me well enough to even notice."

Mom was appalled by my outburst at first, but when I dissolved into tears, she realized how serious I was. She said that if I wasn't happy then maybe I should just quit and come back home. She was so calm, even after I had yelled at her, that it made me calm down, too, and I started to think reasonably about the whole situation. It wasn't Danny and Rhea who were making me miserable; it was my own desire to do something that was closer to my dreams.

Okay. It's clear now that I have to quit the whole nanny stint and start making plans for my future. And I'm not even all that angry that Ryan hasn't noticed how miserable I am. It's obvious that he'll never really know what's going on with me. And it is my responsibility to find someone who'll share my dreams. I think I finally get it now. Now I see why the subtitle of *Women Who Love Too Much* is *When You Keep Wishing and Hoping He'll Change*. Hello? That is what I have been doing. Trying to make him something he is not. What is it my mother always says? You can't make silk out of a pig's ear. Or is it his tail? Anyway, I know this is what I need to do, even though he might always be my "hard habit to break." Oh, great, now I'm quotings songs from Journey. Or was it Air Supply? Chicago? I don't know.

Note to self: Must get out and hear some local bands!

Simply by deciding to leave I felt a jolt of excitement about what lay ahead for me. College? Probably. I had been doing a little research about a college in Oregon with a well-respected nursing program. Since the time I was small, I had a fascination with the medical field, even if it was just to diagnose my own self-concocted potentially life-threatening medical conditions. I thought I would make a good nurse. But how was I going to tell this to Danny and Rhea? This was my chance to practice the assertiveness I knew I'd need in my life as a grown-up.

The opportunity presented itself sooner than I expected. A few mornings later, Rhea asked me to accompany her and the kids to the park. When we got there, we took a stroll on the manicured green grass as the kids played close by on the jungle gym. Rhea turned to me, saying, "We're so happy with you, and I know Max loves you." Just a few short months ago, I would have given anything for that kind of appreciation, but now it made me instantly uncomfortable. I knew that if I didn't have the nerve to tell her then, I would get in deeper, and it would be even harder to break my commitment.

I took a deep breath, and everything I'd been thinking came pouring out in one long speech. I explained that they were the best employers I'd ever had. I said that if I'd worked for them first I'd probably be there forever, but I had come to them already burned out. A twenty-four-hour-a-day job didn't give me time to figure out what I wanted to do with my life, but I thought I wanted to go to nursing school. So I wanted to leave California. But I promised her that I would absolutely stay until they found someone else, and I offered to contact the nanny school to see if there was anyone there to fill the spot.

Rhea said she was so disappointed, but she understood my need to move on and encouraged me to follow my heart.

In the days and weeks that followed, Rhea and Danny still treated me well, although they seemed a little more businesslike. I understood. It was as if they had already started to cut me out of their hearts, just as I had learned to do with the Ovitz children. I kept calling the nanny school, but for two weeks I got no response. It seemed like the pool of nannies had dried up just when I needed a replacement. Finally, after biting my nails to the quick, I heard back from the school about a possible candidate. I told Rhea that there was someone who might work out for her and Danny. She called right away to get a reference, talking to my instructor-friend Mary.

After that, she came back to me and said that Mary had recommended the new girl but had cautioned, "This girl is no Suzy." She smiled and patted me on the shoulder, as if she was truly going to miss me.

That's when I realized that I had actually made an impact on someone besides Max. And even though Danny had listened patiently to Michael, he had never treated me any differently after hearing that I had left the most powerful man in town "high and dry." Even now that I was leaving them, the subject was never brought up. The biggest compliment they gave me was when Danny said to me one day, in a contemplative moment, "I guess ole Michael was wrong after all." I said, "Thanks," and smiled. I have never forgotten those words.

When the new girl came for her interview, Rhea asked if I would help evaluate her. We sat down in the sunny breakfast area, where not long ago I had eaten all of Rhea's special cookies. I wracked my brain for the right questions to ask, ones that would bring the girl out of her shell and force her to reveal everything.

I chided myself for not writing something down, but I saw that Rhea was doing the interview off-the-cuff as well. We talked to her a little about her background and history, which seemed solid enough. She didn't have a ton of experience being a nanny, but she had gone through the program without any problems. I wanted to warn her about getting too attached to the children you cared for, the one topic they had not covered in nanny school, but I couldn't say anything with Rhea next to me. During one of Rhea's questions, the girl said she didn't think she could make a blanket statement that she "loved children" because she had to meet the child first to know.

Later, when Rhea asked me how I thought the interview went, I said I wasn't sure. I figured that someone who wanted to be a full-time care-giver of kids of all ages should be able to say she *loved* children. "It just sounds odd, coming from someone looking to be a nanny," I said.

Rhea told me to go ahead and keep looking. I had contacted the local placement agencies also, but none of them had any promising appli-cants, either. I wished that I hadn't already gotten Tammy a job. But of course she wouldn't leave Sally. Finally Rhea said that she was going to hire the girl we had interviewed since there didn't seem to be anyone else.

I was frustrated by my inability to find a great replacement and sad that I couldn't convince Cindy to move back to Oregon, too. She also had had just about enough of LA life, but she was a stickler for the rules and wasn't willing to break the lease on her apartment or leave her roommates *high and dry*. Ryan's dad, bless his heart, had spent a lot of time on the phone, trying to convince his directionless son to join the armed services. Fortunately, he had been successful. Go Navy! It looked like we were headed home together (but not together).

So many life changes. It wasn't until I started packing that it finally hit me: *I was really, really never going to work in this town again!*

Now, when I look back on some of the things that I didn't do, it is so insignificant compared to having them. Kids change your life in every possible way. They completely turn it upside down. And I am really thankful for that.

—Annette Bening

chapter 23
# back to the future

I was so glad to be home and thankful that Ryan drove twelve out of the fourteen hours. During my short time behind the wheel, however, I managed to receive a speeding ticket, somewhere between Weed and Yreka. It must have been California's way of saying good-bye and please come back soon.

Little did I know how quickly I'd be back. I had barely unpacked when a distraught Rhea called.

"I need to let this girl go," she said. "Is there any chance you could come back, just for a little while?" She said her gut told her something just wasn't right with the new nanny. Max was crying a lot and didn't seem nearly as happy as he had been with me.

Rhea had never sounded so sad, and I agreed immediately. I kicked myself for not finding a better replacement. She said she'd send me a plane ticket right away (thank God I didn't have to drive!).

I called Mandie, who was back home in Montana after sticking it out at the Goldbergs' for two whole years. Turned out that her replacement hadn't lasted long, either, and she would also be heading back to LA to pinch-hit. Would we *ever* move on with our lives?

When I landed at LAX, I dialed the Ovitzes' immediately. Almost before I could speak, Delma suggested sneaking out to the park to meet.

It had been more than a year since I'd laid eyes on Brandon, and when I saw him on the playground, I couldn't believe how much he had grown. He was almost a toddler. No longer a baby, as he had always remained in my mind. He immediately threw his arms around me, and we hugged for a long time. My throat started to form a familiar lump. I was overjoyed to see him, but I knew that this would probably be the last time. Now he could talk. Soon he'd be able to tell his parents.

The two of us plopped onto a swing, and Delma took our picture. I had no idea that someday I would blow up and frame that one snapshot, giving it a place of honor on my dresser for many years. The camera caught so much. Brandon stared ahead with wide-eyed innocence and an enormous smile, showing off those wonderful chubby cheeks. I looked a little like someone whose beloved pet had just died.

Reluctantly I let him jump down and play. Delma and I perched together on the edge of the sandbox, just two of many nannies at the park that day, clucking over the kids.

"I still miss Brandon so much," I said, watching him toddle in the sand. "It's like I've lost a part of me."

"I know you do." Delma patted me on the arm. "He misses you, too."

"Does he even remember me, though?" I asked.

"Take my word for it, you're one of the best things to ever happen to him," she assured me kindly. "He is such a sweet little boy now. I think he'll always remember you in some special way." She always knew just what to say.

"Thank you for saying that." I smiled at my friend.

I could've stayed at that park forever, but I did have work to do. This time I'd be watching Max and both the girls. More work, but it seemed easier in some ways. This time I was in a different emotional space; I knew the gig was temporary, and I had applied to a nursing program that I was looking forward to starting. Max warmed up to me quickly, and this time I let myself enjoy him. Helping fly the kids to Danny's movie set in Sante Fe sounded like a fantastic way to cap off my nanny career. Rhea was not so enthusiastic.

"With your help, we'll make the best of it," Rhea said. "Audrey's ears always bother her on planes, so it's no fun for her to fly. I have a feeling she'll have a hard time."

This turned out to be an understatement. Audrey wailed for nearly the entire five-hour flight, triggering stares and huffs from the other first-class passengers. Just like on my flight to Hawaii. It was as if wealthy travelers thought screaming children only sat in coach. Max sat quietly on my lap, but he *was* a baby, and, of course, he kept trying to crawl onto the lap of the perfectly groomed—and fairly pissed-off—stranger sitting next to us.

To top it off, some passengers recognized Rhea and sent their kids to get autographs: "Daddy told me to tell you he watches your show all the time," they'd say, napkin and pencil in hand. After a while, first class started to look like a kindergarten class.

Worn out by the time the plane landed, we stepped out into the sauna that was Sante Fe. *Hot* was simply not a strong enough word for the weather. We slogged our way to the hotel. I couldn't figure out why on earth the producers had chosen to film Danny's movie—*Twins*, costarring Arnold Schwarzenegger—in a boiling-hot town outside of Sante Fe, when the script didn't even mention New Mexico.

We trekked out to the set to meet Danny for lunch. I briefly got to meet Arnold Schwarzenegger and Kelly Preston, but the actors were on a tight leash. The director's yell carried over everything. "Let's move it, people. We need to get this shot before the sun sets! We are behind schedule. I do not want to pay these extras for another day because we couldn't get it done!" The cast and crew bustled around, corralling the actors and props for each scene.

I don't think they banked on the interfering townspeople, however. The excited residents weren't accustomed to seeing celebrities and quickly mobbed the streets, and apparently the studio hadn't hired enough security to handle the crush of people. The local police were supposed to provide protection, but they seemed to be doing a lot of gawking themselves. On top of that, the crowd became much more unruly than expected, to the point where the director had to cut certain scenes because there wasn't enough room to move on the streets. I'd heard that two bodyguards would safely escort us to lunch, and I was beginning to think they might be necessary.

Soon Danny made his way over and directed us to start walking briskly toward the restaurant. But suddenly I felt like I was in the mosh pit at a rock concert, surrounded by crazed lunging fans. I tried to keep going, to push Max's little stroller forward, but I couldn't even move it because of the swarm of people. "Is that Danny DeVito's baby?" teenagers asked, trying to touch him.

Finally some security guys came by to help, but in all the commotion Audrey lost Rhea's hand. The poor six-year-old started crying out, and suddenly a huge ocean of fans swept between her and the rest of us. I was closest, and Rhea took Max, yelling, "Grab her!" Heart thumping, I pushed through the crowd, ignoring the yells and stares and not making eye contact. It was a weird feeling, to be so close to all those people but so apart from them. I scooped up Audrey frantically.

The private room at the restaurant felt like an oasis. We ate our food in a secluded area, with a guard monitoring the door. I'd never been so thankful to be away from the swarming public. Who was I kidding— usually I was the public! But inside this fishbowl of fame, everything seemed skewed and a little surreal.

For the next five days, we tried to avoid the blistering heat and the hounding autograph seekers. Rhea, the kids, and I mostly stuck to the pool and anywhere with air-conditioning, but Danny had to work in the stifling heat for hours. I never realized how long it took to get the shots right. The actors and actresses had to take and retake the same scenes over and over while the people in charge buzzed over things like which of the eighteen different colors of ties an actor should wear (when the *tie would be hidden by an overcoat*). The shooting of one particular scene lasted an entire day, and that scene was literally in the final cut for six seconds.

I guess that's why movie stars get paid so much. Maybe sitting in the spotlight—or the sun—takes more out of a person than you'd expect.

A few days later, as I sat on the plane headed back to Oregon and to my new life in nursing school, I scribbled in my journal.

> I am truly, finally done. I love the DeVitos, and I hope I stay in contact with them, but going back has made me realize I made the right decision. The past couple of years have given me a lot

of valuable experience. But sometimes I think if I had to do it all over again, I am not sure I would have. The pain of leaving the kids was so much greater than I ever imagined. I just didn't put enough thought into the good-byes.

I am more than ready to start college and just be a student again.

I have really been thinking that moving on from Ryan was the best step in the growing up department. I think it has been hard for me to let go of my memories with him. But he is a chapter in my life that I am finally closing.

So maybe without these experiences it would have taken me longer to see the relationship for what it was . . . an intense feeling of "first love." So I am grateful this helped me come to a much needed—no you really can't change anyone but yourself—obvious realization.

Reminder to self: Stop being so grouchy when Mom's friends ask me all the annoying questions about what life is like in Hollywood, and try to remember that I had a window into a life that most people only see in the movies.

I was bone-tired and thrilled to be back in my own comfortable bed. A letter from Mandie, covered with foreign postage stamps, was waiting for me, and I curled up to get the latest.

*Dear Suzy,*

*Well, the European vacation is amazing in some ways. The whole family and I went on this really big boat, some superyacht or something, and I was so sick I thought I was going to lose my noodles over the side. The water was so rough that I could barely even walk along the deck without weaving all over the place and stumbling into things. People must have thought I was drunk. But maybe they didn't notice, because it seemed like a lot of other people were seasick, too. Or maybe they were drunk!*

*Anyway, I'm out on the deck and this big swell comes up, and suddenly I go crashing into this guy standing by the railing. Luckily I didn't barf on him. He helps me steady myself, and then he kind of squints at me and asks me if I'm all right. I felt like a total loser! But that was nothing. I start to say, "Thank you very much," but before I can get the words out, I whip*

*around and start dry heaving off the side of the deck. Then I'm like OH
MY GOD, because he says, "Ma'am, can I get you anything?" and he
looks at me again, all squinty and stuff, and I realize it's Clint frickin'
Eastwood!!!*

*"Do you need anything?" he says, and I'm thinking, all I need now is a
hole in the earth to disappear into. I've never been so embarrassed in all
my life. (With the possible exception of my falling-down incident with Mel,
remember?)*

*You won't guess who I spent the afternoon with a few days later in
Rome. Demi Moore! The Goldbergs and me and the kids and Demi went to
this museum that must have been a hundred years old, all very boring. But
I finally saw an opportunity to take some pictures with my instant camera—snapshots of Demi to send back to my family and friends in Missoula! (Because you know how excited my dad got when I sent that picture
to him of me and Quincy Jones, it really made his day.) Anyway, I'm
thinking, maybe I can get Mrs. Goldberg to take one of Demi and me
together. As you would expect, that never happened. Nevertheless, I figured
a couple of shots of her with my boss would be proof enough that I spent the
day with her.*

*The only problem is that the three of them were walking together and
mostly they were stopping and staring at paintings, so the first 11 out of 12
pictures on the roll are the back of her head, as far as I could tell. Then,
with only one picture left, she turns to ask a security guy where the ladies'
room is. I quickly pull the viewfinder up to my eye. Demi is smiling at me.
She even preens a bit. But just as I'm about to snap the shutter, the security
guy rips the camera out of my hand and says, "No foto-grahffi in museum,"
and Demi runs off to the bathroom.*

*I don't think I'll even get them developed.*

*Everything's too old here in Rome and nobody speaks English. I can't
wait to get back to Montana and decide what to really do with my life.*

> *Love,*
> *Mandie*

I chuckled. Mandie always made me laugh. But I knew what she
meant. Enough with timidly penciling in the future. It was time to ink
in my plans.

One thing I have learned is that women really can have it all.

—Jada Pinkett-Smith

# almost famous

I was beginning to think that I had a magnetic attraction to Hollywood.

In three years, I'd managed to chug forward on all fronts: I was studying at a respected nursing program at a private college in Portland, and for the last six months I had been dating a great guy named Wes, whom I'd met on a blind date set up by Mary, my nanny school mentor. Ryan had joined the Navy. His family, whom I had always adored, gave me updates every now and then. I was glad to hear that he was doing well, but my heart had definitely moved on. Like Ryan, Hollywood seemed to be a million miles away.

But somehow it always seemed to tug me back.

Out of the blue, Rhea called. I hadn't seen or talked to the DeVitos much since my previous stint in New Mexico, and sure enough they needed another hand again. The itinerary was a working vacation followed by a jaunt to Hawaii, and I didn't have to think twice. I had the time off from school, and I really thought Hawaii deserved another chance. I'd hardly seen any of it during my last visit.

I couldn't be in Hollywood without thinking of Brandon. It had been a good two years since I'd spoken to any of his family, although, thanks to the Lakers, I'd seen them. I often felt incredibly grateful for that one night so long ago when Michael had given Delma and me his tickets; I then knew where to look during an NBA broadcast. In fact, I still recorded Lakers games in an attempt to catch a glimpse of one of the children attending with their dad. It was the only way for me to see how they'd grown, and many times I spotted Josh and Brandon for a split second. Sometimes I'd get a glimpse of Michael and Judy in the court-side seats. She looked as beautiful as ever.

Not long after arriving back at the DeVito house, I called Delma, hoping she still worked there.

"Hello, Ovitz residence," said an unfamiliar voice.

"Yes, may I speak with Delma please?" I said. Even now, years later, my voice shook.

"And may I ask who's calling?"

"Uh, yes, this is Cassandra with Robinson's department store," I said, thinking up the quickest white lie I could come up with. "I, uh, have a question regarding her statement."

"Hold just a moment, please."

"Hello?" Delma said in her charming accent.

"Hi, Delma, it's Suzy. The nanny."

"Soooozy!" she yelled.

"Oh my God, is anyone right there?" I gasped. I didn't want to get her in trouble. "Who's standing next to you?"

"It's okay," she assured me. "They're gone to New York."

"Who answered the phone?" I asked.

"It's Mrs. Ovitz's new secretary, who works here at the house. You know how it is."

"That's good for you; no more phone messages." We both laughed. "Anyway, how are you? How's Carmen? How are the kids? Oh my gosh, how big are they now?"

"Brandon is so big you wouldn't believe it, and Carmen is fine."

"Please tell her I said hello and that I miss her."

"She's off today but I will when I see her. I can't wait to tell her I talked to you."

"Are you still the nanny? Did they ever hire anyone else?"

"No, I'm still the nanny, and I get to wear whatever I want." She giggled, and I laughed, too.

"Guess what, Suzy!" she said excitedly.

"What?"

"I'm pregnant!"

"No way, you're kidding!" I screamed. "Really?"

"Yes, I am," she answered, a touch of pride in her voice.

"Did you get married?"

"No, it's my boyfriend Juan's baby."

"Oh my gosh. How far along are you?"

"Oh, about four months."

"What are you going to do? Are you going to bring the baby to work?"

"I don't know. We'll see," she said thoughtfully. "Mrs. Ovitz has been very nice to me.

"But you know what?" Her tone shifted now into something slightly confidential. "Mr. Ovitz asked me to come down to the office for the second time in my life—"

"Uh-huh."

"He asked me if I was happy that I was going to have a baby, and I said, 'Yes, very happy.' And he said, 'Oh, I see. I was wondering if we could do anything to help you out,' or something like that. And I said, 'I am happy I am having a baby, Mr. Ovitz.' He said, 'Oh right. Of course you are.' And then he put his arm around me."

"Maybe he was just trying to help you out, Delma, since he knows you're not married," I offered weakly.

"You could be right, but it seemed kind of strange," she said. "But I guess maybe I was just scared, being in his big office, you know."

"Oh yeah, I remember that feeling well."

I always thought that Delma would make a great mother.

"Anyway, I'm so happy for you. I wish I could see the kids." I couldn't keep from saying what I knew was never going to happen.

"I know. They're too old now, though, and you know they'd tell."

"I know, Delma. I was just wishing."

"Listen, Suzy, I have to go," she said. "The kids just got home from school."

"Okay." I could hear the kids in the background. Was that Brandon? "Please give the kids a hug from me."

When I hung up, I started sobbing, and I couldn't stop for a very long time. I knew that I'd never see any of them ever again.

I went downstairs to try and forget about my phone conversation. I was pleasantly surprised by something really sweet, an old note I saw on the dining room table.

> *Dear Danny and Rhea,*
>
> *During this time of year we think of all the things we are grateful for, and we realize that we are more fortunate than most people. We live an extraordinary life and have all the comforts we could ever wish for. So, instead of buying gifts for our friends, we have donated money in your honor to a children's charity.*
>
> *With love,*
> *Arnold and Maria*

It was the first time that I had ever known celebrities to acknowledge that the lives they lead are very different from the majority of the American public. My suspicion that Maria Shriver was a person of character was confirmed, and I felt hopeful that all high-profile people weren't as hurried and angry as the ones I had encountered.

Of course, I already knew Danny and Rhea were relaxed and real. They knew that I was going to be with them for only a short while this time, but they still made me feel appreciated. Even though I still worked every minute of the day and never had any "off" time in the evenings, I loved being with them, because they treated me like I mattered. They always invited me to have dinner with them. When they had friends over, they always included me in the adult conversations.

The first stop on our way to Hawaii was San Francisco, where Danny was on a month-long shoot. We tried to do some sightseeing, but nearly everywhere we went, crowds formed around us. It was Santa Fe all over again. Sometimes it made us laugh, like the time we were going to dinner on the Fisherman's Wharf and a guy with a Bronx accent yelled over to us, "Hey, Louie! Everybody tells me I look just like you!" I thought "everybody" must be blind, because the guy was about five foot ten and 250 pounds.

Unfortunately, most of the attention we got wasn't the least bit funny. Mobs of "adoring" fans clamored for autographs. They wanted to take pictures or ask inane questions. Once, on a ferry across San Francisco Bay, a group of kids and their "chaperones" surrounded us, sticking their hands in our faces and insisting on autographs. Rhea said no, that they were on vacation and that she wouldn't be signing anything. Normally, she was pretty accommodating, but she didn't like it when fans demanded things of her. In a short while, the crowd grew rowdy. Audrey, Lexie, and Max were frightened, and there was no way off the ferry, so Rhea finally agreed to sign a few autographs. That seemed to calm the horde a bit. What annoyed me most was that the parents didn't do anything to stop their kids. In fact, they were in on the mayhem, too. At least they didn't invade the set; the actual filming areas were much calmer than the *Twins* set had been. The police and members of the film crew kept the crowds at bay.

One day, the girls said, "Daddy, can't we be in the movie?" Then Max chimed in. "I want to be in it, too." Danny agreed, but then Rhea said, "If Max is in it, then Suzy has to be in it, too." Rhea asked if that was okay with me. I said sure!

I was bustled off to Hair and Makeup, where I was positive the stylists would transform me into a glamorous starlet. Wrong. They put me in a horrible 70s outfit—brown cords, rust-colored top, and a flower-power headband. They brushed my hair into its least attractive state—straight, parted down the middle, and showcasing my forehead like an eight ball. This would be my film debut? I tried to roll up my sleeves, just a small attempt to look better, but the wardrobe lady came rushing over to me, saying, "No, no, no. Roll those back down. You look too hip; they didn't do that in the seventies."

The kids and I were slated for a crowd scene, just four more people in a group watching a puppet show. Not exactly a speaking role. Okay, that's not quite the truth. We were all supposed to yell, "We want the clown! We want the clown!" But as far as I was concerned, in my 70s getup, I was the clown.

Luckily, our time in front of the camera ended up to be less than an hour, since Max was bored with the whole thing after ten minutes, and I spent the next forty begging him to stand still for just a little bit longer.

After filming in San Francisco, we took off on one of the studio jets. I had forgotten how great it was: no shoving carry-ons into overhead compartments, no squeezing past people to get to your seat, no lines for the bathroom. Bliss.

And then we landed in Hawaii. Better bliss.

> The Mauna Lani Bay Hotel is unbelievable. I've never seen such a beautiful place. I'm in the main building, in a huge suite with a balcony, a minibar stocked with Butterfingers, and a TV showing constant movies. Rhea, Danny, and the kids have a house with a private pool just a short walk from the hotel.
>
> The beaches are spectacular, and the temperature is perfect. I went and bought a new swimsuit first thing. I am happy to report I am back to my "pre-nanny-life" weight.
>
> When I got back to my hotel room, there were a dozen roses from Wes. What a surprise! I miss him more than I thought I would. I really like this guy. I woke up wanting to talk to him one morning, so I called him. I was just going to talk for a minute, but next thing I knew, I was on the phone for a half hour. I couldn't believe it when I looked at the clock. I love it here, but I can't wait to see him again.
>
> Mom called this morning to see how the trip's going. She was going on and on, saying she saw my hotel on Lifestyles of the Rich and Famous. She asked if there were a lot of famous people here and if I have my own butler and pool. And do they serve margaritas right on the beach? Yes, Mom, they do, but did you forget about the time change? It's 3 A.M. To which she replied, Oops. Sorry, honey. Talk to you later.

When it was time to leave, I headed over to their private house to help Rhea finish packing up the kids. Danny was seated at the huge marble dining room table saying, "Okay. I see. Uh-huh." And a man from the hotel was standing behind him, waiting for his approval of the bill. When I glanced down at the table, I saw twenty-five pages of charges. Then I saw the bill for my room. On the front page it said "Page one of eight," and the total in the bottom right-hand corner was so high that I'm embarrassed to think about it, even today. I saw the words "Movie Rental" and realized that all those movies I'd watched, and half-watched before getting bored, weren't free at all. How was I supposed to know that they charged for them? They needed a clearer warning on the information channel. I felt like an idiot.

Then I remembered the phone calls to Wes and all those trips to the honor bar. In retrospect, I'm willing to bet those were the priciest Butterfingers on record. I stood there with my bag beside me, feeling sheepish.

I kept expecting Danny to question me about my bill, but he never did. He paid the man and slipped him a big tip, too. Still, I felt guilty. I walked over to the table.

"Danny, I'm sorry about all that. I didn't realize—"

"All what?" he said. "Don't worry about it. We're just glad you came with us."

At first I was consumed with guilt for all the room charges, but when I think about it now, I can see that the hyper-awareness about finances I had learned in my first nanny job automatically kicked right back in. I would've been drawn and quartered at my old gig. But not here. I couldn't believe how generous the DeVitos were. The charges on the bill, combined with the cost of my room, totaled about one semester's college tuition, yet Danny didn't bat an eye. He actually seemed to think I was worth it.

And finally I was beginning to believe I was too.

I had to wait a while for the release of Danny's movie, but I was really looking forward to it. All this time in Hollywood, and I'd hit the silver screen! Or so I thought. My rust-brown glory must not have impressed the film editor. Apparently I only made it to the tiny frames of film on the cutting room floor. Actually I'd probably been swept up and put into the garbage by now.

I took it as a sign that Hollywood was finally giving me the boot.

I know that in the end I wouldn't feel balanced if I didn't have my work as well as motherhood. For a long time I thought I'd only have my work.

—Susan Sarandon

# epilogue

Given that all of this took place in the film capital of the world it's probably not surprising that my story doesn't end there. Too abrupt, too many loose ends. And so the lights dimmed for one final scene, two years later.

I had just earned my nursing degree. From the moment I started studying, I knew I'd made the right decision. By focusing on labor and delivery, I was still working with families, helping them begin the challenge of becoming parents. And in my new career I could also leave any work problems at the hospital *and* sleep in my own bed—two benefits that were not lost on me. Having my own place to come home to every night was even more important now, because I had just gotten engaged to Wes, and we were planning a wedding for the following spring.

Then I got a call from Whitney, the niece of one of my mom's friends. Whitney, who had just graduated from NNI, asked if I could help her find a job in LA. As we talked, it became clear that this was a good excuse for me to take a short vacation between college and my first job. I was *sure* I could help Whitney avoid making the same mistakes I did.

(And somehow I did; she ended up as a nanny to Rick Schroder for many years. But that would come a bit later.)

Before we left, I called Rhea and told her I was coming. As always, she was incredibly generous, offering to put us up at her home.

As it turned out, on the day that we arrived, Rhea and the children were planning to attend a charity event, and she invited us along. It was a fund-raiser for the Elizabeth Glaser Pediatric AIDS Foundation. Besides raising money, the purpose of the event was to allow children with AIDS to meet some of their famous heroes.

Whitney and I quickly realized this was no ordinary outdoor party: a full-fledged carnival, the event was ringed with stars manning game booths, offering kids the chance to win prizes. I spotted a basketball shoot, a bottle-toss, and a chance to sound a gong if you could wallop a fake sledge hammer hard enough, all administered by high-wattage celebs. Certainly a far cry from Cottage Grove's annual Bohemia Days, when the carnies' hands were so greasy I was scared to hand them my ticket because I didn't want to get dirty.

I eagerly shook hands, starting with Magic Johnson. Then a photo op with Paula Abdul (Wes would be thrilled). The celebrity parade seemed never-ending. Whitney gushed over Luke Perry, her personal favorite, but I was sidetracked by a very short and ordinary-looking Mel Gibson. I couldn't get over how different *People*'s Sexiest Man Alive (two years running) looked in person. *This* was Mandie's equivalent to Tom Cruise? If the guy walked into Safeway while I was buying groceries, I don't know if I'd even notice him. He did graciously have his picture taken with Whitney, and she maintained her composure much better than Mandie had.

Maybe I'd been away for too long, but I had some trouble figuring out who all the stars were. I pointed out Yakov Smirnoff to Rhea, who gently told me that the man in question was not the Russian comedian, it was Ringo Starr. And there was one head who towered over the crowd, but I couldn't put my finger on his name. I guessed from his build that he was probably a professional basketball player, so I had my picture taken with him. What the heck. Later, I heard all the kids calling him Shaq. Apparently, taping all those Laker games hadn't made an impression on me.

Then I spotted someone who made my knees weak. I couldn't take in enough air.

Grandpa Ovitz. Standing by the ice cream stand with Grandma Ovitz—and two children. The girl looked about ten and the little boy about six. I quickly did the math. It couldn't be . . . could it? I didn't see any parents and decided to go for it.

I began waving frantically. "Mrs. Ovitz, Mrs. Ovitz! Over here!" I shrieked, trotting toward them while still waving like crazy. Mrs. Ovitz craned her neck a little in my direction, no doubt trying to discern who this crazy person was. She squinted as I approached.

"I know you," she said. "Don't tell me now. Your face looks so familiar. Has it been a long time?"

"It's me. Suzy," I said, hoping that would be enough of a clue.

"Oh my God," she said. "I can't believe it's you. The nanny." She went on to tell me that Michael and Judy were in New York and had given them their tickets to the event. *Whew.*

Amanda and Brandon stood by, looking patient, just as beautiful as ever. I bent down toward them, breathless and grinning. I felt like a long-lost aunt begging for kisses from her nieces and nephews she hardly ever sees.

"Do you remember me?" I asked Amanda.

Amanda's face lit up with a smile of her own. "Yes, I do. You were our nanny."

I couldn't believe it. She wasn't even five years old when I left.

Standing up, I looked back at Mrs. Ovitz and asked if Carmen and Delma were still there. I was amazed to hear that both my friends had stayed. I don't know why I was surprised. I should've guessed, given their patience and the limited career choices they felt they had.

Oh, Delma's baby! I asked Mrs. Ovitz, remembering my last conversation with Delma. She looked genuinely sorry when she said that Delma had lost the baby. My heart sank. Amanda chimed in and said she was really sad because the baby had been born too little to live. It seemed as if the children weren't as spoiled and lacking in compassion as I'd feared.

"Oh yes," Mrs. Ovitz continued, referring to Delma's loss, "Judy gave her time off. You know how good she's always been with the girls." Of course, I couldn't help but agree how generous it was of Judy to let her take time off, but I really didn't agree that women of thirty and forty-five should still be referred to as "girls."

Throughout the entire conversation, Grandpa Ovitz stood silent. He looked at me pleasantly but with a tinge of coldness that I interpreted as, *Shame on you for leaving my son high and dry.*

"How's Josh?" I asked while keeping my fingers crossed that early senility had erased the elder Ovitz's memory of the infamous "butter and stitches" incident.

"He's fine," Grandpa said. "He didn't come with us today because he thought it would be boring."

Out of the blue, Brandon took my hand and asked me to ride with them on the tram back to the cars. I felt tears well up when I squeezed his hand in mine—the hand of a boy, not a baby. I tried to keep the tears in during the ride, which ended all too quickly. I asked Amanda if I could give her a hug. When she said yes, my heart grew three sizes. Then Brandon threw his arms around me and squeezed me, too.

If I was to be truly honest with myself, I couldn't say with conviction that he remembered me. After all, Brandon was less than two years old when I left.

Maybe time has given the memory a warm and fuzzy glow, or maybe I made it what I wanted it to be. But for a brief moment it felt like we were kindred spirits. I could swear that within his hug I felt him saying, "Thank you, Suzy, for loving me."

I should have known. It all started in Hollywood, and here in Hollywood, it would finally end. I now truly felt ready to move on, to my own life, my own home. And hopefully, someday to children I would never have to hug good-bye. My own.

# acknowledgments

I always enjoy reading the acknowledgments page of other books. I flip back and forth between the notes of gratitude and the author's picture—this way, I can accurately make up a story about what I think the author's life is *really* like. If you are anything like me, you might be wondering about my everyday life. I will give you a sneak preview. Most days I don't actually look like my author picture. In fact, I usually show up at my children's school with a baseball cap, no makeup, and sweatpants that could double as pajama bottoms.

Now that the book is complete, I promise my family that I will not embarrass them anymore by leaving the house in my "writing attire," that I will actually put on lipstick, style my hair, and wear something that matches. I will spend more time outside my office than in and, yes, start cooking dinner again— Well, I guess I didn't really cook that much before. But I will start now.

I am extremely blessed with family and friends who have been very patient during this writing process. As I send this off to the publisher, I am happy to report to my loved ones that they will no longer have to hear me say, "I can't talk right now; I'm working on the book."

I extend my heartfelt appreciation to each and every one of you who have lent your patience and support in order to make this book possible.

First and foremost . . .

. . . I want to give a special acknowledgment to the professional nannies who have dedicated their lives to the well-being of children. Thank you for sharing your personal stories with me. May all the families you work for appreciate and recognize the important, loving contributions you make to their children's lives.

Thank you to my publishing support team . . .

. . . Sharlene Martin, Julie McCarron, and Suzanne Wickham-Beaird, thank you for passionately believing in the importance of my story being told.

. . . Shana Drehs, my unbelievable editor at Crown Publishers. The hours you spent, your dedication, and your commitment to make this book the best it could be were phenomenal. I am so grateful you are on this journey with me.

Thank you to my supportive friends . . .

. . . Amy, Christine, Kristi, Missy, and Danette, my forever girlfriends, I love you all very much.

. . . Jason, my life would not be the same without your friendship. Thank you for all you give to me and for being my expert on redneck trivia.

. . . My Goddess Girls, thank you for all the love and laughs.

. . . Dianna Matlock, thank you for all the joy you have brought to our family for so many years. We all love you very much.

. . . Nicole, I pray that you will never have to work for a first-time author again. Your endless patience in keeping me, my family, and my life organized was a true gift.

. . . Sohi, I am grateful to have your guidance in my life.

. . . Ryan Craig, Cindy and I so appreciate your commitment to our project. With your film and my story, Cottage Grove will be sure to get on the map now.

Thank you to my family . . .

. . . My sister Cindy, who should have the title of producer of this book. It would not exist without you and Mark's dedication. Kisses to my sweet little Chance and Ariel.

. . . My sister Traci, for helping me to laugh at all the things that I take *so* seriously. You are one of my dearest friends.

. . . Heath, my mini-me. I thank you for all the fun, love, and laughs you share with us. You are my sun.

. . . My parents, for your neverending love and encouragement. Thank you for always believing in me and my dreams.

. . . Cassie and Yuki, my bonus sisters, I am so glad to have you as part of my family.

. . . Diana and Mandie Ludlam, my life has been greatly enriched by both of you being a part of it.

And most important . . .

. . . Jadyn and Parker. I am thankful every single day that I was chosen to be blessed with your little souls. I love you more than I can ever express. I am honored to be your Mommy.

. . . My husband, Wes, for believing in me and in this huge book project with your whole heart. You are the greatest gift in my life. I don't have big enough words to describe how grateful I am to have you. Of course you are now thinking, "Well, you could *show* me how great you think I am by letting me go play eighteen with Carl, Jay, and Russell . . ." Okay, go get your clubs and get out the door before I change my mind!

# about the author

**Suzanne Hansen** received her Bachelor of Science in Nursing from Linfield College after spending time as a nanny in Southern California. She has been a high-risk labor and delivery nurse, lactation consultant, and childbirth educator. She is now a "stay-at-home-and-work" mom. She lives with her husband and two children in Portland, Oregon. The author's website can be seen at www.hollywoodnanny.com.